BRITISH ISSUES
in Geography

> Corrin Flint and David Flint <

> Consultant Editor: Clive Hart <

COLLINS
EDUCATIONAL

Acknowledgements

The authors and publishers are grateful to the following for permission to reproduce copyright material:

BBC Enterprises (Books) Ltd, *Water moves in*, p66
Collins Longman Atlases, Fig 44.6
Cleveland Co-operative Agency, Figs 36.1, 36.3;
Dorling Kindersley Ltd, Figs 20.3, 21.1, 21.2, 21.3, 27.7, 47.5, 47.6;
Friends of the Earth for cartoons by Philip Thompson (p50), and Ken Pyne (p86) from *Earth Mirth*;
Guardian Newspapers Ltd, Figs 11.3 (19.3.87), 19.5 by John Ardill (1.5.87), 21.5 by Paul Brown (9.7.86), 23.15 by John Hooper and Alan Travis (31.3.87), 23.16 by John Hooper (5.12.85), 25.3 (18.12.87) 27.4 by Anthony Tucker (29.10.86), 31.3 (27.4.87), 32.2 and 32.3 (27.4.88) 39.2 (left) by John Ardill (3.7.87), 39.2 (right) by Andrew Cornelius (27.4.87), 45.2 (3.2.85), 55.1 (24.8.87), 53.3 by Malcolm Smith (9.5.87);
Lightwater Valley Theme Park, Fig 9.2;
Mid Glamorgan Business Team, Fig 33.2;
Mid Wales Development, *Mid Wales Data File*, pp12/13;
North Kent Enterprise Office, Fig 33.4;
The Observer, Figs 15.3 (22.4.84), 15.6 by Geoffrey Lean (19.4.87), 24.8 by Geoffrey Lean (21.4.85), 25.10 by Robin McKie (19.7.87), 26.2 by Robin McKie (3.3.85), 43.5 by Michael Dineen (11.10.88), 45.4 (15.2.87), 50.6 (31.5.87), 52.2 by Graham Smith, (30.7.87);
Ordnance Survey (Crown copyright), Fig 51.5;
Ordnance Survey of Northern Ireland (Crown copyright), Fig 18.2;
L.W.A. Rendell, Director of Planning and Transportation, Warwickshire County Council, Fig 12.3;
Rother Valley Country Park Joint Committee, Fig 12.2;
Dr R. A. Slaughter, material on futures (p180) from *Futures: Tools and Techniques.*

The authors and publishers wish to acknowledge the following photograph sources:

ACE Photo Agency, p2 (top), Figs 8.2, 8.5, 8.6, 20.1, pp94/95; /Beryl Bingel, 24.5, 41.3 (bottom right); /Paul Thompson, 38.1 (top), 46.4, 54.1;/Gabe Palmer, p2 (top); Paul Steel, 38.1 (left);/Graeme Stuart-Turner, 41.3 (top right);/Mike Goss, p179;
John Akehurst, Figs 42.1 (centre), 42.5 (photo 4);
J. Allen Cash, Figs 22.1, 53.2;
F. J. Aldridge, Figs 7.3, 7.7;
Ardea London Ltd/Trevor Marshall, Fig 19.4 (bottom);
Aviemore Photographic, Fig 10.2;
BBC Hulton Picture Library Fig 28.4 (bottom);
Barnaby's Picture Library/Ken Lambert Fig 44.5;
Birmingham Public Library, Fig 44.2 (left);
Janet and Colin Bord/Wales Scene, p6 (photo 2), Figs 2.2, 6.1, 8.1, 8.4;
Martin Bond, Fig 21.4;
Mark Boulton/ICCE, Fig 11.4;
British Airways, Fig 24.6;
British Coal, Fig 23.13 (top and bottom);
British Nuclear Fuels plc, Fig 25.7;
British Petroleum Fig 24.8;
Camera Press, p25 (bottom), p167;
Celtic Picture Agency/M. J. Thomas, cover (bottom left), Figs 3.1, 3.2;
Central Electricity Generating Board, Fig 27.1;
Martyn Chillmaid, Figs 5.2, 14.2, 14.4, 43.1, 43.3, 44.2 (right), 48.9, 49.1, 49.3, 49.4;
City Museum and Art Gallery, Stoke-on-Trent, Fig 31.5;
Chorey and Hendford, Fig 46.7;
John Cleare/Mountain Camera, Fig 7.8;

John Cornwell, p2 (bottom), Figs 23.10, 23.11;
Countryside Commission, Fig 13.8;
Daily Telegraph Colour Library, Fig 47.2;
Chris Davies/Network, Fig 25.2;
Eastleigh Town Council, Fig 45.6;
Mark Edwards/Panos, Fig 15.2;
C. D. Flint, p7 (photo 4), Fig 41.3 (top and bottom left);
Nance Fyson, Figs 2.3, 7.4, 7.5, 15.5, 38.1 (bottom right), 38.2, 38.4, 39.1, 40.4, 42.1 (bottom), 45.3, 46.4, 48.1;
Ford Motor Co Ltd, Fig 30.2;
Format Photographer, Fig 45.1 (top);
Bob Gibbons, Fig 17.5 (bottom right);
Sally and Richard Greenhill, cover (top left), Figs 4.1, 36.2, 42.1 (right), 42.4, 42.5 (photo 3), 45.1 (bottom), 47.7;
Greenpeace/Gleizes, Fig 25.6;
Robert Harding Picture Library, p3 (right, top right), p55 (top); Figs 27.2, 37.2;
Harving Photography Ltd, Fig 37.5;
Highlands and Islands Development Board, Fig 2.1;
Holt Studios Ltd, p 7 (photo 3), Fig 56.1 (top);
D. Horsfield/Nature Conservancy Council, Fig 10.3;
J and P Hubley, Fig 44.1;
Hunting Aerofilms, Fig 37.9;
David Jones, cover (middle right);
Kubiac and Grange Design Associates, Fig 34.2 (top and bottom);
Barry Lewis/Network, cover (bottom right), Fig 42.5 (photo 1);
Michael Manni Photographic, Fig 28.5 (centre, top and bottom right);
Martin Mayer/Network, p3 (centre);
Mercury Press Agency, Fig 55.1;
Mid Wales Development, Figs 3.7, 3.8, 3.9;
John Mills Photography, Figs 35.3, 35.6;
John Mowlem and Co, Fig 46.5;
Mulberry Housing Co-operative, Fig 43.6;
National Trust, Fig 39.3;
Nissan Sunderland, Fig 30.4;
Northern Picture Library, p3 (left), Fig 50.5 (left and right);
Bill O'Connor, p43;
Oxford Scientific Films, Figs 17.5 (top right), 53.1;
Peak Park Tourist Planning Board, Fig 11.2;
Peterborough Development Corporation, Fig 50.3;
Planet Earth Pictures, Fig 56.1 (centre);
QA Photos, p1;
C. M. Rolfe, 17.5 (top left), 31.2, 31.4;
Jackson Coultersay Ronnochman, Fig 16.2;
Rother Valley Country Park, Fig 12.1;
Skyscan Balloon Photos, p6 (photo 1), Fig 19.1;
Frank Spooner, Fig 25.5;
John Sturrock/Network, cover (middle left), p98 (bottom), Fig 42.5 (photo 2);
Topham Picture Library, Fig 56.1 (bottom);
Topix, p3 (bottom);
Tyne and Wear Passenger Transport Executive, Fig 47.8;
A. C. Waltham, Fig 13.9;
Simon Warner, pp4/5, Figs 7.6, 8.3, 13.4, 13.5, 14.3, 28.4 (top) p129;
Welsh Tourist Board, Fig 3.13;
Whinlater Visitors' Centre, Fig 17.2;
Derek D. Widdicombe, Figs 15.4, 28.4 (centre);
John Wildgoose/Observer, Fig 52.1;
Douglas Williamson, Fig 50.2;
Tom Willock, Fig 17.5 (bottom left);
Philip Wolmuth, Fig 38.1 (centre);
George Young, p100

© Corrin Flint and David Flint

First published in 1989 by Collins Educational
8, Grafton Street, London W1X 3LA

ISBN 0 00 326617 6

Designed by Geoffrey Wadsley and Malcolm Young
Cover design by Ted Bernstein
Illustrations by Ann Baum, Gay Galsworthy, Malcolm Porter and Peter Schrank

Typeset by Dorchester Typesetting Group Ltd
Printed in Italy by G. Canale C.S.p. A, Turin.

Contents

Preface

Few people who study the geography of Britain can fail to realise that it is a country of immense geographical variety. Within a relatively small total area, major differences in landscape, population distribution, land use, industrialisation, urban growth and culture are to be found, separated often by only a few kilometres. Different parts of the country are well known for their distinctive characteristics, many of which are vigorously defended and protected by local people at times of change.

British Issues in Geography is about the forces that are changing the geography of Britain. Many factors, some of which are on a large scale and are quickly and widely felt, combine to bring about geographical change. For instance, increasing mechanisation in farming has created readily visible changes in Britain's farmscape through the removal of hedgerows and woodlands. Another example is the impact of motorway development on the economic growth of different parts of the country. The development of 'hi-tech corridors' along some of our motorways, especially those in the south of England, is exerting a strong influence on employment and on patterns of regional wealth and prosperity. In fact, there are precious few aspects of Britain's geography today that are not changing in one way or another, and quite often at a pace that has rarely been witnessed before.

Geographical change is most noticeable when it affects the localities that we know well. But we probably hear and see more about the country's changing geography as a whole through the newspapers, radio and television. Much of this 'news' is presented to us in the form of a geographical or environmental issue, characterised by argument and debate, as different groups of people campaign for the solution that they prefer. Examples of current environmental issues are plentiful. They include where to dispose of nuclear waste, whether or not to build new towns in parts of rural England, where to locate the high-speed railway tracks between London and the Channel tunnel entrance in Kent, and so on.

British Issues in Geography helps students to explore the changing geography of Britain in the closing years of the twentieth century. Rarely do issues come and go, never to be heard of again. The majority rumble on, and what is a problem or a challenge or opportunity for one place today may well be in store for somewhere else tomorrow. However, it is important to recognise that we all take part, in one way or another, in altering the geography of Britain. In this book students will be introduced to some issues that require them to make up their minds on where they stand. They will learn something of the processes through which issues are handled and resolved — if not always to everyone's satisfaction. In the *Conclusion* they have the opportunity to consider the geography of Britain as it will affect their children halfway through the next century!

Clive Hart

Introduction

Building the Channel Tunnel at Folkestone, Kent. This picture was taken in 1988, and the Tunnel administration block on the cliff top is next to the Tunnel entrance site. The Tunnel's traffic capacity will be far greater than all Channel ports combined. What advantages and disadvantages could this development bring to the area?

'We're all in the same boat . . .'

Geographers study places and people. This book focuses on Britain and its people. However, Britain and its people are only a small part of the planet Earth; it is important to remember that what happens in other places can have significant effects on Britain. For example, in 1986 the spread of radioactive fallout from an explosion at Chernobyl nuclear power station in the USSR affected large areas of Britain and Europe.

There are other, less damaging links between Britain and the rest of the world. Many countries supply us with a whole range of goods, from luxury items such as cars and television sets to essentials such as food and clothing. In return, Britain sells its own goods and services to countries around the world. We live in an INTERDEPENDENT world; that is, we all depend on other places and other people, as the cartoon on this page illustrates.

© The Sunday Times, London/Peter Brooks

'All countries are troubled by rising unemployment. In the South, . . . the numbers for whom jobs have to be provided are much greater than in the North, and resources for investment much more modest . . .' *North-South: A Programme for Survival*, the Brandt Report, 1980

The changing face of industry. Coal mines like the one shown below provided mass employment in the Welsh valleys through the first half of this century. Today, the pithead winding gear lies idle, and in this valley, the Rhondda, the last out of the original 66 pits closed in 1986.

New jobs have been created in electronics, over the last ten years in particular. However, these industries employ fewer people, and require particular skills

Within this pattern of interdependence geographers are looking much more closely at how we use the earth's RESOURCES, particularly those within the British Isles. From the nineteenth century onwards factories, power stations and shipyards were built over much of Britain, and little thought was given to their effects on either the ENVIRONMENT or its people. It was only later that problems such as health hazards, air pollution, loss of valuable farmland, and mass local unemployment became apparent.

We have slowly come to realise the importance of looking after the Earth's resources (of which people are an essential element) to ensure we make the best use of them. Geographers are vital to this process; they ask key questions such as, Where is the resource? How extensive is it? Who owns it? Do we really need it? What are the likely effects of developing it? Who will decide about development? How will they reach these decisions?

What makes an issue?

In general, issues arise when people fail to agree on how resources should be developed. Geographers often help to identify and clarify such issues in the early stages. Issues may be local, such as the effects of a new hypermarket on surrounding shopping centres, they may be national – the effects of unemployment for example – or even international, such as the responsibility for acid rain, and its effects elsewhere.

Pollution caused by industrial waste in Britain takes effect elsewhere and meets with protest at home. Pressure has also been applied through the EEC to get Britain to 'clean up'. Why do you think this is important?

A change in land use. Once the Albert Docks in Liverpool bustled with the arrival and departure of cargo ships laden with sugar, timber and wool. As this trade tailed off in the 1960s, the area gradually became derelict (*above*). During the 1980s it was redeveloped to provide a new shopping, residential and business centre (*below*). What changes do you think a local resident may have experienced as a result?

The issues covered in this book are important, both in their own right, and because they are typical of many other similar cases. Behind each issue are people's decisions about which resources will be developed, and for whose benefit. For this reason it is important to understand how individuals and groups make such decisions, and what factors influence the decision-making process. Throughout this book you will have the opportunity to examine the geographical effects of people's different beliefs, values and attitudes. It is important to think carefully about *your own* views on each issue too. Which group do *you* agree with? Is your agreement based on evidence and logical thoughts or on emotion? Do you make up your own mind on issues? How much are you influenced by other students, or by television programmes and newspaper articles? You also need to be able to see other people's points of view, even if you disagree with them.

Although this book will introduce you to a number of important British geographical issues, there will be many others, often particular to your own area, which you will be equipped to study and evaluate using the methods applied here. These will be your own British Geographical Issues.

Managing rural environments

Rural deprivation

Leisure and the countryside

Buttercup meadow and oak trees, Yorkshire Dales. Areas of fallow land like this are fast disappearing from Britain's landscape. What do you think are the major threats? What are the possible results for plants and wildlife?

1   What makes a rural area?

Everyone has their own image of RURAL areas or 'the countryside'. Often this mental picture shows a thatched, stone cottage, against a background of small fields, hedges and narrow lanes. In fact it is difficult to define rural areas because they vary so greatly. Look at photographs 1-4 here, which illustrate four different rural areas.

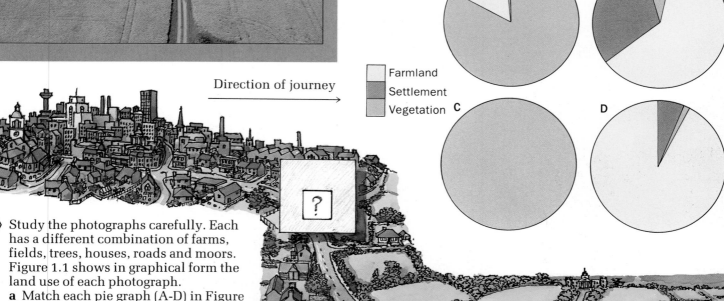

Direction of journey →

FIGURE 1.1
Land use

A   B

Farmland
Settlement
Vegetation   C   D

1 Study the photographs carefully. Each has a different combination of farms, fields, trees, houses, roads and moors. Figure 1.1 shows in graphical form the land use of each photograph.
  a Match each pie graph (A-D) in Figure 1.1 with its corresponding photograph and justify your decisions.
  b Now arrange all the photographs (1-4) in a sequence to show the changes you would see on a journey from the edge of an urban area into a region of wild moorland, as shown here.

It is important to remember that there is no clear, sharp line dividing rural areas from town and cities. Rather, there is a gradual change away from houses and factories towards farms and fields. However, most rural areas do have features in common such as these:

- Fewer people than towns and cities.
- Few factories, roads and houses.
- Most land is farmed or left as forest or moor.
- Often many streams, rivers or lakes.

Some rural areas have other features, for example:

- A lot of old or retired people.
- A higher proportion of people working in farming or forestry.
- People leaving the area to live in towns and cities.

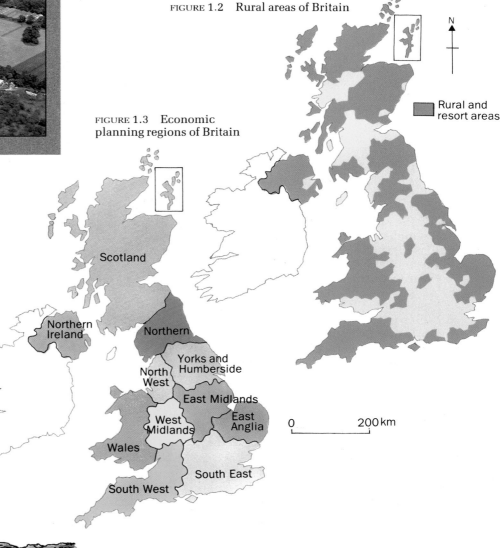

FIGURE 1.2 Rural areas of Britain

Rural and resort areas

FIGURE 1.3 Economic planning regions of Britain

0   200 km

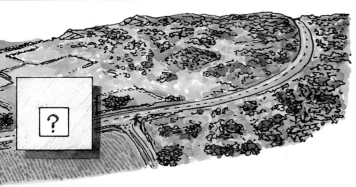

2. Study Figures 1.2 and 1.3 together with a regional atlas map. Use them to describe the distribution of rural areas within each of the economic planning regions. The following points will help you:

- How much (percentage) of each region can be classified as rural?
- Where are the main rural areas within each region? (mainly in the north-west/south-east, etc.)
- Name the major towns, cities and rivers, close to the rural area.

Conflict and control in rural areas

Rural areas have many RESOURCES, that is, things people find useful. Grass becomes a resource when farmers use it to feed their animals. There are many different resources in rural areas, such as soil, weather, rocks, plants, animals and scenery. The problem is that the resources are in limited supply. Yet there are many different groups of people who all want to make use of them. For example, bird watchers may want to keep an area of open moorland in its present wild state. However, the Forestry Commission may want to plant trees on that same moorland. This would dramatically change the numbers and types of birds to be seen. These two groups may therefore disagree on how best to use the moorland resource.

In order to resolve such conflicts, rural resources have to be carefully *managed*, to try and balance the demands of different groups. The problem is how to preserve the beauty of the scenery and the wildlife and still allow people to earn a living from such activities as farming, quarrying or forestry.

 Study the picture on this page (Figure 1.4) which shows some of the competing claims for rural resources.
  a Do you agree that all the 'needs' in Figure 1.4 are *essential* while the 'desires' are *optional*? Answer for each claim in turn.
  b Which of the claims might compete most strongly in the following rural areas? Make a copy of the table below and complete it with your choices and reasons.
  c Compare and discuss your answers.

FIGURE 1.4   Competing claims on the countryside

Rural area	Competing claims	Reasons
A. Fertile river valley, 30km from major town		
B. Agricultural land bordering on small village (pop. 150) situated halfway between major port and growing new town		
C. Limestone area, rich in rare wildlife		
D. Open heath, undeveloped, unpopulated, nearest town 80km		

2 Leaving the countryside

In 1951 there were 10.4 million people living in rural Britain. By 1971 this figure was 12.8 million, by 1981 it was 14 million and by 1987 it was 15 million. It seems as if more and more people are living in rural areas. However these are only average figures, they conceal large differences between places. In some areas, such as the remote islands of Shetland, people have been leaving the cottages and villages for over a hundred years and this RURAL DEPOPULATION continues today. In other areas, such as parts of Cornwall and Devon, the population is increasing with the SETTLEMENT of retired people from other parts of the country. In parts of East Anglia and the West Midlands, the population is also increasing as COMMUTERS move into the countryside. These are families who choose to live in the villages and who often have long journeys commuting to and from work and school.

FIGURE 2.1   Loch Broom in the Scottish Highlands. Remote, hard-to-farm areas such as these have sometimes lost entire populations

Why do people leave the countryside?

North-west Scotland is an area which until recently suffered severe population decline as the graph on this page (Figure 2.2) illustrates. The traditional ways of earning a living were by farming, fishing or by producing tweed cloth or whisky.

Farming has always been difficult here because of the large areas of steep slopes, high mountains and thin soils. Worse, some areas receive over 1 500mm rainfall each year. This high, mostly wet, area has always been remote from the main centres of British population, so farmers concentrated on rearing sheep and growing a little oats and barley.

The traditional farms, or crofts as they are called, used to cover a much larger part of the Highlands and employed more people. During the nineteenth century the large landowners drove many of these crofters away from the land because they wanted to create large open pastures for big herds of sheep. As a result of these Highland clearances many people left the area altogether and were forced to look for work in the towns of southern Scotland, England or to emigrate to other countries, such as Canada.

Figure 2.3 gives some of the other reasons why people have left the Highlands since. The movement of people from one area to another is called MIGRATION. This migration is generally a combination of PUSH factors which drive people away (such as the lack of jobs) and PULL factors (such as better services) which attract them to other areas. Study the model (Figure 2.4) of this migration process shown here. You will notice that there are more negative ('push') forces in the rural area and more positive ('pull') forces in the urban area, which reflect the reasons given by the Highland people themselves.

FIGURE 2.2   Population change in the Highlands and Islands of Scotland

500 000 —
400 000 —
300 000 —
200 000 —
100 000 —

1851   1861   1871   1891   1911   1931   1951   1971   1991

1. Use the information you have studied in this unit so far to produce a list of 'push' and of 'pull' factors operating in the Highlands.

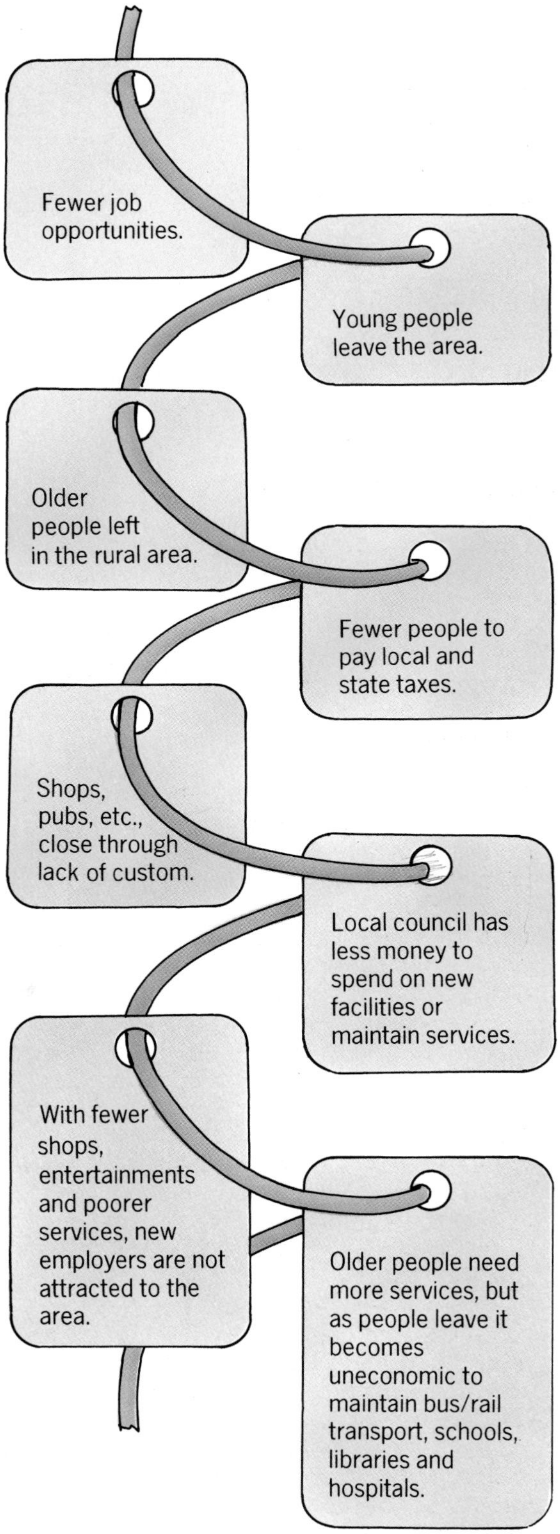
Fewer job opportunities.
Young people leave the area.
Older people left in the rural area.
Fewer people to pay local and state taxes.
Shops, pubs, etc., close through lack of custom.
Local council has less money to spend on new facilities or maintain services.
With fewer shops, entertainments and poorer services, new employers are not attracted to the area.
Older people need more services, but as people leave it becomes uneconomic to maintain bus/rail transport, schools, libraries and hospitals.

FIGURE 2.5 The downward spiral of migration

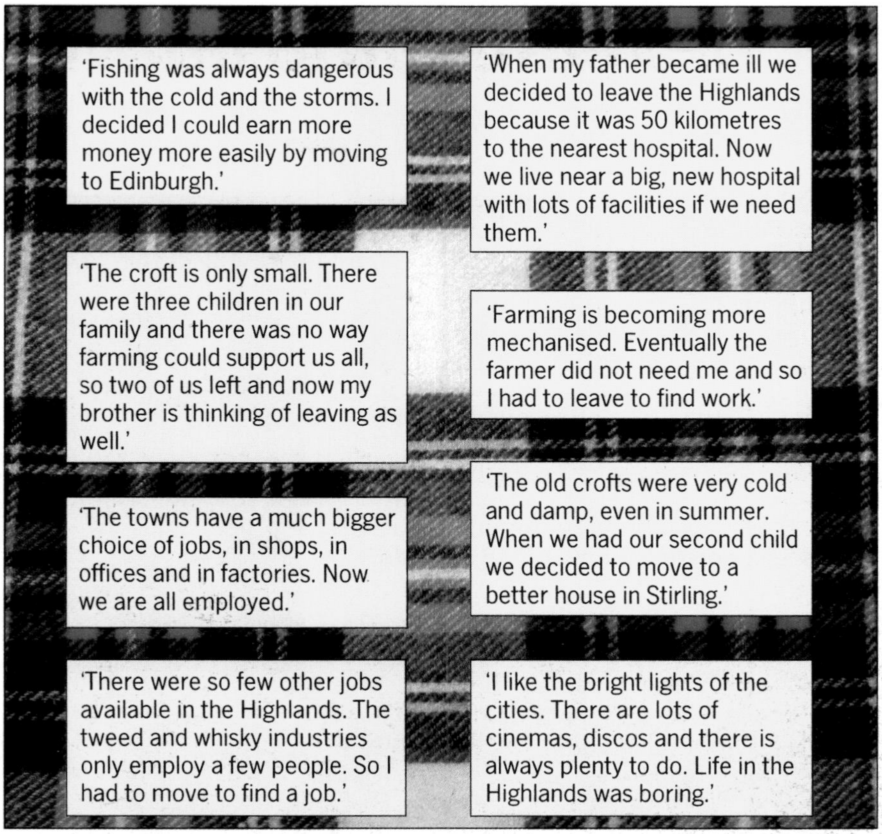
'Fishing was always dangerous with the cold and the storms. I decided I could earn more money more easily by moving to Edinburgh.'
'When my father became ill we decided to leave the Highlands because it was 50 kilometres to the nearest hospital. Now we live near a big, new hospital with lots of facilities if we need them.'
'The croft is only small. There were three children in our family and there was no way farming could support us all, so two of us left and now my brother is thinking of leaving as well.'
'Farming is becoming more mechanised. Eventually the farmer did not need me and so I had to leave to find work.'
'The towns have a much bigger choice of jobs, in shops, in offices and in factories. Now we are all employed.'
'The old crofts were very cold and damp, even in summer. When we had our second child we decided to move to a better house in Stirling.'
'There were so few other jobs available in the Highlands. The tweed and whisky industries only employ a few people. So I had to move to find a job.'
'I like the bright lights of the cities. There are lots of cinemas, discos and there is always plenty to do. Life in the Highlands was boring.'

FIGURE 2.3 Leaving the Highlands: what the people think

FIGURE 2.4 Model of Highland migration

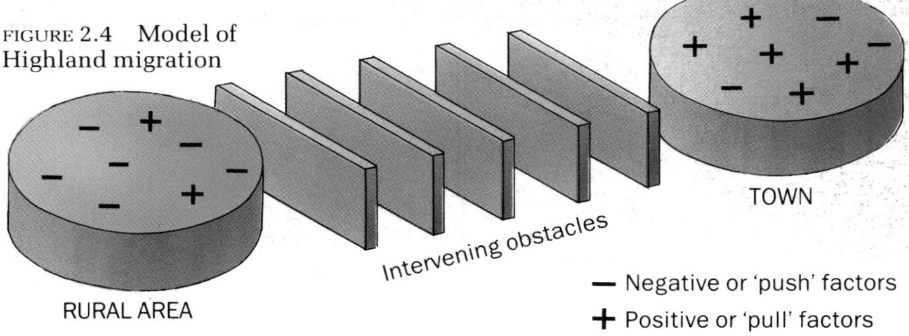
RURAL AREA
Intervening obstacles
TOWN
— Negative or 'push' factors
+ Positive or 'pull' factors

2. Migration is never simple, and Figure 2.4 above indicates 'intervening obstacles' between the rural and the urban area. List as many of these obstacles as you can. They could include the problem of selling a house or croft, and the high costs of housing in the city.

3. Put forward the arguments you might have used to persuade each of the people in Figure 2.3 to stay in the Highlands.

Once people start to leave an area permanently, a downward spiral starts. As more people leave, so there are fewer customers for shops and services which often close. This means there may be fewer jobs and fewer entertainments so even more people are encouraged to leave. This process is shown in Figure 2.5.

4. Study Figure 2.5, then suggest as many ways as possible in which this downward spiral could be reversed. For example, the government could subsidise bus services to retain links with the outside world. Or new roads could be built to try and attract new firms to the area. What could local people do to help themselves? (They might run their own minibus service, for example.)

3 Reversing the outflow

Rural Mid Wales: the problem

From 1901 to 1971, 42 000 people left Mid Wales. They left because farming was difficult and becoming more mechanised, so it employed fewer people. Also there were few other job opportunities. In the past, slate was mined at Blaenau Ffestiniog and limestone in the Brecon Beacons, but this had largely ceased by 1971. Other local industries such as wool manufacture, forestry and brewing, employ few people today. Hydro-electric stations in the area and the nuclear power station at Trawsfynydd also require few workers.

The strategy

In 1976 the government set up the Development Board for Rural Wales to try to halt the population decline. The Board now operates under the name *Mid Wales Development*.

 Look at the data file on Mid Wales shown here. You have been asked to write a report on the area by a foreign company that is thinking of building a factory in Mid Wales. Your report, based on the information in the data file, should consist of the following sections:
   a Introduction to Mid Wales, including its size (area and dimensions), the percentage of Wales it covers, and its general characteristics of weather and scenery.
   b Communications with the rest of the UK – including main motorways and journey times to London, Manchester, and Birmingham.
   c Population changes in the area this century, especially since 1971, and overall population structure compared to the rest of the UK.
   d Traditional occupations and characteristics of the workforce.
   e Factories provided by Mid Wales Development since 1977, and the advantages claimed by other firms who have located in the area.
   f Other incentives offered.
   g General conclusions as to the advantages and disadvantages of locating a factory in Mid Wales.

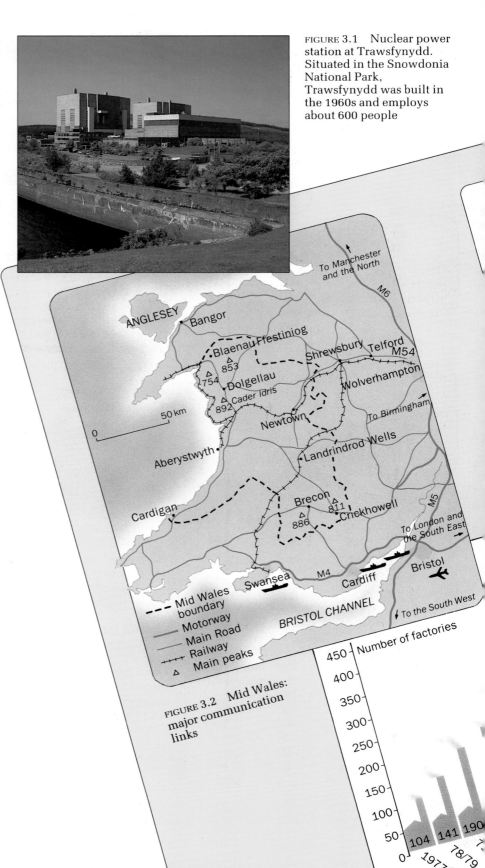

FIGURE 3.1 Nuclear power station at Trawsfynydd. Situated in the Snowdonia National Park, Trawsfynydd was built in the 1960s and employs about 600 people

FIGURE 3.2 Mid Wales: major communication links

Mid-Wales Data File

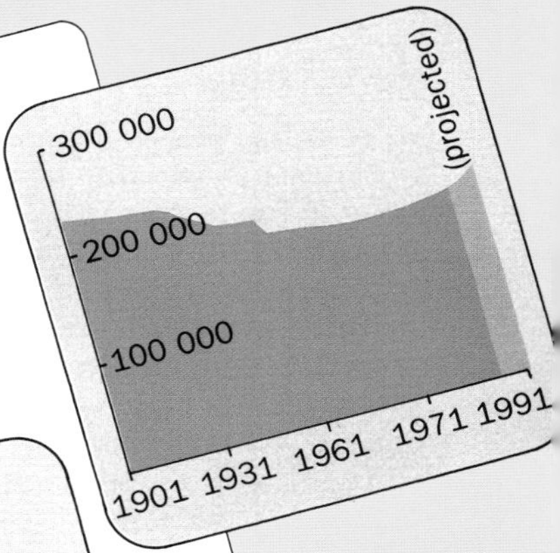

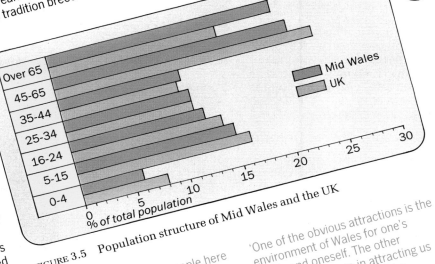

...d Wales can boast some of the ...est, most spectacular mountain ...cenery in Britain ... much of it ...designated National Park or areas of ...outstanding natural beauty.

Aberystwyth, for example, gets less rainfall on average in a year than Falmouth in Cornwall ... fewer foggy days than Croydon in Surrey ... as many sunny days as Great Yarmouth in Norfolk ... average annual temperatures on a par with such sun-spots as Brighton in Sussex.

Thanks to its direct traffic-free trunk roads and fast motorway links, transport problems shrink. In reality, Mid Wales is no further than three hours from London's M25, one hour from Birmingham and two from Manchester. Average journey times are a third less than in the crowded conurbations you're used to.

By rail the story is the same. Express services direct to London and Birmingham will speed you in comfort to urgent meetings and back.

Mid Wales has been a sheep-farming region for generations, so many of the workforce come from communities that are traditionally sheep-rearing or cloth-making. This tradition breeds reliable, responsible and resourceful individuals. Positive, enthusiastic, well-motivated people, with precisely the attitudes and skills you need to be successful today.

FIGURE 3.5 Population structure of Mid Wales and the UK

'We have found that the people here have adapted very readily to high technology.

We have the M54 ... and that links up to all the major motorways ... no problem.

We now have three units and we have tailor-made them to suit ourselves with again a lot of support from Mid Wales Development.'
GEOFF HAINES – KTK (Newtown) Ltd. Part of Control Techniques PLC Group.

'There's a karate club, a squash club, the swimming baths, all the amenities are here and just one set of traffic lights.

... The standard of education is superb, very good ... my little girl was twelve months ahead of the children in Blackpool in the classes.'
KEVIN SALTER – Powys Printers Ltd.

'One of the obvious attractions is the environment of Wales for one's family and oneself. The other obvious advantage in attracting us here is the low rents and the purpose-built factories and all the other facilities we require to run our business.'
JOHN MALLON – Brook Thompson Ltd.

'When we moved up here it was a vast improvement ... the whole attitude of the people round here, collection and delivery, they'll put themselves out ... I for one would not move back to London for all the tea in China.'
DAVID MARGETTS – Conblock Electrical Ltd. Manufacturers of electrical components for industrial and domestic use.

FIGURE 3.3 Factories provided by Mid Wales Development, 1977-86 (includes those sold to tenants)

5   303   339   371   471

31/82   82/83   83/84   84/85   85/86

Mid Wales Development (MWD)

MWD has tried to reverse the loss of population in the following three ways:

Developing industry

MWD offers grants, loans, ready-built factories and freedom from rent for between five and ten years to attract new firms. There are also training schemes for the workforce and, between 1977 and 1984, 275 new factories were built creating 2000 new jobs. Growth is concentrated in nine Growth Areas, ten Special Towns and eight Key Towns (see Figure 3.6). The new industries include clothing, packaging, food, drink and electronics. Most factories are small but, in 1985, 102 new firms created 2000 jobs. The result can be seen in the POPULATION TURNAROUND of Mid Wales. It has now become an area of population *increase*, with a projected total of 194 000 for 1991, compared with 184 000 in 1931: 2000 new jobs must be created each year to achieve this population target.

Building facilities for the community

MWD recognises the need to create an attractive quality of life for people as well as to provide jobs. Village halls and community centres receive grants for improvement and development as do theatres at Aberystwyth, Harlech and Newtown. New sports centres, often built alongside secondary schools, are providing more facilities for leisure and recreation. Typically, the 3000th social grant from Mid Wales Development was to a project to improve TV reception in part of this mountainous region.

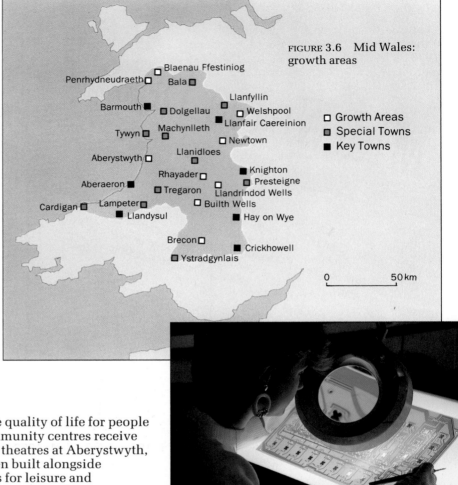

FIGURE 3.6   Mid Wales: growth areas

□ Growth Areas
▨ Special Towns
■ Key Towns

0   50 km

FIGURE 3.7   Checking circuit boards at an electronics company in Ystradgynlais

FIGURE 3.8   Sports hall, Bro Dysynni, Tywyn

FIGURE 3.9 Community hall at Merthyr Cynog

Encouraging tourism

Figure 3.10 shows that the number of tourists to Mid Wales has fluctuated since 1978 but now seems to be increasing. Attractions such as the Ffestiniog railway, spa towns like Llandrindod Wells, historic towns such as Hay-on-Wye all draw in visitors. However MWD's plans require tourism to create 600 new jobs each year and so support is given to projects such as the development of Aberystwyth harbour, and the marketing of 'Welsh Gold Hotels' in the USA. The canals, the railways, the mountains and the coast remain important tourist attractions.

FIGURE 3.10   Tourism in Mid Wales: visitors to the top 20 attractions

FIGURE 3.12

FIGURE 3.11   Ffestiniog Railway. Originally built to carry slate from Blaenau Ffestiniog quarries to Porthmadog for export. The steam railway and its scenic route are now a major tourist attraction in the area

FIGURE 3.13   The slate crags of Blaenau Ffestiniog dominate the town

BLAENAU FFESTINIOG: TOURISM PROFILE

The drawbacks

• Not enough tourist accommodation
• Few recreational facilities
• Lack of entertainment centres

The potential

• Attractions in local area:
   Ffestiniog Railway
   Slate mines and caverns
   Trawsfynydd power station
   Beautiful lakes and mountain scenery
• 330 000 visitors to local area each year

Local employment

Tourism 10%
Slate industry 4%
Unemployment 13%

 Study the tourism profile of Blaenau Ffestiniog in Figure 3.12. Imagine you are submitting a project for Blaenau's Enterprise Scheme to attract more tourists to the town. If your project is accepted, MWD will provide a grant to help finance it, so make sure you (i) describe your project carefully and (ii) list the benefits you think it will bring to the town.

4   *The newcomers issue*

When people are at work they usually choose to live quite close to their place of employment. However when they retire they can move wherever they like. At present 10 per cent of people in Britain move when they retire, and the numbers are increasing every year.

The map on this page (Figure 4.2) shows the places people in a recent survey chose for their retirement. Generally people are attracted to areas which they think have a pleasant climate, and offer a high QUALITY OF LIFE. They often look for unspoilt rural areas with few large urban or industrial settlements.

Use an atlas and Figure 4.2 to answer the questions which follow.

1. Name the four counties which receive the largest number of retired people from Greater London.

2. Name the county and three towns in the area chosen by retired people from Nottingham and Leicester.

3. Where do most people from Greater Manchester choose for their retirement? Is the pattern the same in West Yorkshire?

Retired people moving into a rural area do not always mix with the local people. Sometimes they form separate groups. Retired people also create a demand for services for the elderly such as special transport. They can also put a strain on the local health service because many more people will need treatment.

Most retired people buy a house or flat in the new area. This may cause house prices to rise beyond the price that locals can afford (see also Unit 5 on the effect of commuters). Often the retired newcomers find difficulty in getting gardeners or cleaners to work for them because many young people have been forced to leave by high house prices.

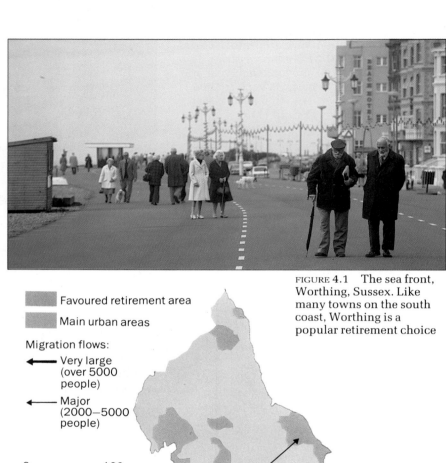

FIGURE 4.1   The sea front, Worthing, Sussex. Like many towns on the south coast, Worthing is a popular retirement choice

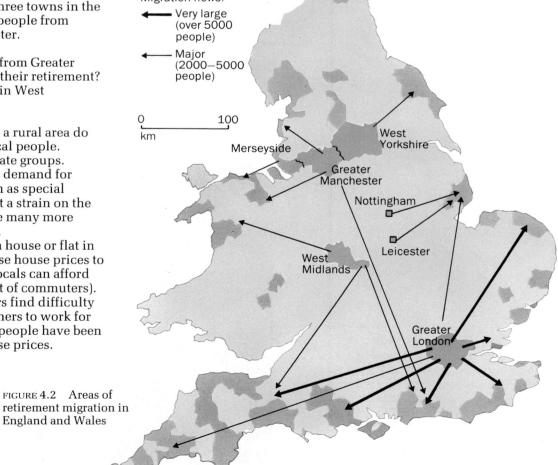

FIGURE 4.2   Areas of retirement migration in England and Wales

The picture below (Figure 4.3) shows what two couples think about their retirement to North Yorkshire. As you can see, their views are very different.

 4 What advice would you give to an elderly couple from Halifax thinking of retiring to North Yorkshire? In particular point out both the advantages and disadvantages of living in North Yorkshire. Use the evidence to help you.

 5 How do you think the following local people would feel about increasing numbers of retired people moving in to an area like North Yorkshire:

a A young couple, who want to buy or rent a small house?
b A builder, specialising in bungalows and flats?
c The owner of a mobile disco which is not doing well?
d A coach tour operator?
e A doctor?
f A couple thinking of opening a private nursing home?

 6 What research about an area should people complete before they make a retirement move? For example, find nearest hospital, nearest doctor's surgery, closest shop, frequency of bus and/or train services, etc.

FIGURE 4.3   Retirement to North Yorkshire

The Walkers

The Pages

5 Town into countryside?

Commuter villages

Many villages in rural areas near large towns and CONURBATIONS are growing rapidly as newcomers move in. These commuter villages are usually close to a main road (often a motorway) or railway linking them to the nearby cities. Many commuters spend up to four hours each day travelling to and from work, although the average journey time is about two hours.

People think that living in the countryside is healthier and house prices are cheaper, so they put up with long

journeys. During the 1980s more and more people were attracted to commuter villages by the idea of unpolluted air, rural peace and quiet, and the slower pace of country life. The effect of these new arrivals on traditional villages has been considerable. The two pictures here (Figure 5.1) show the changes in one typical village between the 1930s and the present.

1 Study Figure 5.1, then list all the changes you can identify in the village between the 1930s and the present. Suggest reasons for these changes.

FIGURE 5.1   Then and now

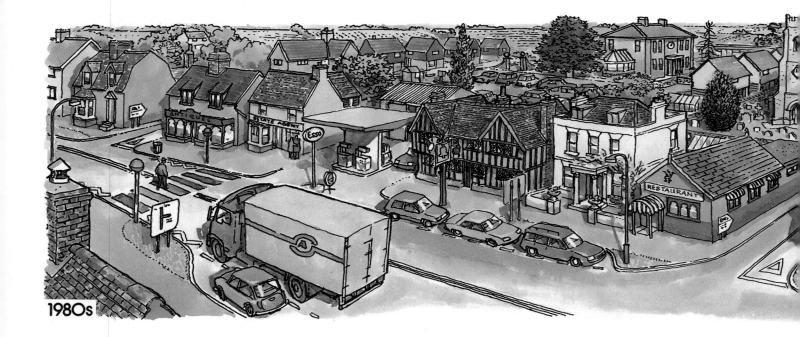

Figure 5.1 shows the physical changes which have taken place in a commuter village. There are also important economic and social changes which result from an influx of commuters. Belbroughton (Figure 5.2) is a commuter village 17 kilometres west of Birmingham. One pensioner describes the social and economic changes she has seen there since the 1930s.

 Using the pensioner's account, add to your list from question 1 to include more social and economic changes. Which groups have become more important in the village, and which less important? Which groups have become richer and which poorer? Why?

FIGURE 5.2 (*Above*) Belbroughton High Street. (*Below*) An older resident remembers

I can remember when nearly all the people who lived in the village also worked here. We had a blacksmith as well as a carpenter, a butcher, a baker, a saddle maker, a doctor and an innkeeper. Some of the houses in the village were working farms and we used to see the horses and cattle going up and down the road. The doctor, the vicar and the squire were the important local people. We often used to go and ask their advice.

Everyone knew everyone else in the village, and many families had ancestors who were buried in the churchyard. We did not go to Birmingham very often as there was no bus service and we did not have a car. Besides we could get virtually everything we needed at the shops in the village. Shopping was a chance to meet and talk as well as a means of getting provisions. If someone was in trouble all the village would try and help out.

But all that has changed now. The new people began to arrive in the 1960s. At first there were not many of them so it did not cause a problem. Later, local farmers made a lot of money by selling their land for the new housing estates. Now I don't know most of the people I see in the village. The newcomers don't mix much with us older residents. They usually have one or even two cars and they do their shopping in hypermarkets out of the village.

We have better roads now, but on a morning lots of people leave early for work and then the village is very quiet until they return about 6 p.m. Most of the old crafts like the saddlemaking, baking and carpentry have died out. A lot of the newcomers own horses but they are shod by a travelling blacksmith so even that trade has gone. Today it is the bankers, estate agents and financial people who are the important locals, but they may charge for advice. We do have new shops and even a restaurant but their prices are too high for us.

FIGURE 5.3   (*Above*) Belbroughton: a commuter village in the West Midlands

FIGURE 5.4   (*Below*) Model of commuter village development

The map opposite (Figure 5.3) shows Belbroughton as it is now. Study it and then compare it with the model below (Figure 5.4) which explains how commuter villages develop over time. This model is based on what happened in many villages in southern England.

3 Study the information in Figure 5.2 on the previous page. Use it to describe three ways in which Belbroughton follows a similar pattern to that shown in the model. In what ways does Belbroughton *differ* from the model?

4 The data opposite was collected in a recent survey of Belbroughton. Use it for the following:
   a Draw a pie graph of the main reasons given for moving to Belbroughton.
   b On an outline map of the standard regions of Britain, draw circles of different sizes, proportional to the numbers of people who have moved to Belbroughton.
   c Draw a bar graph of where people in Belbroughton work.

5 Now carry out a survey of a commuter village you know. In what ways is it similar to Belbroughton? In what ways is it different? Use the data on Belbroughton to guide you in your survey and comparison.

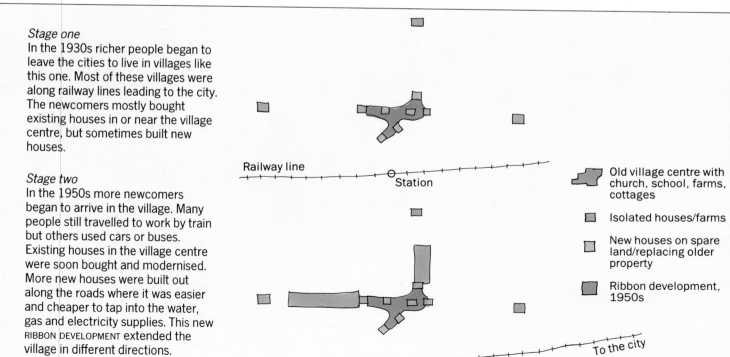

Stage one
In the 1930s richer people began to leave the cities to live in villages like this one. Most of these villages were along railway lines leading to the city. The newcomers mostly bought existing houses in or near the village centre, but sometimes built new houses.

Stage two
In the 1950s more newcomers began to arrive in the village. Many people still travelled to work by train but others used cars or buses. Existing houses in the village centre were soon bought and modernised. More new houses were built out along the roads where it was easier and cheaper to tap into the water, gas and electricity supplies. This new RIBBON DEVELOPMENT extended the village in different directions.

Railway line   Station

To the city   Station

Old village centre with church, school, farms, cottages

Isolated houses/farms

New houses on spare land/replacing older property

Ribbon development, 1950s

BELBROUGHTON SURVEY

A 38% of people said they moved to Belbroughton for cleaner air and more open space.

32% of people said they moved to Belbroughton to a better house.

20% of people said they moved to Belbroughton as a result of a change of job.

10% of people said they moved to Belbroughton for its other advantages such as peace and quiet.

B Seventy per cent of people who had moved to the village in the past ten years came from the West Midlands; 10% came from the London area, 5% from Yorkshire or Northumberland, 1% from Scotland and the remainder from Cumbria and north-west England.

C 60% of heads of households worked in Birmingham.
30% of heads of households worked elsewhere in the West Midlands.
5% of heads of households worked in Kidderminster.
5% of heads of households were retired.

D 95% of families did some shopping in the village.
80% of families did their main food shopping away from Belbroughton.
70% of families had bank accounts in Birmingham.
30% of families had bank accounts in other local towns.

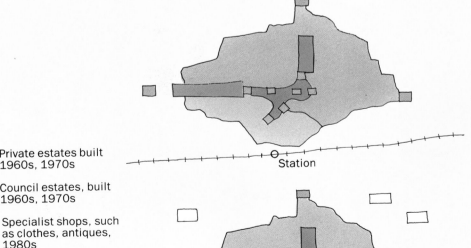

Private estates built 1960s, 1970s

Council estates, built 1960s, 1970s

■ Specialist shops, such as clothes, antiques, 1980s

R Restaurant, 1980s

S Leisure site, such as riding centre, 1980s

Large new houses, 1980s

Station

Stage three
The villages became more compact between 1960 and 1980. Houses were built on open space in the village to provide new, planned estates. Some were estates of council houses, others were private developments. Parts of the old village centre were demolished to make way for new shops or big new houses.

Stage four
In the late 1980s small craft workshops opened on the edge of the village. Leisure sites such as riding stables were opened towards the village outskirts, whilst in the centre antique shops, clothes shops and specialist restaurants opened. Fewer estates were built, but large new houses were built away from the village.

6   Second homes: winners and losers

Second-homes claim proved false

Sir – As a Welshman, and the owner of a second home in Gwynedd, I am not against Plaid Cymru wanting home rule for Wales, or the efforts of the Welsh Language Society to get my language more widely spoken and used in Wales. But for the life of me, I cannot see how their campaign against second homes can do anything but damage their image and put the clock back . . .

Surely the great problem for Plaid Cymru is the grave unemployment in Wales. The campaign against second homes only aggravates that. Fire sends terror into people's hearts, and this is to be seen by the marked reduction in the numbers of tourists in Wales. Apart from the large amount of money that second-home owners paid to local contractors, who in turn paid their workers, they are still pouring large sums of money into the coffers of local councils every year as well as paying locals to maintain them . . . I cannot see local councillors responsible to the rate-payers doing anything that will chase second-home owners out of Gwynedd to leave their properties to become once again unoccupied and paying no rates.

L. Jones, Birkenhead

FIGURE 6.1   Letter to the *Liverpool Daily Post* (Welsh Edition), 23.12.1981

FIGURE 6.2   Second homes: what the people think

Many townspeople have bought a house or flat in the countryside as a second home. They use this second home on weekends and at holiday times to get away from the stresses of living in town.

Seventy per cent of second homes in England and Wales are at or near the coast. The other 30 per cent are in attractive inland rural areas. In addition most second homes have to be within easy reach if their owners are to keep journeys as short as possible. So second home areas like North Wales are close to conurbations such as Manchester and Merseyside. They are also often linked by motorways such as the M56.

The number of second homes in Britain has increased dramatically as the table on page 23 shows. There are 33 000 second homes in Wales alone. This represents 3 per cent of *all* Welsh houses. However, the second homes are not spread evenly across Wales, but concentrated in the north and west. In Gwynedd one in every seven houses is a second home. The situation is even more acute in particular villages, such as Rhyd, which is on the edge of the Snowdonia National Park. Here, 14 out of 20 houses are second homes.

What are the effects?

 Figure 6.2 shows a variety of views held by some people about second homes. Use this to draw up a list of advantages and disadvantages of second homes.

 The newspaper extract on this page (Figure 6.1) shows a letter in support of second homes written to a local newspaper. Write a letter to a newspaper complaining about second homes as if you were one of the following people:
a   A village school teacher whose classes were becoming smaller as locals left and their houses were bought for second homes.
b   A bus driver, made redundant when services were cut in the area. Most second home owners use their cars.
c   A farmer with many footpaths across her land whose animals suffer in summer by eating abandoned plastic bags or standing on broken bottles, or being chased by uncontrolled dogs.

We want to start a family but cannot afford a house or a flat in the village. Prices of property have gone sky high since the newcomers arrived.

I have been able to open a chain of small restaurants in these villages because many second-home owners like to eat out.

My garage does good business from the newcomers between Easter and October.

3 Use the data in the table below (Figure 6.3) to draw a line graph of the rising number of second homes in England and Wales.

FIGURE 6.3 Second Homes in England and Wales.			
1955	50 000	1975	250 000
1960	72 000	1980	310 000
1965	98 000	1987	370 000
1970	160 000		

a When did second home numbers increase most rapidly?

b If present trends continue how many second homes will there be by the year 2000?

The following factors suggest that the number of second homes in Britain will rise:

- More and more people are able to afford a second home.
- People generally have more leisure time.
- The motorway network continues to make new areas accessible such as places near the M25 motorway.

 4 What other factors might lead to an increase in second homes?

Coping with the demand

Some countries, such as the Netherlands, build special chalets for use as second homes. This avoids the problems of driving up house prices, and of depriving local people of housing. Other solutions seem to have more problems. Developers might agree to build basic low-cost housing for locals but these could still be bought by outsiders, as second homes. In Wales and the Lake District, the Planning Boards have tried to reserve some new houses solely for local people. The government has stopped this practice.

The National Agricultural Centre Rural Trust (NACRT) is a charity which sets up housing associations to provide houses for locals. These associations can provide a few houses, but they still need to buy land very cheaply to keep costs down. This can lead to conflict when commercial developers are bidding for land in the same village.

The introduction of the Local Community Charge (or Poll Tax as it is sometimes called) makes things more difficult. The tax is based on the number of people *permanently* living in an area. Many villages with second homes will therefore have even less income to spend on services.

 5 Should people who own cottages or property in villages be free to sell to anyone, including outsiders?

The council gets rates from these second homes. In the past many of these houses were empty, so we received no rates.

Some second homes look terrible. They have been renovated but they do not blend in with the rest of the houses in the village.

I have been able to sell my grandfather's cottage for a good price so I am glad people want second homes.

It is nice to meet people from towns in other parts of the country. It broadens our outlook.

Our water supply, electricity and sewage systems were designed for a village of 800 people. It is OK in winter when we have only 250, but in summer it can be 1500! The systems just will not cope.

I have been able to find part-time work as a gardener and my sister is a cleaner. If there were no second homes we would probably be unemployed.

With so many newcomers the paths are being worn away, and people drop litter all over the area.

Second-home owners do not mix much with the local people. They are only concerned with material possessions like boats and cars. This seems very strange as we think people are more important than possessions.

7   *Providing services*

The problems

Even in rural areas which are not losing population, providing services such as public transport, shopping, education and health care can be difficult.

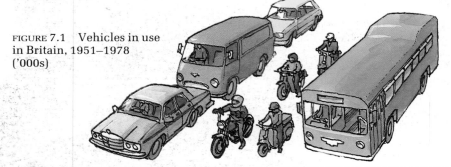

FIGURE 7.1   Vehicles in use in Britain, 1951–1978 ('000s)

Year	Private cars and private vans	Motor cycles, scooters and mopeds	Public transport vehicles
1951	2380	823	136
1956	3888	1290	99
1961	5979	1790	91
1966	9513	1406	94
1971	12062	1021	106
1976	14047	1220	113
1982	15642	1370	111
1987	16789	1520	103

FIGURE 7.2   Methods of transport used in South Oxfordshire

	10–24 yrs	25–60 yrs	Over 60	Total
Method (%)				
Walk	23.2	13.0	30.1	16.9
Car driver	20.5	59.5	44.7	50.7
Car passenger	28.2	18.2	18.1	19.9
Public transport	13.7	5.2	3.6	6.4
Other	14.4	4.1	3.5	6.1
Purpose (%)				
Home	41.5	41.1	46.6	42.0
Work	11.9	18.6	4.4	15.4
Employer's business	3.0	6.1	1.8	5.0
Personal business	6.4	5.1	12.2	6.2
Entertainment/sport	4.3	2.8	4.4	3.5
Social	17.7	10.5	12.3	12.0
Shopping	7.3	10.3	16.3	10.5
Education	6.1	0.2		1.2
Medical	0.3	0.7	1.0	0.7
Escort	1.5	4.6	1.0	3.5

Transport

On average 60 per cent of all households in Britain have the regular use of a car. In rural areas the figures are higher, for example 74 per cent of all households in Devon have access to a car. Men are twice as likely to be car owners in rural areas than women. Similarly the wealthier households are likely to have more than one vehicle.

As more people own their own transport the demand for bus services declines. Faced with fewer passengers, bus companies are forced to raise fares and reduce the frequency of the service. This leads to a vicious circle of higher fares and poorer services, leading to even fewer passengers.

1) Use Figure 7.1 to draw line graphs which illustrate the changes between 1951 and 1987, for all three types of transport.

2) **a** During which five years was there the largest increase in private cars?
b Describe the changes in the numbers of motor cycles, scooters and mopeds. (Mention such points as when numbers increased most, how and when numbers have fallen and risen.)
c In what year was there the largest number of public transport vehicles in Britain?

3) What advantages do you think there are of car transport over public transport in the rural areas? What disadvantages are there?

4) Study Figure 7.2 which shows the methods of transport employed by people in rural South Oxfordshire, then answer these questions.
a Which age group depends most on public transport?
b Which age group depends least on public transport?
c Which age group is most likely to walk to their destination?
d Which age group is least likely to walk to their destination?
e Describe how dependence on the private car varies between age groups. Use your answers to **a-d** as a basis for your description.

Railway transport declined in the 1960s. The government closed many unprofitable lines, most of which were in rural areas. Norfolk, for example, has lost 70 per cent of its rail network since 1962.

Rural bus services developed in the 1920s as a rival to the trains. Until the 1950s Britain had a dense network of these. The decline in bus services began with the rise in car ownership and continues to the present. Ten per cent of all villages in rural England and Wales now have no bus service.

FIGURE 7.3   Steventon, Hampshire. The weekly bus service to Basingstoke is a lifeline for these pensioners. There are no shops or services nearby

FIGURE 7.4   Newsagent, Sissinghurst, Kent, one of the few remaining shops . . .

Other services

As bus services in the countryside have declined so have the numbers of schools, doctors' surgeries, hospitals and shops. It has recently been calculated that 20 per cent of all villages in rural England and Wales have no food shop, 65 per cent have no doctor's surgery and 80 per cent have no chemist.

Small village schools are expensive to run. People also argue that with only two or three teachers such small schools can only offer a limited curriculum. However, villagers trying to keep their schools open argue that the school is often at the centre of village social life. It is a meeting place for many groups, not simply pupils, teachers and parents. Closing the school can badly affect the whole village.

More doctors are working in group practices. These require a large population to be economic and so such group practices concentrate in the larger villages. Other doctors cover several different villages, operating a surgery on particular days of the week in each place.

Many small cottage hospitals have also been closed. It is argued that larger hospitals can give better specialist care and they can afford expensive new equipment. The problem is that by concentrating services in a few hospitals, groups such as mothers and babies, the old and the poor suffer most. Yet these are the people *most* in need of health care.

FIGURE 7.5   Former village butcher's, Wadhurst, Sussex. This has since become an antiques shop. Can you suggest reasons for the change?

FIGURE 7.6   Oldfield First School, Yorkshire (enrolment, 20-25 pupils). Parents won their appeal against closure in 1982. Can you think of possible reasons for this?

Solving the problems?

In order to provide services in rural areas a number of solutions have been tried. Some services such as shops and libraries can be made mobile in large vans. These call on different villages throughout the week.

Some rural areas have used minibuses to replace normal public bus services. This system has not saved much money because 75 per cent of all the running costs are the wages of the bus drivers and of the people maintaining the buses and organising the service. Post buses have been established for a long time in countries such as Switzerland and Austria, and in 1971 were introduced in Scotland. In other places a community car service is run by a rota of village car owners who provide a service for those people without a car.

In the 1970s a KEY SETTLEMENT POLICY was tried in some areas such as Devon. The idea was to concentrate services in the more accessible or easy-to-reach villages. This has certainly helped these villages to grow, but only at the expense of the other villages which have lost people and services. Since 1981 Devon has changed its policy to help the smaller, more remote villages.

The VILLAGE CONSTELLATION (see Figure 7.9) is another possible solution. Here a number of villages group together to provide the services between them. So one village may have the bank, another the post office and so on.

FIGURE 7.7 Mobile library service in Hampshire

FIGURE 7.8 This Scottish post bus carries mail and passengers to remote areas and has proved a great success

⑤ Which groups of people suffer most from the lack of services in the rural areas?

⑥ How far do you think the various solutions might be helpful to these groups? Are there any further problems involved?

FIGURE 7.9 Model of a village constellation

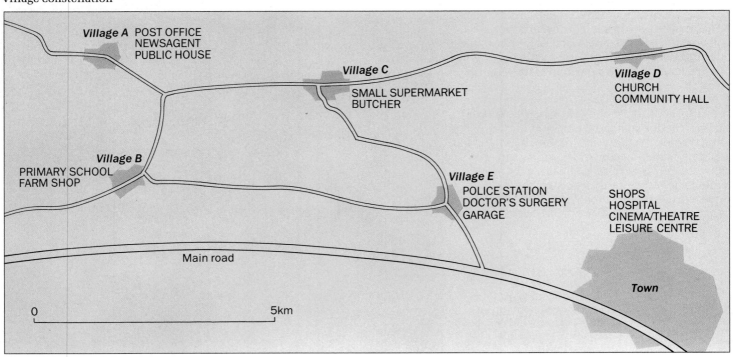

Village A POST OFFICE NEWSAGENT PUBLIC HOUSE

Village C SMALL SUPERMARKET BUTCHER

Village D CHURCH COMMUNITY HALL

Village B PRIMARY SCHOOL FARM SHOP

Village E POLICE STATION DOCTOR'S SURGERY GARAGE

SHOPS HOSPITAL CINEMA/THEATRE LEISURE CENTRE

Main road

Town

0   5km

KEY POINTS

- Rural areas consist of RESOURCES which are in limited supply. There is competition and sometimes conflict between different groups who want to make use of these resources.

- People leave the countryside for a variety of reasons which combine both 'push' and 'pull' factors. Once started, this process of RURAL DEPOPULATION may become a downward spiral.

- As people leave the cities and move to villages in the countryside, problems such as rising house prices, pressure on services and conflicting values may arise.

- Many more people are buying second homes in the countryside. Some rural groups such as builders and shopkeepers may gain from second homes, but others suffer, such as young couples unable to afford the new, higher house prices.

- People living in rural areas are suffering a decline in services such as shops, transport, schools and health care, which are expensive to provide over such large areas. Developments such as post bus services and VILLAGE CONSTELLATIONS may ease the problems but do not necessarily solve them.

IDEAS FOR COURSEWORK

 Carry out a survey of parents and grandparents of pupils in your class.
- How many were born locally?
- How many moved into the area?
- When did they move in?
- Where did they come from?
- Why did they move?

In this way you could also identify both 'push' and 'pull' factors that had affected the people in your survey.

 If you are close to a rural area, or if you visit one on fieldwork, carry out a survey of what services are available in one or more of the villages. Collect information such as:
- bus timetables,
- the number of shops, pubs, churches to be found,
- the nearest dentist, doctor and hospital used by most of the villagers,
- the visiting days and times of any mobile services such as shops or libraries.

Do larger villages seem to have more services?
Are larger villages more accessible by public transport?
Do certain age or gender groups find it particularly difficult to obtain services? Why should this be the case?

 You may visit or live close to a rural area which has villages where more and more houses and flats are becoming second homes. Try to establish what percentage of housing in a particular village is made up from second homes. Look for clues (maybe the lack of a garden or an overgrown garden, the city of origin on car number plates and tax discs of vehicles parked outside, houses and flats left empty).

Local planning departments often keep records of how many second homes are to be found in which villages. Local estate agents are another useful source of information. You might also politely ask local people for their views on second homes.
- How many are in favour? Why?
- How many are opposed? Why?

 Commuter villages are to be found in many parts of Britain. Carry out a survey to establish the following:
- Why did people choose to move to one particular village?
- Where did most people move from?
- Where do most newcomers work?
- Where do newcomers go for services such as shops, banking and entertainment?
- What do people who have lived in the village for many years feel about the newcomers?

8 Changing holiday patterns

For some people today, work takes up less time than it used to. Many people have more LEISURE. This is time free from paid work or other, unpaid work, such as looking after an elderly relative or a young family. The pictures on this page all show different ways people use their leisure time to have holidays. Study each photograph in turn and discuss the questions raised by each one.

FIGURE 8.2 (*Left*) Riding on the beach, Isle of Wight. Activity holidays such as this are increasingly popular in Britain. Why do you think this is so?

FIGURE 8.3 (*Below*) Sailing on Ponden Reservoir, Yorkshire. Why do you think inland sailing is so popular? What other leisure activities might be possible here?

FIGURE 8.1 (*Above*) Brighton beach, 1937. How do you think people travelled to Brighton in those days? Some would have stayed for the day, others for a week. What would they have needed in the town?

FIGURE 8.4 (*Left*) Permanent caravans at Llanelltyd, Wales. For many people a fixed caravan serves as a second home. Why do you think people would want to return to this area over a number of years? What would they need from the local community while staying here? What effects would they have on the local community?

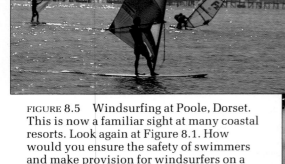

FIGURE 8.5 Windsurfing at Poole, Dorset. This is now a familiar sight at many coastal resorts. Look again at Figure 8.1. How would you ensure the safety of swimmers and make provision for windsurfers on a busy beach?

FIGURE 8.6 (*Right*) Heading for the sea: holiday jam on the M25. What significance does this have for anyone planning or developing a resort?

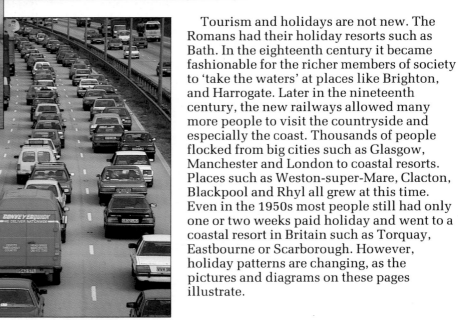

Tourism and holidays are not new. The Romans had their holiday resorts such as Bath. In the eighteenth century it became fashionable for the richer members of society to 'take the waters' at places like Brighton, and Harrogate. Later in the nineteenth century, the new railways allowed many more people to visit the countryside and especially the coast. Thousands of people flocked from big cities such as Glasgow, Manchester and London to coastal resorts. Places such as Weston-super-Mare, Clacton, Blackpool and Rhyl all grew at this time. Even in the 1950s most people still had only one or two weeks paid holiday and went to a coastal resort in Britain such as Torquay, Eastbourne or Scarborough. However, holiday patterns are changing, as the pictures and diagrams on these pages illustrate.

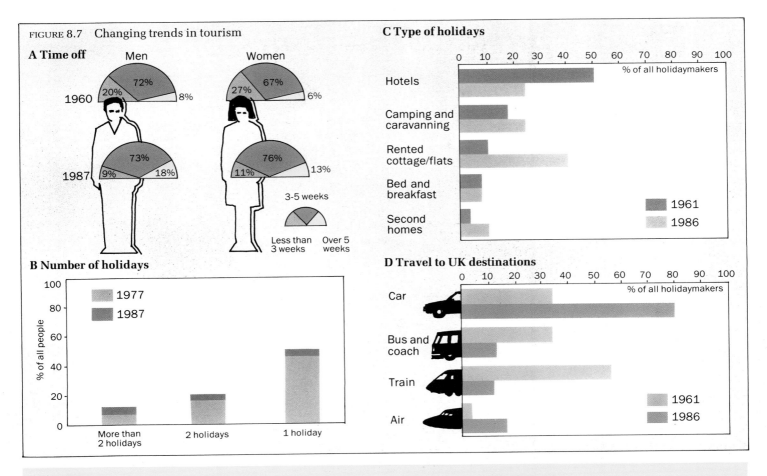

FIGURE 8.7   Changing trends in tourism

A Time off

Men — 1960: 20%, 72%, 8%; 1987: 9%, 73%, 18%

Women — 1960: 27%, 67%, 6%; 1987: 11%, 76%, 13%

3-5 weeks

Less than 3 weeks   Over 5 weeks

B Number of holidays

1977
1987

% of all people

More than 2 holidays   2 holidays   1 holiday

C Type of holidays

% of all holidaymakers

Hotels
Camping and caravanning
Rented cottage/flats
Bed and breakfast
Second homes

1961
1986

D Travel to UK destinations

% of all holidaymakers

Car
Bus and coach
Train
Air

1961
1986

1 Study the data A-D in Figure 8.7 then write a short summary with the title *Changing Trends in British Tourism*. In particular you should mention the following:

a The percentage of men and women in 1960 with less than three weeks paid holiday and the changes by 1987.

b The percentage of men and women with over five weeks holiday in 1987 and the change this represents since 1960.

c The percentage of people taking one holiday in 1977 and in 1987.

d The greatest increase in numbers of holidays taken between 1977 and 1987.

e The main changes in the types of accommodation used between 1961 and 1986.

f The main changes in the types of transport used for holidays between 1961 and 1986.

2 Imagine you are a planning adviser for a British coastal holiday resort such as Scarborough, Weymouth, Blackpool or Ayr. On the basis of your summary *Changing Trends in British Tourism* (see question 1 above) you have been asked to write a report pointing out the implications of these trends for traditional seaside resorts. In particular you are asked to advise the town council on their future attitudes towards:

a *Car parking*   Will they need more? Should they build more? Should it be multi-storey?

b *Traffic flow*   Is there likely to be a problem in the future? Will this be a problem for the whole year or only part?

c *Second homes*   Should the council encourage outsiders to buy second homes?

d *Holiday accommodation*   Should the council encourage more hotels? Should it allow hotels to be converted into self-catering flats? Should it allow cottages to be converted into self-catering properties?

e *Different types of holiday*   Should the council advertise more varied holiday patterns such as weekend breaks, reduced price off-peak bargains, flower festivals etc?

f *Attractions*   Can some existing attractions be developed further (for example, using an old building to make a museum)?

9 Theme park on the doorstep

Because traditional holiday patterns are changing, so too are the demands placed on the countryside. More people are seeking outdoor recreation. A recent survey produced the following list of most popular outdoor activities. They are numbered here in order of popularity.

1 Visits to theme parks
2 Visits to a zoo
3 Picnic
4 Pleasure drive
5 Short walk or jog in Country Park
6 Swimming
7 Skiing
8 Angling
9 Horse riding
10 Visits to historic site
11 Observing wildlife

What other types of outdoor recreation can you think of, which are not mentioned in the list?

Figure 9.1 below summarises the main facilities available for tourism in Lancashire. Study the map and its key carefully for a few moments before you use them in the question which follows.

1 a On a tracing of Figure 9.1 mark the coastline, main rivers and the towns of Lancaster, Morecambe, Blackpool, Preston, Blackburn, Accrington, Burnley, Colne, Ormskirk and Skelmersdale.
 b On the same tracing, mark in any theme parks in Lancashire.
 c Then mark on the tracing zoos, picnic sites, Country Parks, ski runs, historic houses and castles and nature reserves.
 d Which of the three most popular attractions does Lancashire seem to lack?
 e Which of the eleven most popular attractions are well provided in Lancashire?

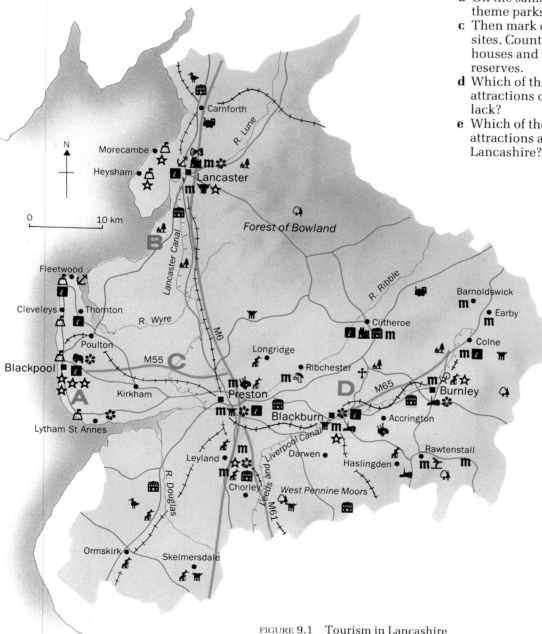

FIGURE 9.1 Tourism in Lancashire

Key

🏰 Castle
🏛 Historic house
🐘 Zoo
⚓ Maritime museum
m Museum
🚂 Steam museum
Textile museum
Steam-powered mill
Roman museum
✝ Abbey/church
✋ Art gallery
— Main route

FIGURE 9.2
Lightwater Valley
Theme Park: what
it offers

Sports centre

Nature reserve

Picnic site

Country Park

Access area

Parks and gardens

Seaside resort

Ski slope

Playhouse

Rare breeds survival unit

Tourist information centre

Other attraction

⊢—╂ Railway

Theme parks such as the one pictured here at
Lightwater Valley near Ripon in North Yorkshire,
are now very popular for day outings. They aim to
provide lots of different activities for the whole
family. There are various factors which influence
the location of theme parks, for example:
- They must be accessible to a lot of people. This
  usually means being close to a motorway or
  other main road.
- They need a lot of space so are not usually
  found within towns.
- Sites near the coast which include beach
  activities are particularly popular.
- They are usually situated away from rival
  recreation attractions such as Country Parks,
  zoos or seaside holiday resorts.

 Imagine you have been asked to
recommend one of four possible sites in
Lancashire on which to build a park

similar to Lightwater Valley. The four
possible sites are marked A B C and D on
the Lancashire tourist map.

Complete a copy of the table below for
each of the four possible sites. For each
location factor, score the sites out of 10,
on a scale where 1 is poor and 10 is
excellent.

a which site did you find the most
suitable?
b Are there any special features you
would wish to include in the theme
park as a result of your choice?

Factors	A	B	C	D
1 Accessible (near motorway)				
2 In countryside to give more space				
3 On the coast				
4 Away from other recreation facilities (over 5 km)				
Total				

10   Conflict in the Cairngorms

Outdoor recreation is increasing in popularity each year, and this brings its own problems. Skiing, for example, is one of the fastest growing sports in Britain, yet there are only a limited number of sites where real snow skiing is possible. One of these is in the Cairngorm mountains of Scotland near Aviemore (see Figure 10.1).

Aviemore is a purpose-built centre for many types of activity including swimming and ice hockey as well as dancing, saunas and visits to the cinema or the theatre. However, one of its main functions is as the centre for skiing on the nearby mountains (see Figure 10.2). Throughout the winter, skiers flock to the area. This creates traffic jams on the roads and long queues for the chairlifts.

In order to overcome these problems caused by the popularity of the sport, the Cairngorm Chairlift Company wants to expand its operations westwards into the Lurchers Gully area. This would mean building a new 2 kilometre road together with car parks and new ski-lifts. The proposal is opposed by groups such as the Nature Conservation Council who are worried about the damage such a project would do to the delicate local environment.

In order to investigate this issue of expanding skiing in the Cairngorms you need to consider in detail the views of each interested party. The following role play exercise will help you.

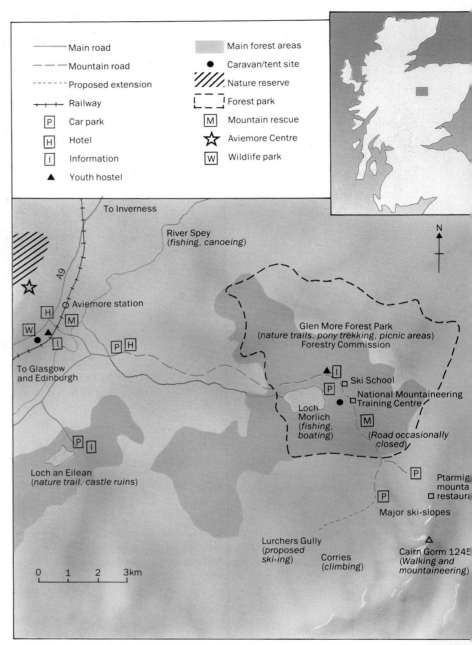

FIGURE 10.1   The Cairngorms

① Hold a mock planning inquiry in the class as to whether the extension of skiing to Lurchers Gully is to be allowed.

a *Phase One*   Divide into pairs. Each pair will assume the role of one of the groups listed in the box on the page opposite. Produce a series of reasons based on the map and the text as to why you think the project should, or should not go ahead.

b *Phase Two*   Elect a neutral chairperson who will control the enquiry. Each pair in turn will put forward its arguments. Other pairs can challenge these arguments at the discretion of the chairperson, and comments from the rest of the class can be raised during this phase.

c *Phase Three*   Summarise, in note form, the main arguments that have been put forward both for and against the scheme. Which arguments seem to be the most persuasive? Are most of the class sympathetic to the Cairngorm Chairlift Company or to the environmental groups? Take a class vote on whether you think the project should go ahead.

FIGURE 10.3   Lurchers Gully

FIGURE 10.2   Skiing in the Cairngorms

The Cairngorm Chairlift Company
You have applied for planning permission to expand into the Lurchers Gully area. Present facilities can only handle a maximum of 5000 skiers. At weekends during the season this is frequently exceeded and leads to long queues for chairlifts. Some skiers go abroad because of the overcrowding, and so their money is lost to Britain. Skiing is a rapidly growing sport and the new ski-lifts would allow another 4000 people to come to the area.

The Highlands and Islands Development Board
Your job is to promote the economic health of the area and stop people leaving the region. You favour this project as it will create a lot of new jobs – constructing new roads, car parks and ski-runs, as well as in the hotels, restaurants, cinemas and discos which will grow up to cater for the extra tourists.

The Scottish Skiing Association
You object to your members being seen as vandals destroying the environment. Many of your members are keen conservationists and do not want to harm the environment. You have members travelling to the Cairngorms from all over the UK and they spend over £4.5 million in the area every year. This gives a big boost to the local shops and hotels and protects many jobs. You are in favour of the scheme as it would bring in more wealth to a relatively poor rural area.

The Royal Society for the Protection of Birds (RSPB)
You are against the project because this is a unique area for bird watchers. The ptarmigan (a type of grouse), the snow bunting, the golden eagle and the osprey all live around Lurchers Gully. Any expansion of skiing would disturb these birds, destroy their habitat and drive them away. They might be lost for ever.

The Countryside Commission for Scotland
You oppose the project because Lurchers Gully is the largest arctic alpine area in the UK. It has rare alpine plants and mosses, together with lichens, and bogs. You believe all this would be destroyed by the expansion of skiing. In the existing ski area the heather has been so badly eroded that in some places the bare soil has been exposed. Soil erosion has taken place despite attempts at sowing quick-growing grasses during the summer. You do not want the same to happen in Lurchers Gully.

The British Mountaineering Council
You oppose the project because your members enjoy the beauty and the wilderness of the area as it is. You also support the world mountaineering association (UIAA) which has identified Lurchers Gully as one of the places most in need of protection from development. The construction of chairlifts, roads and buildings would destroy the peace and beauty of the landscape for ever. It would also make mountaineers go to other, quieter places, taking their money with them.

11 *Honeypot sites*

FIGURE 11.1   Getting away from it all . . .

FIGURE 11.2   Three Peaks area

The cartoon above shows what different people expect from a summer's day spent on the hills. Some people clearly feel that the area is too crowded! This can be a problem for many rural areas. As some people have more leisure time, they use the countryside more. Particularly attractive areas which draw in many visitors are called HONEYPOT SITES, because people flock there like bees to honey. The danger arises because the sheer numbers of people may destroy the very special attractions of the site, as in the case of the Three Peaks area in North Yorkshire (see Figure 11.2).

1 Study Figures 11.2 and 11.3. What is the problem in the Three Peaks area? What solutions have been attempted? Which solution do you think is most likely to solve the long-term problem?

Campaign to save Three Peaks wearing thin from popularity

THE Three Peaks in the North Yorkshire Pennines are wearing out. The summits of Ingleborough (725m), Whernside (740m) and Pen-y-ghent (694m) attract thousands of walkers annually—some out for a day's stroll, others passing by along the Pennine Way – and the footpaths are being worn away.

In places, the paths are now 20 metres wide or more, eroded in the centre and yielding gently at the edges. The grass, moss, reeds, rushes, and heather that survives at these cold altitudes are suffering, too.

Various remedies are being tested. One path has been dug out by about 15 cm and filled with aggregate, with smaller chips to make the top surface. But it is not easy to carry aggregate to the high places of the Pennines – and every metre of footpath can take two-thirds of a tonne.

Another section reduced to a muddy trail has been treated with a consolidating agent to stabilise the peat and create a firm surface.

On the higher slopes of Pen-y-ghent, a third experiment is under way: for about 200 metres, a path has been covered with a boardwalk of planks laid on baulks of timber.

FIGURE 11.3

(2) There are many honeypot sites throughout Britain. Some are on the coasts (see Figure 11.4 for example), some along rivers, some on lakes, others in mountains or moorlands. There are also smaller honeypot sites often within towns at places such as popular parks or beauty spots. Make a study of a honeypot site near you, to include:

a Details of the attractions of the site (both *natural attractions* such as open space, trees, streams, waterfalls and *other attractions* made for people, such as a BMX track, nature trail, or tennis courts).

b How does the site try to cope with the large numbers of visitors? (Are some areas set aside for certain activities, for example?)

c How have visitors changed the place over the past few years. (How do local residents feel about the changes?)

d Where do most of the visitors come from?

FIGURE 11.4   Lulworth Cove and nearby Durdle Door are both spectacular limestone cliff formations in Dorset. This area receives thousands of visitors annually. What advantages and disadvantages do you think the visitors bring to the residents of the small village of West Lulworth?

Capacity: how many is too many?

The problem is to establish at what point the site becomes overcrowded. In theory each honeypot has a CAPACITY, that is a number of people who can arrive without spoiling it. However there are different types of capacity:

ECOLOGICAL CAPACITY is the number of people who can visit a site without causing environmental damage. When the capacity is exceeded, erosion takes place, as on the Three Peaks.

PHYSICAL CAPACITY is simply the total number of people who can get on to the honeypot site.

PERCEIVED CAPACITY is the numbers who can use a honeypot before people's level of satisfaction and pleasure begins to fall. This varies a lot from person to person.

FIGURE 11.5   Two views of 'capacity'

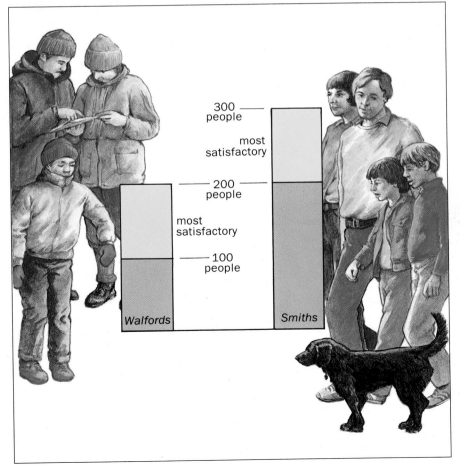

(3) Study the capacity graphs in Figure 11.5. Describe the different reactions of the Walford and Smith families to a day on the hills.

(4) What is the perceived capacity of the area for each family?

(5) Draw a similar graph to show your views of a day on the hills.

12 *Country Parks: a solution?*

In 1967 and 1968 the Countryside Commissions for England, Scotland and Wales created COUNTRY PARKS. They were created because the increasing numbers of visitors to the countryside were causing environmental damage and erosion. The solution was to set aside areas for recreation, and provide facilities such as car parks, toilets, picnic sites and other attractions.

These Country Parks vary greatly in size from 7 to 1300 hectares. They also vary with regard to the attractions they offer, as the brochures in Figures 12.2 and 12.3 illustrate.

FIGURE 12.1   A visit to a Country Park may be to pursue a hobby such as birdwatching or simply to enjoy a family stroll

FIGURE 12.2   Rother Valley Country Park: visitor's plan

How to get there

To Barnsley
To Rotherham
Aughton
M1
A57
Aston J31
B6084
Swallownest
Woodhouse
A618
ROTHER VALLEY COUNTRY PARK
MAIN ACCESS
A816
Beighton
B6058
B6053
Killamarsh
Mosborough
Renishaw
Eckington
B6053
B6419
To Staveley

Rother Valley   Country Park

Rother Valley Country Park

BEIGHTON
River Rother
P
M P
Chesterfield Canal Towpath
A618
N
KILLAMARSH
B6058
0   0.5km
Area: 287 hectares

Symbol	Meaning
)	Angling
⛵	Watersports
/	Family boating
♩	Model boats
🎿	Grass ski slope
✈	Nature reserve
🏃	Sports
🎪	Events
—	Internal roads
-----	Paths and bridleways
⛺🚐	Camping and caravans

M   Bedgreave Mill (cafe & toilets) Information Centre
P   Car parks

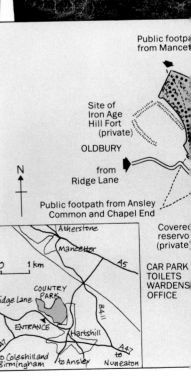

Hartsh

Public footpath from Mance

Site of Iron Age Hill Fort (private)

OLDBURY

from Ridge Lane

Public footpath from Ansley Common and Chapel End

Covered reservoir (private)

CAR PARK TOILETS WARDENS OFFICE

Atherstone
Mancetter
A5
N
0   1km
to Ridge Lane
COUNTRY PARK
B4111
ENTRANCE
Hartshill
A47
A47
to Coleshill and Birmingham
to Ansley
to Nuneaton

FIGURE 12.3   Hartshill Hayes Country Park: visitor's plan

1 a Study the information given on Rother Valley Country Park, and Hartshill Hayes Country Park. Make a copy of the comparison table shown here on the right. Complete it for each Country Park.
  b Which Park seems to have more attractions?
  c Which Park would you most like to visit? Give reasons for your choice.

2 Study the map of Country Parks (Figure 12.4). Name those areas of the UK which have few Country Parks. Suggest reasons why there are so few in these areas. (Remember why they were originally set up.)

	Rother Valley Country Park	Hartshill Hayes Country Park
1 Total area of each park	287 ha	
2 Parking		
3 Toilets		
4 Information centre		
5 Footpaths		
6 Bridleways (horse riding)		
7 Grass ski-slopes		
8 Sports pitches		
9 Percentage of total area covered by woodland		
10 Viewpoints	none	one
11 Angling		
12 Watersports		
13 Percentage of park as nature reserve		
14 Camping Picnic areas		
15 Events centre		
16 Other attractions		

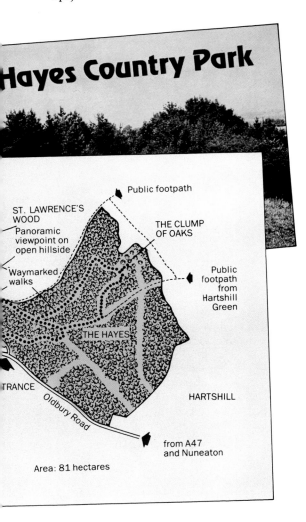

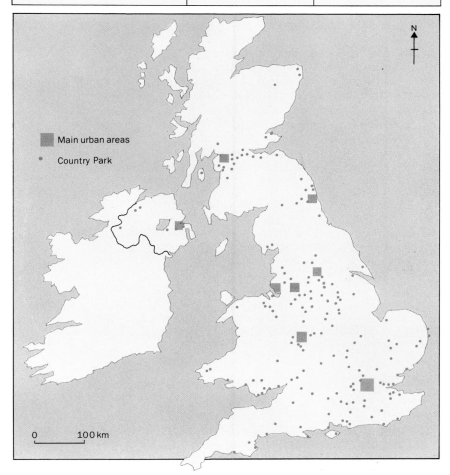

FIGURE 12.4 Country Parks in the UK (right). These have helped to reduce the problems of many visitors to rural areas, but on busy summer weekends, some Parks still cannot cope. The problems arise from too few parking areas, overcrowding on lakes, and disturbance to wildlife reserves.

13 Conflict in the Yorkshire Dales

NATIONAL PARKS were created in Britain in 1949 by the National Parks and Access to the Countryside Act. At that time, the government felt there was a real danger that some of Britain's most beautiful countryside would be destroyed. As a result, ten National Parks were set up, to:

preserve and enhance the landscape;
provide facilities for public, open-air recreation;
preserve wildlife and historic buildings;
ensure that the local economy could continue to function.

The idea was to protect areas of countryside for future generations to enjoy. Figure 13.1 shows the distribution of the National Parks in Britain.

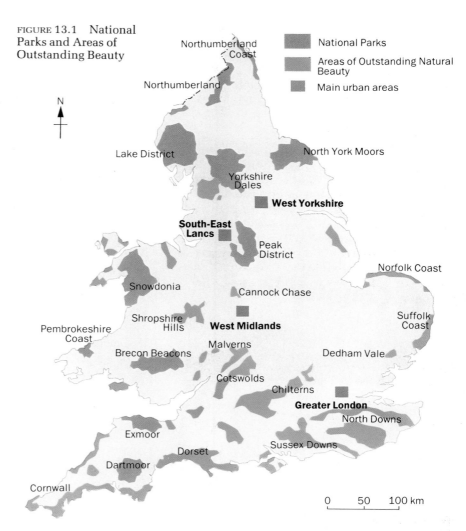

FIGURE 13.1   National Parks and Areas of Outstanding Beauty

 1 Study Figure 13.1 and use the information to answer the following:
 a Which is the nearest National Park to each of these urban areas:
 London;
 The West Midlands;
 West Yorkshire?
 b Name three Areas of Outstanding Natural Beauty near the West Midlands.
 c Which three Areas of Outstanding Natural Beauty are most likely to be visited by people from London?
 d Make a rough estimate of the total area covered by the National Parks.

 2 Most National Park land is privately owned, as Figure 13.2 indicates. This means that the National Park Authority (NPA) has to persuade the different landowners to follow its guidance. Study Figure 13.2 and then answer the following:
 a In which Park is the National Trust the second largest landowner?
 b In which Parks does the Ministry of Defence own land?
 c Which is the only Park where the National Trust does not own any land?
 d In which Park is the area Water Authority the second largest landowner?
 e Which Park has the lowest percentage of privately owned land?

3 On an outline map of Britain, draw pie graphs for each National Park, based on the statistics in Figure 13.2. Describe the varying pattern of land ownership in the four most northerly Parks.

FIGURE 13.2   Land ownership in Britain's National Parks (% of total area)

Park	National Trust	Forestry Commission	Water Authorities	Min. of Defence	National Park	Other	Private
Brecon Beacons	4	7	4	—	2	—	83
Dartmoor	2	2	—	5	3	1	87
Exmoor	9	2	—	—	2	4	83
Lake District	20	5	7	—	2	—	66
Northumberland	1	18	1	23	—	—	57
North York Moors	—	12	—	1	1	—	86
Peak District	5	1	14	—	2	—	78
Pembrokeshire Coast	3	1	—	5	—	—	91
Snowdonia	9	11	1	—	—	6	73
Yorkshire Dales	1	—	—	—	—	—	99

(Source: Countryside Commission)

The Yorkshire Dales National Park

The Yorkshire Dales Park (see Figure 13.3) is the seventh Park to be established in Britain, and covers 176 153 hectares of the Pennines. It is a mixture of open hills covered by moors or farmland. Very little of the Park is forested. It has two types of scenery: the millstone grit areas (see Figure 13.4) with their dark, sombre landscape, and the limestone areas with their distinctive 'scars' such as Malham Cove (pictured in Figure 13.5) and Gordale Scar.

The Yorkshire Dales has a unique group of resources, namely land, water, wildlife, scenic beauty and sites of architectural interest. As you saw earlier (Unit 1 page 9), the number of groups of people wanting to use these resources is large, and they are frequently in competition and conflict. This is because the resources are in very limited supply. The role of the National Park is to manage the resources to meet as many of the conflicting claims as possible.

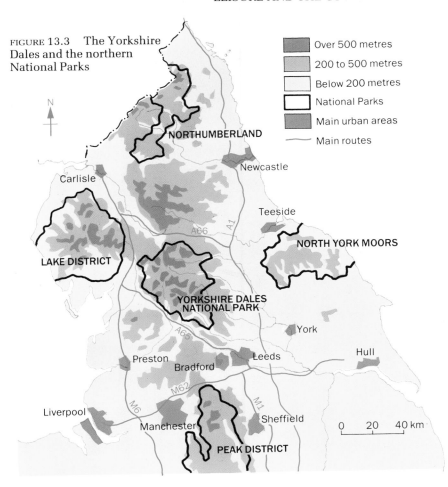

FIGURE 13.3   The Yorkshire Dales and the northern National Parks

FIGURE 13.4   Millstone grit area in the Yorkshire Dales. What evidence is there of farming on these slopes? What sort of farming would it be, in this environment?

FIGURE 13.5   Area around Malham Cove, Yorkshire Dales. Malham Cove itself (seen here in the background) is a spectacular limestone cliff nearly 80 metres high. Notice that the barn in the foreground is built from the local stone. Such barns are a typical feature of the Dales

Recreation in the Yorkshire Dales National Park creates many problems. Eight million people live within 90 minutes travelling time of the Dales. On a summer Sunday, there may be over 100 000 people in the Park. Figures 13.6–13.8 give detailed information about these visitors.

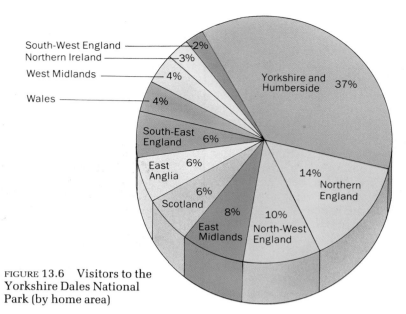

FIGURE 13.6   Visitors to the Yorkshire Dales National Park (by home area)

4 **a** Study Figure 13.6. On an outline map of Britain, draw flow lines to the Dales National Park from each region. Make the flow lines broader or narrower, in proportion to the percentage of visitors from each region.
b Try to explain the pattern of visitors shown on the map you have drawn. (Think of distance, motorways, other National Parks, attractions not present in this Park.)

FIGURE 13.7   Reasons given for visiting the Yorkshire Dales and Pembrokeshire National Parks

	Yorkshire Dales (% of total interviewed)	Pembrokeshire (% of total interviewed)
Fishing	6	0
Sailing	0	15
Beach	0	32
Coastal scenery	0	15
Potholing	14	0
Shopping	3	7
Climbing	15	0
Walking	32	11
General sightseeing	28	17
Other reasons	2	3

5 Use the data in Figure 13.7 on reasons for visiting the Dales and Pembrokeshire Coast Parks to draw two pie graphs.
a In what ways are the two Parks similar?
b How do the two Parks differ?

6 Study the graph in Figure 13.8 showing the flow of vehicles in the Dales Park. Try to explain the traffic flow at the points labelled A B, C and D.

FIGURE 13.8   Vehicle flow in the Yorkshire Dales (Spring Bank Holiday)

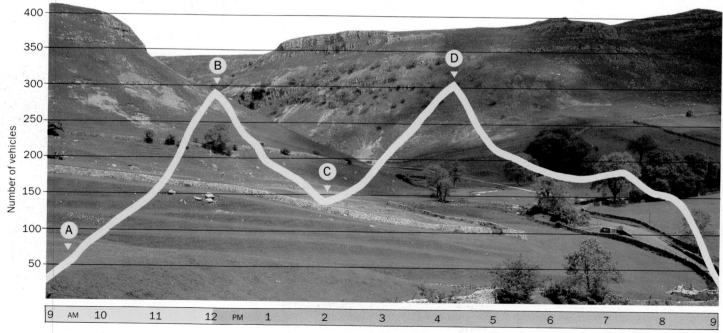

Unfortunately, the visitors to the Dales Park are not spread evenly over the whole area. They concentrate on honeypots such as Pateley Bridge, Bolton Abbey, Grassington and Malham Cove. The result, in some cases, is litter, pollution, traffic jams, erosion of footpaths and even the destruction of underground stalactites and stalagmites in the cave systems, as shown in Figure 13.9.

The visitors also need places to stay, so certain sites have spread across the fields. Many farmhouses now offer bed and breakfast to the visitors, and old cottages and barns have been converted into holiday homes. Opinions on these different recreation uses vary, as the statements on this page show.

 7 Study the opinions given in Figure 13.10. What do you think the following people would say about visitors to the Dales:
  a A pub owner in Pateley Bridge?
  b An RSPB warden?
  c A coach tour operator?
  d A farmer wanting to sell land for a caravan park?

 8 Make a list of the groups of people who benefit from tourism. (Think about the visitors who need food, a place to stay, entertainment, etc.) Make a second list of groups who suffer as a result of tourism.

The National Park Authority (NPA) wants visitors to enjoy themselves and bring money to the area, *without* spoiling its beauty. By providing car parks, litter bins, toilets and information centres, the pressure of so many visitors can be channelled into sections of the Park where least damage is likely. The NPA also provides funds towards rebuilding drystone walls, repairing bridges and re-routing footpaths. A ranger service to advise farmers, landowners and visitors is another attempt by the NPA to manage its resources for the benefit of all groups.

FIGURE 13.9 The stalactites and stalagmites in the underground cave systems in the Dales are constantly at risk from cavers and potholers. Though they may take years to form, they can be broken in a moment by a careless visitor. How would you resolve this problem?

I am fed up with all these tourists. They scare my sheep, leave gates open and drop litter. Some of my sheep have died because they ate plastic bags and ring pulls from canned drinks.

Caravan sites are an eyesore. You can see them for miles and they spoil the view. They also cause traffic jams on the narrow lanes, so we locals find travelling difficult in summer.

I came here to walk in the beautiful surroundings, but the motorists spoil things. They leave their cars all over the place and drop litter. The only way to get some peace is to come in winter or mid-week.

It is hardly worth opening the café in winter because there are so few customers, but in summer we do really well.

We came here to get away from it all in a quiet place, but we are tired of people peering in through the cottage windows. It's like living in a goldfish bowl.

We love driving around the country lanes, and finding new pubs and cafes. We can park in the fields and go for a walk across the hills. It's a shame there are not more car parks.

FIGURE 13.10 What the people think

KEY POINTS

■ Holiday patterns are changing. People now have more leisure time. They tend to take more frequent holidays, often by car, to self-catering accommodation in Britain and abroad.

■ Because so many people want to take part in different outdoor recreations, some special areas have come under intense pressure. There is a danger that the sheer numbers of people will destroy the very things they came to see.

■ HONEYPOT SITES attract large numbers of visitors, and careful management is necessary to conserve the attractions of each site. Country Parks, created by the Countryside Commission, are one response to the pressures.

■ Britain's NATIONAL PARKS are particularly important areas of countryside which must be conserved for the future. The Parks are managed with the aim of allowing visitors to enjoy themselves without spoiling the natural beauty.

IDEAS FOR COURSEWORK

 Carry out a class or school survey of holiday patterns. Some of the questions you might ask are:
- How many holidays away from home do you have each year?
- Where do you go for long holidays?
- Where do you go for shorter holidays?
- How do you travel to your destinations (a) on long holidays (b) on short holidays?
- What type of accommodation do you stay in (a) on long holidays (b) on short holidays (guest houses, hotels, caravans, self-catering flat, etc.)?

You might then investigate questions such as:
- What percentage of pupils have over two holidays each year?
- What are the most popular destinations for (a) long holidays (b) short holidays?
- Do people stay in different types of accommodation on long holidays compared to short holidays?
- Why do some people have no holidays?

 Refer to Unit 9 (pages 30-31). How far do the pupils in your class agree with the order of most popular outdoor activities? Try to explain any differences you may find.

 Make a study of a honeypot site such as a Country Park, an abbey, a river, or a section of coast.
- Where do most visitors come from?
- How have they travelled to the honeypot site?
- How long was their journey?
- What is the main purpose of their visit (walking, climbing, sight-seeing, photography, etc.)?
- What do they particularly like about the site?
- How would they like to see the site improved or developed in the future?

You could map the facilities on the site built specifically for tourists, such as car parks, litter bins, cafés, information centres, picnic sites, toilets and special paths. Look for evidence that the site may be over-used (overflowing car parks, erosion of slopes and footpaths due to visitor pressure, much litter and pollution, and destruction of newly planted trees, etc.).

You could also map the extent of efforts made to cope with visitors, such as separate paths for walkers and horse-riders or motor cyclists, tree planting to prevent or reduce erosion, creation of new hard-core paths, presence of wardens to advise and direct people, etc.

Managing natural resources

Oil rigs in the Brent field. The deposits under the North Sea have made Britain self-sufficient in oil with a daily production of 2.5 million barrels. Hundreds of oil rig workers are flown in 400 kilometres from the mainland on shifts which last for several months. However, the North Sea is a dangerous, stormy environment: How do you think this affects the cost of oil production? What are the human costs?

14   *All change on the farm*

British agriculture has undergone great changes in the last 30 years. The effects can be seen by studying a typical British farm in the West Midlands.

Hagley Hill farm is run by Mr Rose and his son. The map (Figure 14.1) shows its position, 18 kilometres south-west of Birmingham. Mr Rose describes the changes he has seen.

Key

- ▨ Permanent pasture
- ▨ Barley
- — Field boundaries
- ═ Roads
- ▨ Temporary pasture
- ▨ Sugar beet
- ▨ Woodland
- ▨ Wheat

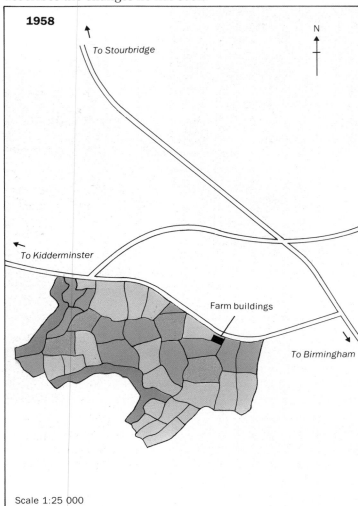

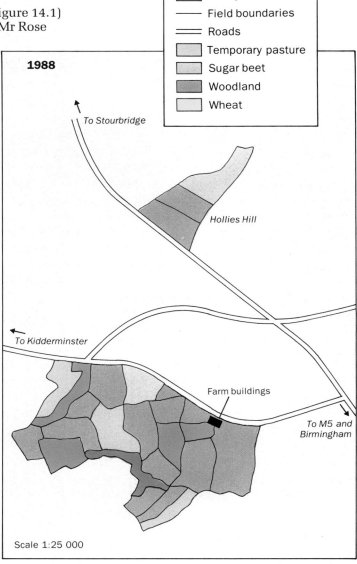

FIGURE 14.1   Hagley Hill Farm: then and now

'Thirty years ago the farm was only 72 hectares in size, but in the 1970s we were able to buy another 31 hectares to the north. This farm used to rear beef cattle and most of the fields were permanent or temporary grass. We did grow some barley to feed to the animals, and manure from the cattle improved the quality of the grass. We had smaller fields in those days, separated by hedgerows and fences.

We had four full-time workers to look after the cattle and help with all the jobs around the farm. A number of tasks such as carrying bales of straw or maintaining hedgerows were still done by hand,

and we also kept two horses for some of the heavier work.

All that changed because the government has been keen to persuade farmers to produce more food. We've gone over to cereals and sugar beet now. The ploughing and tilling is all done by tractors, of course. We use a combine harvester to gather in the wheat and barley and we also use machines to spread fertilisers, or to spray pesticides and herbicides. The sugar beet harvester saves a lot of time as does the muck spreader. All these machines mean we don't need the number of workers we had in the old days, and

FIGURE 14.2   Pig rearing at Hagley Hill. Space is saved by keeping the animals in pens under cover

we only have one part-timer now, in addition to myself and my son, that is. The machines also need large fields to work more efficiently so we have taken up about 15 kilometres of hedgerow and created bigger fields.

We still rear about 40 Hereford/Friesian cross cattle each year for sale at the local Kidderminster market. But the 1800 hens in the two battery units are important because they produce low-cost eggs. The hens are kept in individual cages and supplied with food, water and fresh air. A conveyor belt beneath the cages removes the waste. We also have 600 pigs which are sold to the local abattoir when they are 17 weeks old. In this way I have several products to sell – wheat, barley, sugar beet, eggs, pigs and cattle. I believe in spreading the risk and not relying on just one or two products.

For a long time the government gave us guaranteed good prices for meat, eggs and cereals, so this encouraged us to expand. We bought new equipment, built the battery unit and put drains in several fields. We use artificial fertilisers to get a high yield from the wheat, barley and sugar beet, and we spray pesticides, fungicides and herbicides to protect the crops. All these chemicals are very expensive. We also have to buy food for the livestock. We sell the sugar beet to the factory at Kidderminster. The wheat and barley we sell for cattle food. Recently prices have fallen, so we may have to think again about what we produce.

Some people say that farming has become AGRIBUSINESS, in other words, a very intensive form of agriculture using chemicals and machines to produce the maximum output of crops or animals at the lowest cost. They see farming as being just another industry, like making steel or cars. I don't see it that way. I only use chemicals and machinery to produce low-cost food. If people were prepared to pay more for their food we would not need all the chemicals and machines.'

FIGURE 14.3   Clearing the hedgerows: what results will this bring for the farmer, and for animal and plant life?

1 Hagley Hill Farm is typical of many other farms in Britain. Use the information on this page to write short paragraphs summarising the main changes that have taken place on this farm since the 1950s. The following headings will help you.

Products
Farm size
Land use
Field size and hedgerows
Equipment
Labour force
Use of chemicals
Buildings

FIGURE 14.4   Ploughing-in the stubble after harvesting, in preparation for the next crop

Like all farms, Hagley Hill Farm is a SYSTEM, that is it consists of a series of INPUTS (such as rain, sunshine, seeds and fertilisers), PROCESSES (such as ploughing, harvesting and spraying) and OUTPUTS (such as wheat, eggs and pork). Figure 14.5 below shows this system in detail.

 Use the information in Figure 14.5 to prepare the following:
a A list of the inputs over which Mr Rose has little or no control.
b A list of the hazards which might affect the processes on the farm. (Think about hazards to animals and to crops; prices, the weather, etc.)
c Divide each list into those items that are natural, and those created by people.

3 Draw a systems diagram for Hagley Hill Farm in the 1950s to show inputs, processes, outputs and feedback at that time.

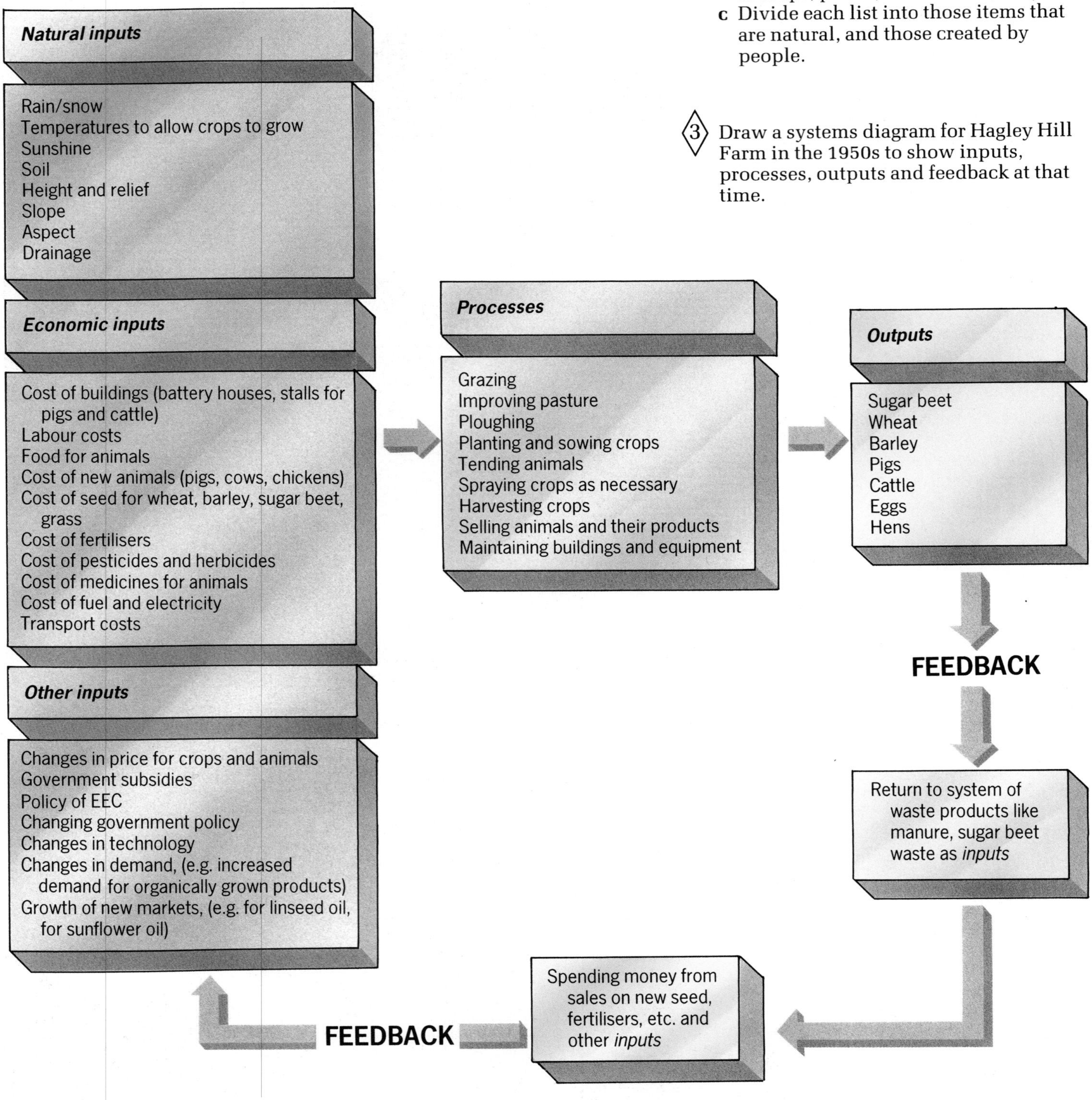

Natural inputs

Rain/snow
Temperatures to allow crops to grow
Sunshine
Soil
Height and relief
Slope
Aspect
Drainage

Economic inputs

Cost of buildings (battery houses, stalls for pigs and cattle)
Labour costs
Food for animals
Cost of new animals (pigs, cows, chickens)
Cost of seed for wheat, barley, sugar beet, grass
Cost of fertilisers
Cost of pesticides and herbicides
Cost of medicines for animals
Cost of fuel and electricity
Transport costs

Processes

Grazing
Improving pasture
Ploughing
Planting and sowing crops
Tending animals
Spraying crops as necessary
Harvesting crops
Selling animals and their products
Maintaining buildings and equipment

Outputs

Sugar beet
Wheat
Barley
Pigs
Cattle
Eggs
Hens

FEEDBACK

Return to system of waste products like manure, sugar beet waste as *inputs*

Other inputs

Changes in price for crops and animals
Government subsidies
Policy of EEC
Changing government policy
Changes in technology
Changes in demand, (e.g. increased demand for organically grown products)
Growth of new markets, (e.g. for linseed oil, for sunflower oil)

Spending money from sales on new seed, fertilisers, etc. and other *inputs*

FEEDBACK

FIGURE 14.5   The Hagley Hill Farm system

4 Study Figures 14.6 to 14.9 and refer back to Mr Rose's description of Hagley Hill Farm. Then answer the following questions under the title, *Changing British Agriculture: the Rise of Agribusiness.*

  a What was the yield of (i) wheat and (ii) barley in Britain in 1986? How did these figures compare with 1970?

  b How many British farm workers were there in 1960? In 1970? In 1986?

  c British farms of 2-20 hectares in size decreased in number between 1961 and 1986. What happened to the number of farms over 300 hectares in the same period? What happened to the number of farms between 40 and 100 hectares in the same period?

  d How many combine harvesters were there in Britain in 1960? In 1970? In 1980? In 1986?

  e What is agribusiness?

  f Why do many farmers use so many chemicals and machines?

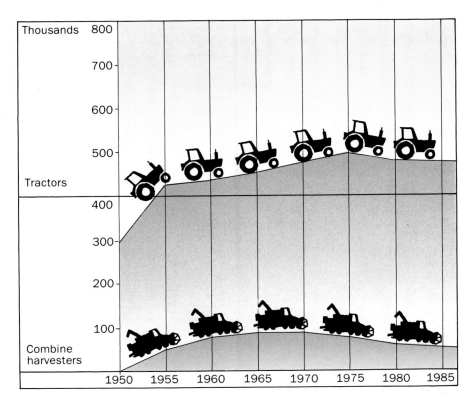

FIGURE 14.6   (*Above*) Tractors and combine harvesters in use in the UK (1950–86)

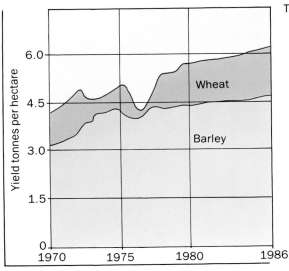

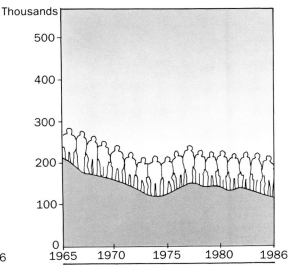

FIGURE 14.7   (*Far left*) Yields of wheat and barley (1970–86)

FIGURE 14.8   (*Left*) Number of UK farm workers (1965–86)

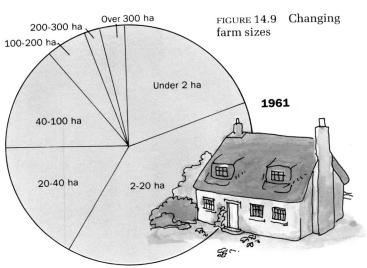

FIGURE 14.9   Changing farm sizes

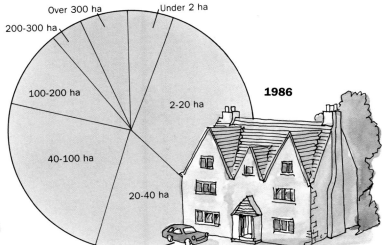

15   *Our countryside: going, going . . ?*

The government, the EEC and farming

In 1939 Britain was having to import 60 per cent of all its food. The Second World War showed that it was strategically dangerous to rely on too much imported food. Since 1945 until recently, governments have encouraged Britain's farmers to produce more.

The British government helps agriculture by the following policies:

- Increasing output through SUBSIDIES on the cost of draining fields or through grants to buy new machinery.
- Advertising to increase consumption of some foods such as milk.
- Regulations to protect the environment, for example through pollution control.

Since 1973, Britain has been a member of the European Economic Community (EEC) and so has to adopt the Common Agricultural Policy (CAP). This policy is designed to give all farmers a fair standard of living and to ensure a reliable supply of food at reasonable prices for Europe. The policy works by setting a minimum price. Farmers are guaranteed this price, so they know they will be able to sell their goods and make a profit.

In the early 1980s, the EEC wanted to encourage farmers to grow more cereals, so high prices were set for these crops. As a result many British farmers began to grow wheat, maize and barley. If farmers produced more than was needed by the EEC, the surplus was stored in warehouses, grain stores or freezers (for meat). As a result 'mountains' of SURPLUS grain, milk and meat built up in the EEC. The size of these surpluses is shown in Figure 15.1 on this page. The storage costs for wheat alone in 1987 were £3100 per minute!

In order to reduce these surpluses the EEC has given away products such as butter, cheese and beef to pensioners and other selected groups. In the longer term, output has been reduced by two methods:

1 Establishing an agreed maximum amount or QUOTA of a product such as milk that a country is allowed to produce. By reducing the milk quota for countries such as Britain and Eire, the surplus is being reduced.
2 Reducing prices for crops such as wheat and barley where there was already overproduction.

Both these methods have meant changes for many British farmers. Unfortunately the change in policy came too late to save much of the countryside from the effects of large-scale farming.

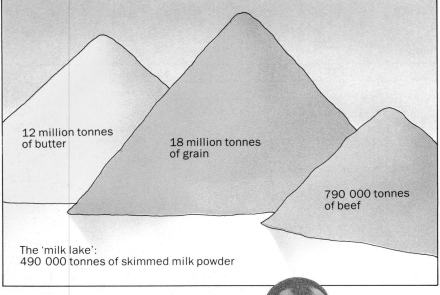

12 million tonnes of butter

18 million tonnes of grain

790 000 tonnes of beef

The 'milk lake':
490 000 tonnes of skimmed milk powder

FIGURE 15.1   'Mountains' and 'lakes' in EEC agriculture: surpluses in Britain at the end of 1986

FIGURE 15.2   Many people feel that Britain could put its surpluses to good use, as shown here. Butter is made into oil to be used as a basic food and cooking ingredient in an Ethiopian relief camp

Environmental consequences of CAP

Figure 15.3 below shows just how much Britain's countryside has changed since 1945. When cereal prices were high many farmers ploughed up marginal land, took out areas of woodland and hedgerow and used chemicals to increase output. In the early 1980s many parts of Britain in August looked like the prairies of Canada, with huge wheatfields stretching away to the horizon. Between 1945 and 1985 Britain lost nearly 60 per cent of its heathland, 90 per cent of its ponds, 25 per cent of its hedgerows and 80 per cent of its ancient woodlands.

The larger fields created for the new machinery are at greater risk from soil erosion, and some gullies have formed in East Anglia which are now so wide and deep vehicles cannot cross them. Hedgerows also provided shelter for animals in winter, and a HABITAT for thousands of insects, birds and small animals. In the past, hedgerows helped to keep animals away from crops they might eat, and hedge trimming was an important winter task for farm workers.

The increased use of artificial fertilisers with a high nitrogen content has been necessary to obtain high yields. Not all the nitrogen is absorbed by the crops and some may pollute drinking water supplies. Similarly the use of herbicides, pesticides and fungicides has killed many 'innocent' plants and insects and animals.

As the countryside has changed, so the wildlife has suffered. There are now over 300 plants and wild flowers officially listed as endangered. At least four types of butterfly are close to extinction and the otter has vanished from much of the country. Even the common frog has almost disappeared in some parts of Britain.

FIGURE 15.3   Britain's disappearing countryside (1945–85)

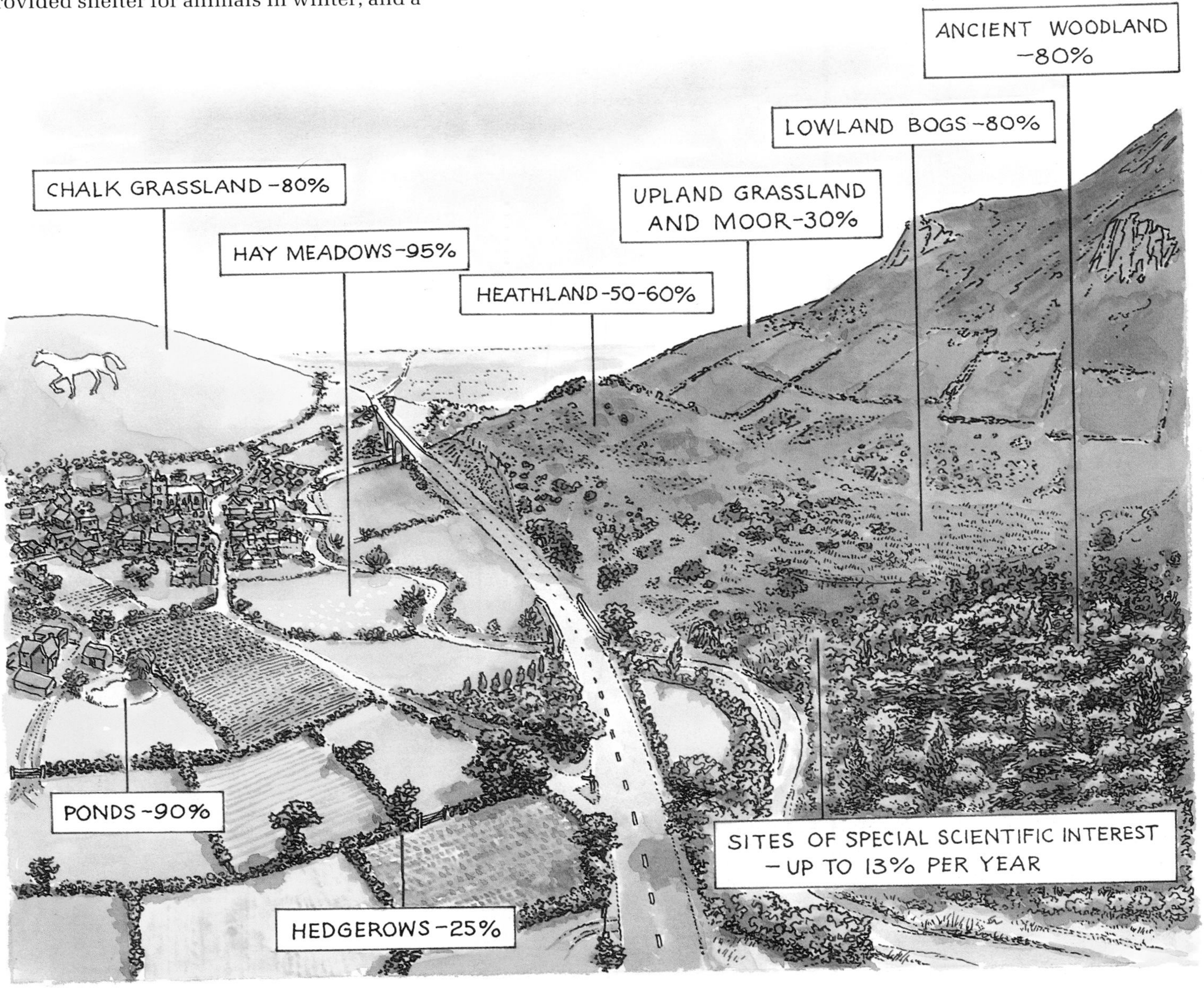

ANCIENT WOODLAND −80%

LOWLAND BOGS −80%

CHALK GRASSLAND −80%

HAY MEADOWS −95%

UPLAND GRASSLAND AND MOOR −30%

HEATHLAND −50-60%

PONDS −90%

SITES OF SPECIAL SCIENTIFIC INTEREST − UP TO 13% PER YEAR

HEDGEROWS −25%

Other consequences

The rise of AGRIBUSINESS has gone hand in hand with the growth of FACTORY FARMING, that is the intensive rearing of animals such as pigs or poultry. Many pigs, chickens and turkeys spend their whole lives inside the special rearing units where food, water, light and temperature are carefully controlled. Many people oppose factory farming because they feel it is wrong to confine animals to very small cages for their entire lives and they point to the aggressive behaviour of some animals when restricted in these ways.

Farmers agree that battery rearing is the only way they can produce eggs and poultry at prices people can afford. However, more shops and supermarkets are beginning to stock 'free-range' products from farms where the animals are allowed to wander over a wider outdoor area. Although slightly more expensive, such products are showing increased sales.

 In order to examine the consequences of these recent large-scale agricultural changes, copy and complete the table below. The main agricultural changes have been identified for you. Use the data in this unit and Unit 14 to complete the other columns. In the final column give your own opinion of the effects of the change (good or bad) and list any possible alternatives.

FIGURE 15.5 Chickens reared in the traditional way. What problems does this method have for large-scale chicken farming?

FIGURE 15.4 Battery chickens in conditions like these have their beaks clipped short, have no room to move either backwards or forwards, and never see natural light. They spend their entire lives in a space about half a metre square

RECENT AGRICULTURAL CHANGES IN BRITAIN

Agricultural change	Reason for change	Effects of change on production and yield	Environmental effect	Is there an alternative? If so, what?	My view of the change and of the alternative
A Removal of hedgerows	Larger machines need bigger fields	Increased output at lower cost	Loss of wildlife habitat, soil erosion, loss of species	Replant hedgerows	
B Ploughing up areas of grassland, e.g. Chalk Downs or Cotswolds					
C Draining marshlands and bogs					
D Uprooting trees and small areas of woodland					
E Use of artificial fertiliser					
F Use of pesticides, herbicides and fungicides					
G Battery animal rearing					

... Pesticides accelerate the development of resistant strains ...

Philip Thompson 85

British farming in the future

A number of trends in British farming are likely to influence the 1990s and beyond.

1 *Changing eating habits.* People are becoming more health conscious and are generally eating less fattening foods. Vegetarianism is increasing, together with the demand for fresh vegetables.

2 *Increasing importance of ORGANIC FARMING.* This method of farming uses no chemicals, and emphasises the natural methods of rearing crops and animals. As people become more aware of the possible harmful side-effects of chemically treated foods, the demand for organic produce has risen, and a number of supermarkets now deliberately stock organic products.

3 *Changing patterns of crop/animal production.* As EEC quotas and prices change, farmers are switching to alternative crops. Bright yellow fields of oilseed rape, used in margarine manufacture are now a common sight. The area under evening primrose (also grown for its seed oil) is increasing, and more scarlet poppies are being grown for their seeds to be used in breadmaking. Willow trees are grown to produce wood fuel for the increasing number of wood-burning stoves around Britain. Wood fuel is also used by tomato growers in Eire, who found that heating their greenhouses that way over three years saved 60 per cent on fuel bills.

4 *Alternative Land Use and the Rural Economy (ALURE).* By 1987 it became clear that reducing EEC food mountains meant that Britain no longer needed as much farmland as previously. Various alternative land uses have been suggested:
   a Some land could be converted to forestry (up to 37 000 hectares each year), with farmers being paid to plant trees.
   b Golf courses, riding schools and other recreations could be set up on land near towns.
   c Farmers could be paid to cultivate land in traditional, less destructive ways, using fewer chemicals.
   d Use land to develop small rural industries, providing local employment.
   e Use land for building new housing.
   f Farm less intensively with more land given over to sheep, deer and cattle grazing in areas planted with oak woodland.

All these proposals would affect about 3 million hectares of surplus farmland.

The newspaper extract below (Figure 15.6) describes a farm which is faced with a number of these competing proposals for its future. Read the extract first and then work in pairs to answer the following question.

 Which of the following people do you think made comments A, B, C and D on the future of Lower Kingcombe Farm? Why?
the National Farmers Union　　a building firm
the National Trust　　British Organic Farmers
   a Explain carefully which of the four views *you* would support, using arguments from this unit and from Unit 14.
   b List other possible views on how the land might be used (such as tourism).

A "We now have surplus farmland in Britain, but a shortage of houses, so it is logical to convert the existing cottages and some of the land into homes."

B "We want to grow thatching straw, harvest the seeds from wild flowers and raise edible snails for sale abroad. This will prevent the area being spoiled."

C "This is high quality farmland which as a nation we cannot afford to waste. We should farm in a more modern way to increase output."

D "We want the area to remain exactly as it is, otherwise we may lose the rare birds, insects and plants."

FIGURE 15.6

Bid to preserve time-warp farm

Conservationists are mounting a desperate bid to save as much as possible of a 1,515 hectare estate in West Dorset, which is thought to be the last of its kind in the country. By a quirk of fate, the farming revolution of the twentieth century has passed it by and it looks much the same as it did centuries ago.

Yet, until a couple of years ago, environmentalists and wildlife experts did not even know it was there.

Even now, to go there is to enter a lost world. Fragrant hay meadows, studded with rare flowers, nestle between hedges up to 10m tall. Fallow roe and sika deer hide in ancient woods. Buzzards and sparrowhawks soar overhead. Rare butterflies abound and the grass is rich in orchids.

It remains like this because the Wallbridge family, which farmed the land for generations, deliberately turned their back on the farming methods that have transformed the rest of lowland England.

They left the hedges in place and cut and laid them by hand, refusing to hack at them with mechanical flails. They made hay in summer, and stocked their fields lightly with animals.

So Lower Kingcombe looks almost exactly as it did 100 years ago, and is little changed since mediaeval times.

To conservationists' dismay, the farm has been split into 15 lots which will be auctioned in Dorchester on 15 May. A glossy brochure has been produced showing how the farmhouse and five cottages, some ruined, could be turned into bijou homes.

Mr Masters says: 'The introduction of fresh interests is going to help the preservation of this area.' He claims that the buyers will want to conserve the land, and will have the money to do so.

But the conservationists argue that just one unsympathetic owner could ruin the whole area.

16   *Can you make farming decisions?*

The pattern of fields, hedges, ponds and woodland typical of most rural areas is the result of decisions taken by farmers. These decisions are essentially about
- what to produce
- how much to produce
- where to produce
- how to produce (i.e. the methods to be used).

There is an increasing number of complex factors which influence the farmer's decisions as the diagram on this page illustrates.

FIGURE 16.1   Factors influencing a farmer's decision

SOCIAL FACTORS

1 Land ownership
People who own their own farm tend to put more effort into their work.

2 Information
Farmers need advice and information from magazines, TV, radio, computers.

GOVERNMENT POLICY
Government policy may be to encourage the cultivation of some crops in short supply and discourage production of other crops (e.g. wheat, barley).
Government policies affect what crops are grown and what prices are paid.

PERSONAL FACTORS

1 Risk
Some farmers are prepared to take higher risks than others.

2 Efficiency
Some farmers are better managers than others.

3 Work
Some farmers work harder than others.

4 Choices
Some farmers have a wide choice of what to produce, others do not.

5 Preference
Some farmers *prefer* to produce certain goods.

ENVIRONMENTAL FACTORS

1 Conservation
In areas of special environmental importance, the government may encourage conservation more than agriculture.

2 Locations
Relief, aspect, soil type, and climate affect what can be produced.

TECHNOLOGY
Is the latest technology available?
Is it too expensive to use?

ECONOMIC FACTORS

1 Profit
The amount of profit dictates how much can be put back into the farm as investment.

2 Labour
The costs and availabilities of skilled labour.

3 Markets
Some markets are high risk (e.g. fruit), others are secure (e.g. vegetables). Some offer higher prices than others.

4 Capital
Farmers may borrow from banks to finance improvements or receive grants and subsidies.

Making decisions: Case 1

Farmers on the island of Islay off the west coast of Scotland, used to be very poor. They have used fertilisers to improve the grassland pastures for their 10 000 cattle and 14 000 sheep. Barnacle geese, a rare and endangered species, also like the improved grass, and thousands spend the winter on Islay. This reduces the food available for cattle and sheep. The farmers want to shoot the geese but an EEC directive forbids this.

 1 Give your view on each of the alternatives below. Choose the solution you think is the best one and give reasons for your choice.

   a Should the farmers shoot these rare birds and so create a court case to establish their legal rights?

   b Should the farmers tolerate the geese and accept a lower standard of living to preserve the birds?

   c Should the EEC or the British government compensate the farmers of Islay if they do not kill the geese?

FIGURE 16.2   Barnacle geese and local farmers lay rival claims to the improved grassland on Islay

Making decisions: Case 3

Bob Munroe farms 100 hectares of fertile land near Flamborough on the Yorkshire coast. With his wife, Pauline, Bob rears 100 sheep, 50 beef cattle, 200 pigs, 50 chickens, as well as growing some barley. Unfortunately, livestock are not very profitable, but Bob enjoys the work and Pauline keeps the chickens as a hobby. They regularly take school parties on tours round their farm, and the children enjoy seeing and stroking the animals. Their bank manager is urging them to get rid of the animals and concentrate on more profitable crops such as oilseed rape and wheat which would grow well on their land. This would also mean grubbing out hedgerows to create larger fields for new machines. Bob and Pauline have a large bank loan and so listen carefully to the advice.

 3 Should Bob and Pauline sell all their animals and concentrate on growing more profitable crops? Or should they sell some of the animals? If so, which ones should they keep?

 4 Redraw the plan of Bob and Pauline's farm (Figure 16.3) to show your suggestions. How has the land use changed? Compare your answers.

Making decisions: Case 2

Pat and Mary Donahue are tenant farmers near Ballymena in Northern Ireland. They rent 42 hectares of land which is only suitable for dairy or beef cattle. The EEC has imposed QUOTAS on milk output which means that the Donahues have to produce less milk. This will mean a drop in their income, which was never large anyway. Because they do not own the land, they cannot sell up and use the money to start again elsewhere. Pat is fifty and feels that he is too old to find another job. Both their MP and Euro MP say there is nothing they can do because farm policy is decided in Brussels.

 2 Pat wants to take a small EEC grant to retire early. They could live in Ballymena. Mary does not want to leave the farm and thinks they should offer bed and breakfast to attract tourists who do visit the area. Work in pairs and explain what you think they should do. What do other groups in the class think?

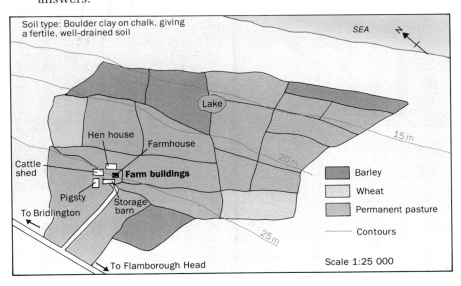

FIGURE 16.3   Plan of the Munroe farm

KEY POINTS

- British agriculture has experienced a revolution since 1945. Large new machines, higher yielding types of seed and animals, together with the intensive use of chemicals are some of the key features of the revolution.

- The changes in farming have had significant effects on the countryside, resulting in the destruction of many wildlife HABITATS.

- ORGANIC FARMING, which uses no chemicals and stresses the rearing of animals in 'natural' conditions, is becoming more widespread. This is so because people are becoming more concerned about the possible harmful effects of AGRIBUSINESS.

- Farming is a business like many others. It depends on people making correct decisions.

IDEAS FOR COURSEWORK

 Visit a farm and use a questionnaire to produce a systems diagram for your farm similar to the one on page 46.
- Where do most economic inputs come from?
- Which inputs are largely beyond the control of the farmer?
- Where are the outputs sold?
- Which outputs become feedback?
- What are the most important processes on your study farm?

 You could use the same questionnaire to identify the main changes on your sample farm over the past five or ten years, such as
- changes in crops grown
- yields obtained
- destination of crops
- animals reared (types and numbers)
- animal food
- destination of animals
- machinery used (including computers)
- numbers of employees (full and part-time)
- number of fields
- field boundaries (hedgerows, fences)
- use of chemicals, fertilisers, insecticides, etc.
- farm size, number and type of buildings

 You could compare two farms under such headings as these:
- crops produced
- animals reared
- machinery and equipment employed
- labour force
- effect of government and the EEC
- use of chemicals
- markets for produce
- links with other farms
- number of fields
- other factors

17 Britain's forests: use or abuse?

Britain's forests have always been very important; 6000 years ago almost all the country, except the highest peaks, was covered by trees. On the lower land deciduous species such as beech, birch, oak and ash were dominant. Higher up the slopes where conditions were harsher, evergreen trees such as pine, fir and spruce took over. The trees protected the soil from EROSION, slowed the rainfall run-off on the steep slopes and provided shelter for a great variety of wildlife.

The case of Thornthwaite Forest

Thornthwaite Forest in the Lake District is pictured on this page. Its story is typical of many areas of Britain. The Stone Age settlers in this part of the country lived by hunting and fishing, mainly along the coast. Later some people moved inland and used stone axes to clear parts of the forest for cattle grazing.

Thornthwaite Forest suffered little from Bronze Age people or the Romans. However things changed when the Vikings arrived via Ireland and the Isle of Man. They cut down large areas of the higher forest as grazing for their sheep, cattle and pigs. 'Thwaite' means valley clearing.

The Normans cleared even more land for sheep and cattle. The growing wool trade encouraged people to cut down trees and let sheep graze the grass covered hillsides. Even

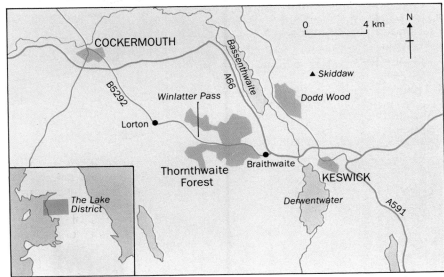

FIGURE 17.1   Thornthwaite forest, in the Lake District

more timber was cut in the sixteenth century to provide charcoal which was a fuel in homes and industries. Local mines also needed timber for pit props and for homes.

The result of this tree felling by the nineteenth century was bare hillsides and a shortage of timber. Some local landowners for the first time began to replant fast-growing larch trees. The famous poet Wordsworth disliked these larch trees, calling them 'a sort of abominable vegetable factory.' In other parts of Thornthwaite, oak trees were planted. Unfortunately many of the replanted trees were once again felled, to supply Britain during the First World War.

FIGURE 17.2   Walking in Thornthwaite. Can you identify the trees? Are they broad-leaved or conifers?

The Forestry Commission

At the time of the First World War, only 4 per cent (one million hectares) of Britain was forested, of which half was deciduous and half evergreen. By 1919, the German submarine blockade had almost succeeded in starving Britain of wood, so in the same year the Forestry Commission was established. Its task was to create a 'strategic reserve of timber' so that Britain should not again be vulnerable to blockades.

Over the next 70 years the Forestry Commission doubled the amount of land under forest to nearly 2 million hectares. The Commission's main tasks are now:

1 To provide wood as economically as possible, bearing in mind amenity and landscape considerations.
2 To protect and enhance (improve) the environment.
3 To provide facilities for recreation.
4 To stimulate the local economy by developing forests and wood-using industries.
5 To further the integration of forestry and agriculture.

FIGURE 17.4   Wood production ('000s cubic metres)

	1973	1982	1987
Forestry Commission	1600	2900	3600
Private	2100	2500	2800
Total	3700	5400	6400

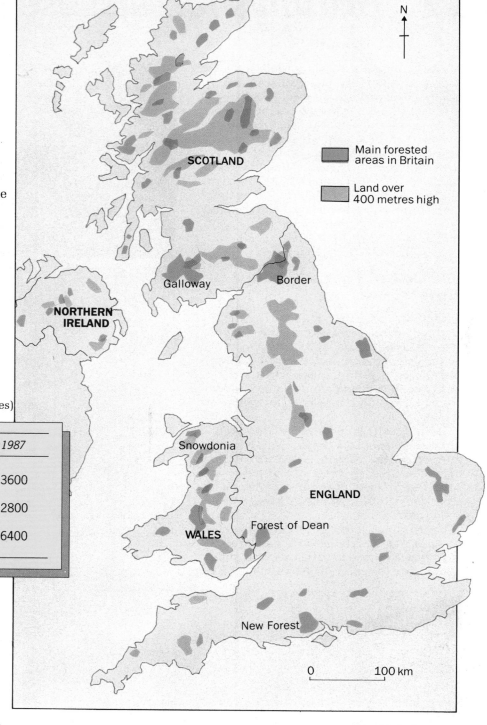

FIGURE 17.3   Main forest areas of Britain

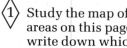 Study the map of Britain's main forest areas on this page (Figure 17.3). Then write down which of the following statements are *true*.
  a The largest areas of forest are in Scotland.
  b All forests are on land over 400 metres high.
  c All areas over 400 metres high are forested.
  d There are important forests below 400 metres.
  e There are no forests in Wales.
  f Most forests are on land over 400 metres.
  g Most forests are in northern and western Britain.

 Use the data in Figure 17.4 to draw three pie graphs for each year showing the relative output of private forests and Forestry Commission lands.
  a Is output greater in private forests or Forestry Commission areas?
  b In which sector has output increased most since 1973?

Two of the problems facing the Forestry Commission in the 1930s were which trees to grow and where to plant them. Figure 17.5 below illustrates some of the natural restrictions on tree growth.

Choosing which trees to grow was easier, because conifers can survive in harsh conditions. They have springy branches which bend but don't break in the wind or under the weight of snow. They also have small, needle-shaped leaves to cut down water loss in winter when the ground is frozen, cones which protect the seeds, and long, shallow roots which get water and nutrients from the thin, acid soils.

Finding suitable places to plant the new

FIGURE 17.5 Trees and altitude

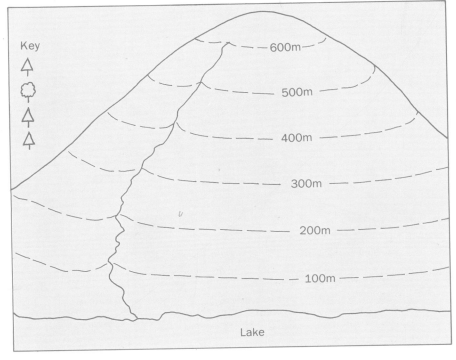

conifers was more difficult. The only large amounts of cheaper land available for afforestation were in areas of high, steep slopes. Most plantations are therefore found in these areas today.

3. Make a copy of the diagram shown on the left. Then use the data from Figure 17.5 above to draw and colour in suitable tree symbols, for the following areas:
   a Where beech will grow.
   b Where douglas fir trees will grow.
   c Where European larch will grow.
   d Where sitka spruce will grow.
   Complete the key for your diagram.

18 Opening up the forests

Fifty years ago, the public were excluded from many forests in Britain, but after the Second World War, and particularly since the 1960s, the policy has changed. FOREST PARKS have been designed to help people enjoy the forests. One such Forest Park is at Castlewellan in Northern Ireland (see Figure 18.1). Study the detailed map of Castlewellan Forest Park (Figure 18.2) then answer the questions below.

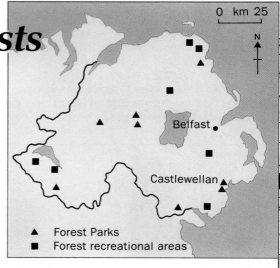

FIGURE 18.1 Location of Castlewellan Forest Park

▲ Forest Parks
■ Forest recreational areas

FIGURE 18.2 Castlewellan Forest Park (Scale 1:10 000)

1 a What is the highest point in the Park?
   b What is the lowest point in the Park?
   c How deep is Castlewellan Lake?
   d How long is Castlewellan Lake?
   e At its widest point how many metres is Castlewellan Lake from north to south?

2 How far would you travel if you walked or took a pony trek between these points:
   a From the Rangers' Hut to the Icehouse?
   b From the site of the old Brewery to Mitchell's Lake?
   c From the castle to the Mountain Lake?

3 Describe in detail what you would see to your right and to your left on a walk from the Rangers' Hut to the Moorish Tower along the south shore of Castlewellan Lake. (Mention fishing points, types of woodland, open spaces, shelter huts etc.)

4 a How many caravan sites are there in the Park?
   b How many camping sites are there?
   c Where are the main picnic sites?

5 Prepare a route for a pony trekking group who are starting from the Pony Trek entrance near Mitchell's Lake. Your route should include the following:

Mountain Lake	The Winter Garden
A viewpoint	The Castle
Cypress Pond	Crow Road
Castlewellan Lake	Finnegan's Hollow

Produce your route as a tracing of the main map on this page to show the main lakes, the points listed above and interesting things to look out for on the journey.

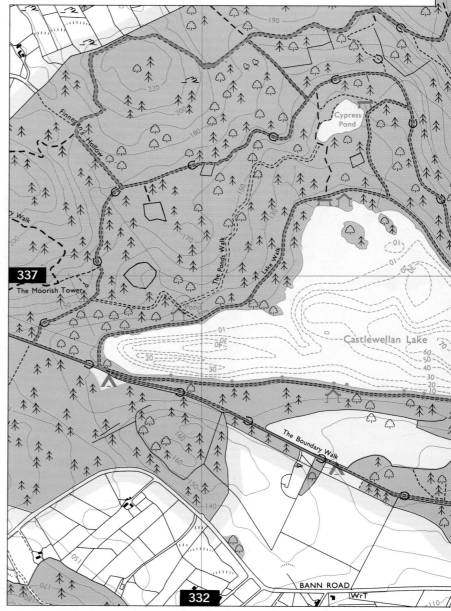

© Crown Copyright Reserved

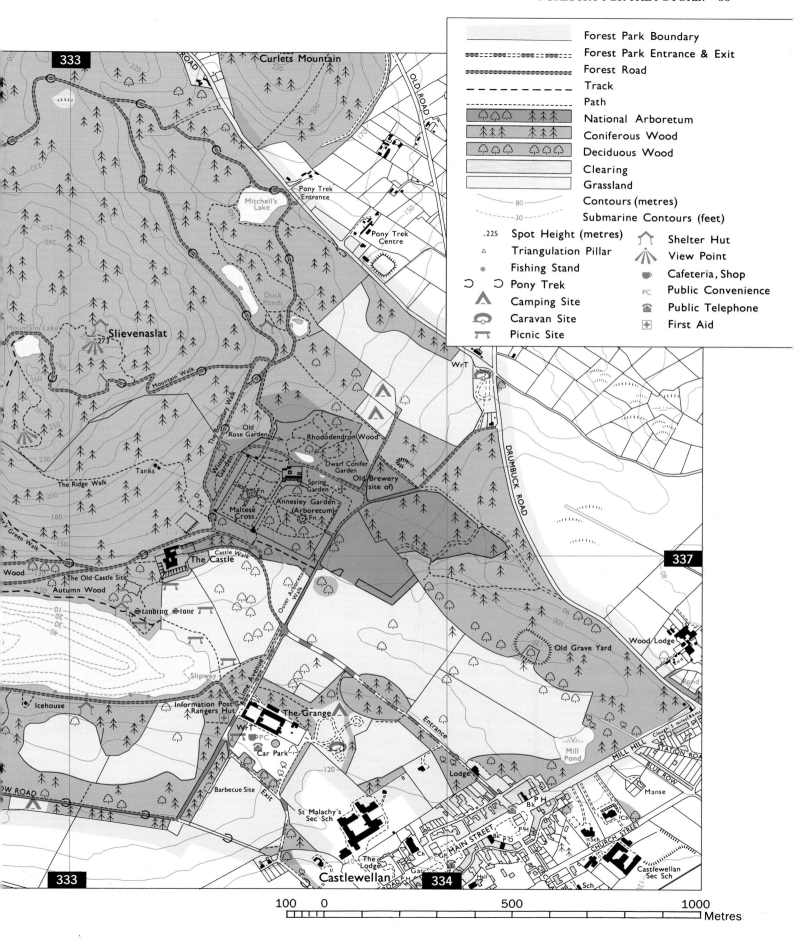

Legend:

Forest Park Boundary
Forest Park Entrance & Exit
Forest Road
Track
Path
National Arboretum
Coniferous Wood
Deciduous Wood
Clearing
Grassland
Contours (metres) — 80
Submarine Contours (feet) — 30

.225 Spot Height (metres)
△ Triangulation Pillar
● Fishing Stand
⊂⊃ Pony Trek
⋀ Camping Site
Caravan Site
Picnic Site

Shelter Hut
View Point
Cafeteria, Shop
PC Public Convenience
Public Telephone
First Aid

333
Curlets Mountain
OLD ROAD
Pony Trek Entrance
Mitchell's Lake
Pony Trek Centre
Duck Ponds
Mountain Lake
Slievenaslat 273
Mountain Walk
The Boundary Walk
Old Rose Garden
Rhododendron Wood
Winter Garden
Dwarf Conifer Garden
Old Brewery (site of)
Spring Garden
Tanks
The Ridge Walk
Maltese Cross
Annesley Garden (Arboretum)
Fn
WrT
DRUMBUCK ROAD
337
Green Walk
Castle Walk
The Castle
Wood
The Old Castle Site
Autumn Wood
Standing Stone
Outer Arboretum Walk
Old Grave Yard
Wood Lodge
Pond
Slipway
Icehouse
Information Post Rangers Hut
The Grange
Lime Avenue
WrT
PC
Car Park
Entrance
Mill Pond
MILL HILL
STATION ROAD
BLUE ROW
Barbecue Site
Exit
Manse
W ROAD
333
Castlewellan
334
St Malachy's Sec Sch
The Lodge
MAIN STREET
CHURCH STREET
Castlewellan Sec Sch
PH
Bk
Ch
Hall
Sch

19 Forestry in conflict

The Forestry Commission has created massive plantations in areas like Wales and Scotland on land where there were few people, and which was of little agricultural value. Recent government policy foresees another million hectares of coniferous forests in the next 50 years. The Forestry Commission argues that we need to plant trees now, in order to reduce the 91 per cent of our timber we have to import. It also argues that demand for timber will rise by 90 per cent over the next 50 years, and that Britain has only 9 per cent of its area forested compared with an average 22 per cent in the rest of the EEC.

Because the Forestry Commission wants to increase wood production quickly, fast-growing coniferous trees are still often preferred. However, some people feel that plantations such as the one shown in the photograph (Figure 19.1) with long straight rows of identical trees, are spoiling superb views and creating a dark, boring landscape. The Forestry Commission has responded by trying to create a more interesting and varied landscape using a more selective planting policy.

FIGURE 19.1 This hillside has been planted entirely with conifers

1 Study the picture below (Figure 19.2) of a landscaped forest using selective planting. Then match up numbers 1 to 8 on the picture with the list here:
Curving firebreaks/forest roads
Trees planted in natural formation
Conifers planted away from villages
Deciduous trees left next to the river
Curved edge of plantation
Summits not planted
Use of different types of conifers
Deciduous trees planted along road.

FIGURE 19.2 Landscaped plantation

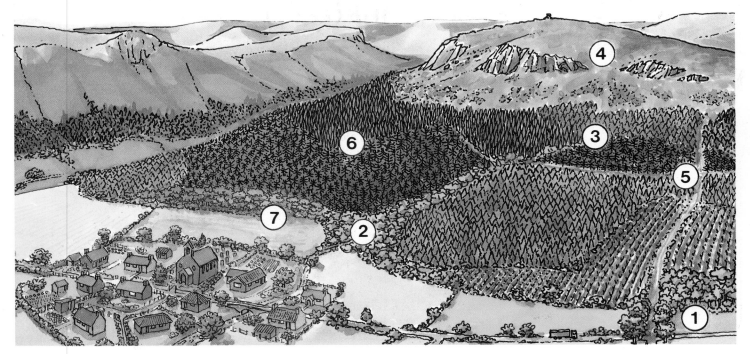

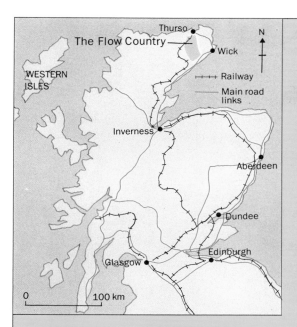

FIGURE 19.3   Location of the Flow Country

For and against forestry

The case of the Scottish Flow Country

AFFORESTATION has raised other issues besides the appearance of the landscape. These are well illustrated in the Flow Country of Scotland (see map opposite). This large part of north-east Scotland is covered by about 10 metres of peat which has been accumulating over the past 9000 years. It is a wild, bare landscape with many lakes and bogs. The main plant is sphagnum moss with many other species of plants in this varied sub-arctic ECOSYSTEM.

FIGURE 19.4   Lichens and mosses in the Flow Country (*above*) give it a pinkish hue when viewed from the air. Greenshanks such as the one pictured here (*left*), have already decreased by about 24 per cent since 1982. There are no alternative nesting sites for these birds in Britain

Forests threaten golden eagle

Blanket afforestation in the Scottish Highlands is destroying the long-feeding grounds of golden eagles and threatening their survival, the Nature Conservancy Council said yesterday.

In summer, eagles feed mainly on mountain hare, rabbit, ptarmigan and red grouse; in winter they live on carrion, mainly dead sheep and deer. All the predatory species are habitants of open terrain, which is disappearing as forestry takes over from sheep farming, the NCC says.

FIGURE 19.5

The balance of plants, insects, birds and animals in the Flow Country is unique and very fragile. Red deer graze in the area, and birds such as greenshank, golden plover and dunlin nest here. However in this area twice the size of Isle of Wight one third was planted with coniferous trees between 1982 and 1987. This is change on a massive scale which is destroying the fragile ecosystem. Local people feel strongly that because the Flow Country is a long way from London and Edinburgh where decisions are made, they are being ignored.

Firms such as Fountain Forestry plan to plant 25 000 hectares using huge machines to break up the soil and install drains. The area then becomes virtual MONOCULTURE of sitka spruce and lodgepole pines. The resulting loss of bird and animal life from this kind of planting is described in the newspaper extract (Figure 19.5). However, the foresters argue that the Nature Conservation Council (NCC) has identified the important wildlife sites in the Flow Country, so the rest is available for tree planting. Some local people feel that outsiders are simply coming in to make money out of planting trees, but do not really care about the future of the region.

FACTS ABOUT FORESTRY

1 Coniferous trees provide a HABITAT for birds new to an area such as chaffinch, wren and woodpigeon.

2 Timber imports cost £3000 million each year.

3 Plantations have cut across ancient paths and routes.

4 Moorland heath and vegetation is replaced by a covering of pine needles and mosses. The whole ecosystem changes.

5 The Forestry Commission employs 8000 people.

6 Forestry Commission timber production:

Year	Production (thousand cubic metres)
1955	300
1980	1500
1987	17000

7 Deer move away from plantations.

8 Trees help to prevent soil erosion and flooding.

9 Imported timber is cheaper than that grown in Britain.

10 £9 million has been spent the government encouraging forestry in the Flow County, but few jobs have been created.

11 Main uses of British timber:

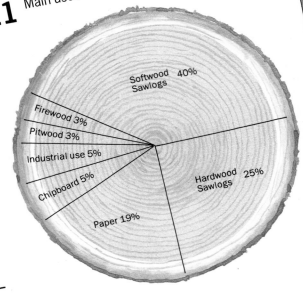

Softwood Sawlogs 40%
Firewood 3%
Pitwood 3%
Industrial use 5%
Chipboard 5%
Paper 19%
Hardwood Sawlogs 25%

12 Forests increase the risk of fires.

13 It costs £30 million to run the Forestry Commission. This cost must be set against import costs.

14 Large areas of single tree species are prone to attack by pests and diseases.

 2 Using the information about the Flow Country and the Facts about Forestry outline the arguments each of the following groups might use for or against planting more trees in the area:

a The RSPB
b Fountain Forestry
c A paper factory owner
d An unemployed local person
e The government (also refer back to Unit 16)
f The Ramblers Association

KEY POINTS

■ At one time most of Britain was covered by forests. Over time, many trees were felled until Britain became short of timber. The Forestry Commission was set up to replant large areas of the countryside with trees.

■ Early Forestry Commission plantations specialised in quick-growing conifers. Unfortunately these plantations created a drab, dull landscape, so now deciduous trees are interplanted to give more variety.

■ The Forestry Commission is opening up more and more forests to provide space for outdoor recreation.

■ Planting trees can be controversial. Some people want to prevent planting trees on open land, with its special types of plants, insects, birds and animal life. Others argue that planting trees saves the cost of imported timber.

IDEAS FOR COURSEWORK

 On a visit to an area of Forestry Commission plantation, map evidence of attempts to make the area more interesting, such as:
- interplanting of deciduous trees with coniferous trees,
- planting deciduous trees along through roads,
- not planting trees in square blocks,
- curving edges to plantations,
- leaving hilltops unplanted,
- using different types of coniferous trees

 Study a Forest Park, and map the location of tourist facilities such as car park, picnic areas, information centre, forest walks, toilets, caravan or camping sites, litter bins etc.
- Look for evidence of over-use by tourists, such as car parks overflowing, excess of litter, too many people on paths, erosion of grassland, unofficial paths through the trees etc.
- How well is the Forest Park coping with its visitors?

Carry out a survey of visitors.
- Have most visitors come over 20 kilometres?
- Where have most visitors come from?
- How have most visitors travelled to the Park?
- What is the main reason for visiting the Park? (bird watching, walking the dog etc.)

20   *Wasting a precious resource*

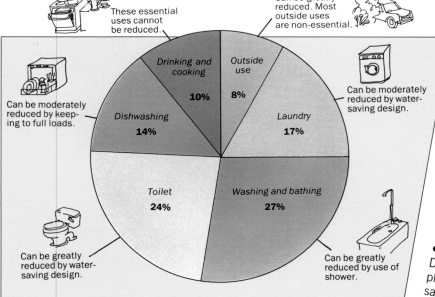

FIGURE 20.1   Earth viewed from space: white clouds of water vapour surround much of the planet

Sun

Evaporation

Rainfall

Water seeps through the soil and forms streams

Streams join together, gradually becoming rivers

River mouth

Sea

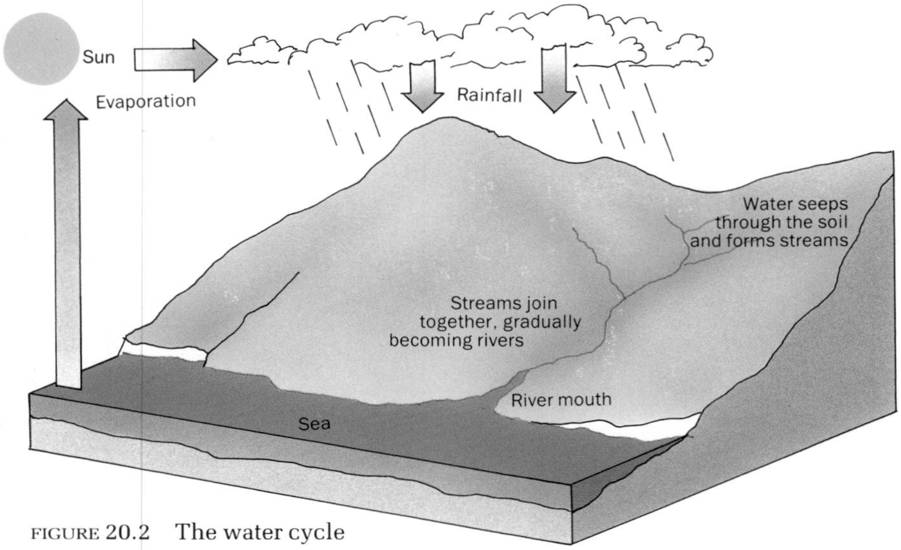

FIGURE 20.2   The water cycle

Water makes Earth different from all other planets that we know of. Earth could be called the 'water planet': water covers two thirds of its surface. This is why it looks blue from space (see Figure 20.1). All life on Earth depends on water. Without it we would die.

Ninety-seven per cent of Earth's water is salt water. It is evaporated from the seas by the heat of the sun and leaves its salt behind. Winds and clouds carry the fresh water inland where some of it falls to the ground as rain. Then it joins together to form streams and rivers which return it to the sea. Here it is mixed with salt again. This is known as the WATER CYCLE (see Figure 20.2).

People interrupt this natural cycle. We collect water somewhere on its passage from the clouds to the sea in order to make use of it. Then we send it on its way again.

The problem is that the amount of water we divert from the natural cycle is getting greater every year. This is because we are using more and more water. Figure 20.3 shows how people use water in their homes, and how we could all save water.

1 Write an article as if for a newspaper pointing out to people how much water we use, and how we could save this resource by simple actions. Use a style designed to shock and persuade people, such as *Twenty things you never knew about water!*

These essential uses cannot be reduced.

Can be greatly reduced. Most outside uses are non-essential.

Can be moderately reduced by keeping to full loads.

Drinking and cooking
10%

Outside use
8%

Dishwashing
14%

Laundry
17%

Can be moderately reduced by water-saving design.

Toilet
24%

Washing and bathing
27%

Can be greatly reduced by water-saving design.

Can be greatly reduced by use of shower.

Source: *Blueprint for a Green Planet* by John Seymour and Hubert Giradet

FIGURE 20.3   Water consumption in the home

POSITIVE ACTION
Simple ways to save water

● *Choose water-efficient appliances*
There are large differences in the amount of water used by different brands of washing machines and dishwashers. Choose appliances that are sparing with water to reduce your consumption.

● *Cut down on car-washing water*
Although a car that is regularly washed will generally last longer, nothing is to be gained by overdoing it: obsessive car-washing just wastes water.

● *Recycle your kitchen water*
Dirty washing-up water is generally harmless to plants. Using it to water your vegetable garden will save tap water in summer.

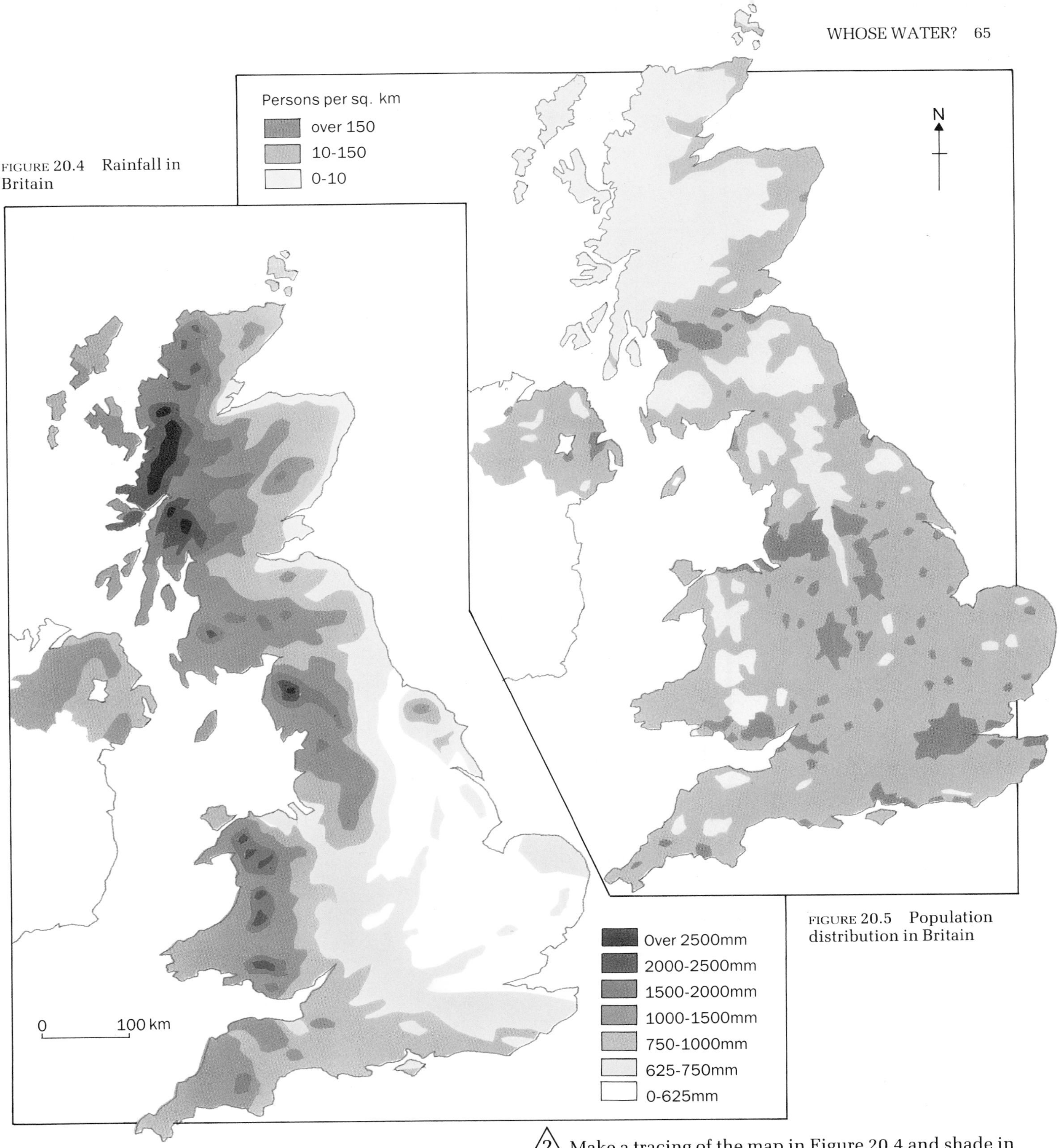

FIGURE 20.4 Rainfall in Britain

Persons per sq. km
- over 150
- 10-150
- 0-10

N

FIGURE 20.5 Population distribution in Britain

0   100 km

Over 2500mm
2000-2500mm
1500-2000mm
1000-1500mm
750-1000mm
625-750mm
0-625mm

Britain's water: supply and demand

Britain's water falls from the clouds as rain, hail, sleet or snow. Figure 20.4 shows those areas of the country which receive most rainfall. Figure 20.5 shows where most people in Britain live. If you look at Figure 20.5, you will see that demand for water is greater in those areas with over 150 people per square kilometre.

2 Make a tracing of the map in Figure 20.4 and shade in all those areas with over 1000mm of rainfall. On the same tracing use Figure 20.5 to mark areas with over 150 people per square kilometre.

a Name four areas of Britain with over 150 people per square kilometre which have *more than 1000mm* of rain each year.

b Name the areas of Britain with over 150 people per square kilometre which have *less than 625mm of rain each year.*

Storing water

Because the areas with the highest demand for water often receive least rainfall, we depend on water storage to maintain supplies.

Aquifers

The diagram opposite (Figure 20.6) shows an AQUIFER. This is a natural water store where the water is trapped underground in a layer of porous rock, sandwiched between layers of impermeable rock.

Demands on these underground water supplies are increasing. In the 1970s the River Stour began to run very low because so much water was being taken to wash cars and flush toilets in growing towns like Colchester. So extra water had to be pumped from the aquifers to increase the flow of the river. The water stored in these aquifers has taken hundreds of years to build up. Now more water is being removed than is being returned, so the aquifers could run dry.

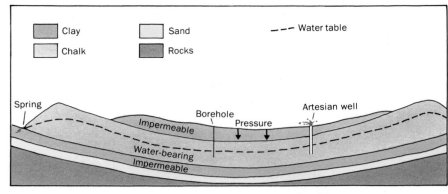

FIGURE 20.6   An aquifer. These are most common in East Anglia and the South East

Surface reservoirs

Since 1900, storing water in reservoirs has been a very important method of ensuring that people in towns always have adequate supplies. Birmingham, for example, built a series of huge reservoirs 160 kilometres away in Wales, where rainfall is usually heavy. People in Birmingham are glad that the reservoirs guarantee their water supply but people in Wales, and other parts of Britain where reservoirs have been built, are not so happy.

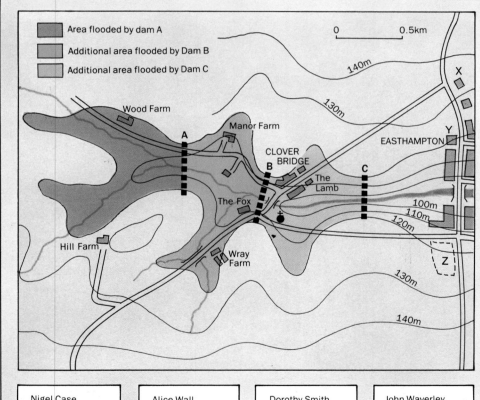

③ The map opposite shows an area where it is planned to build a dam and flood part of the Clover Valley. There are three possible sites for the dam, marked A B and C on the map. Study the map, and read through the profiles of ten local people who are to be interviewed for their opinion on it.

a Work in pairs and choose one of the ten people. Write a few sentences summarising what you think would be their view of the plan.

b Hold a mock public enquiry in the class, taking on the roles of the ten people. Appoint a chairperson to control the enquiry, and include other characters who might have a say, (for example, local planners keen to preserve farmland, councillors for a large city keen to ensure future water supplies). After all the views have been expressed, take a class vote on (i) whether to proceed with the plan, and (ii) what site is preferred.

Nigel Case, power-boat and water ski enthusiast of 'X' Easthampton.

Alice Wall, runs village shop and Post Office, Clover Bridge.

Dorothy Smith, retired teacher. Just bought cottage in Clover Bridge.

John Waverley, unemployed building worker living in Easthampton.

Mary Rivers, landlady of The Lamb at Clover Bridge: worried that The Fox is becoming more popular.

George Atkins, just converted the Old Mill at Clover Bridge into a restaurant.

Rev. J. Waters, vicar of beautiful mediaeval church in Clover Bridge.

Fred Dale, Town Clerk, Easthampton. Keen to develop industrial area at 'Z', which needs a local source of electricity.

Arthur Mudd, managing director of Mudd and Co. civil engineers based at 'Y' Easthampton, hopes for more work building the dam.

Pat Old, member of Easthampton Archaeological Society. Helping with a 'dig' at newly discovered neolithic village near Wray Farm.

21 Polluting our water

Pollution in the countryside

When the rain falls on to Britain it starts to be POLLUTED. Figure 21.1 shows some of the ways this can happen in the countryside.

① List the changes that would be necessary in the countryside to reduce present water pollution.

② Refer back to Unit 16. Are these changes in the countryside likely to take place?

FIGURE 21.1 Water pollution and wastage in the countryside. (Source: *Blueprint for a Green Planet* by John Seymour and Hubert Giradet)

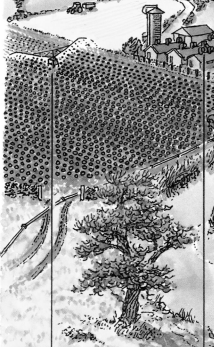

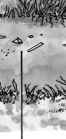

Soil erosion
When heavy rain falls on modern prairie-style fields, many tonnes of topsoil can be washed into rivers, silting them up and ruining the land.

Polluted rain
Atmospheric pollution from factories can make rain water acid before it ever reaches the ground.

Water treatment
Water is pumped out of rivers and chemically treated to prevent us being poisoned by the waste that it carries. Chlorine and copper sulphate are two of the toxic chemicals which may be used to sterilise it.

Irrigation
Using large quantities of water on the land can lower the water-table content and increase the soil's salt content.

Factory farm slurry
Huge amounts of liquid animal manure seep from the farm into rivers, and contaminate the water.

Fertilisers and pesticides
Small amounts are washed out of the soil and carried into the water we drink.

The polluted river
After water has flowed through intensively worked farmland, its quality and wildlife balance are seriously upset.

The land and water storage
Underground water reserves are being used up, and more prime farmland is flooded for water storage.

Pollution in the town

Water is taken from rivers, and filtered and chemically treated to remove all impurities, then it is sent into homes and factories for use. Filtering and purifying the water is very expensive. The picture below (Figure 2.2) shows how this pure, expensive water is rapidly polluted again.

FIGURE 21.2   Water pollution and wastage in the town. (Source: *Blueprint for a Green Planet* by John Seymour and Hubert Giradet)

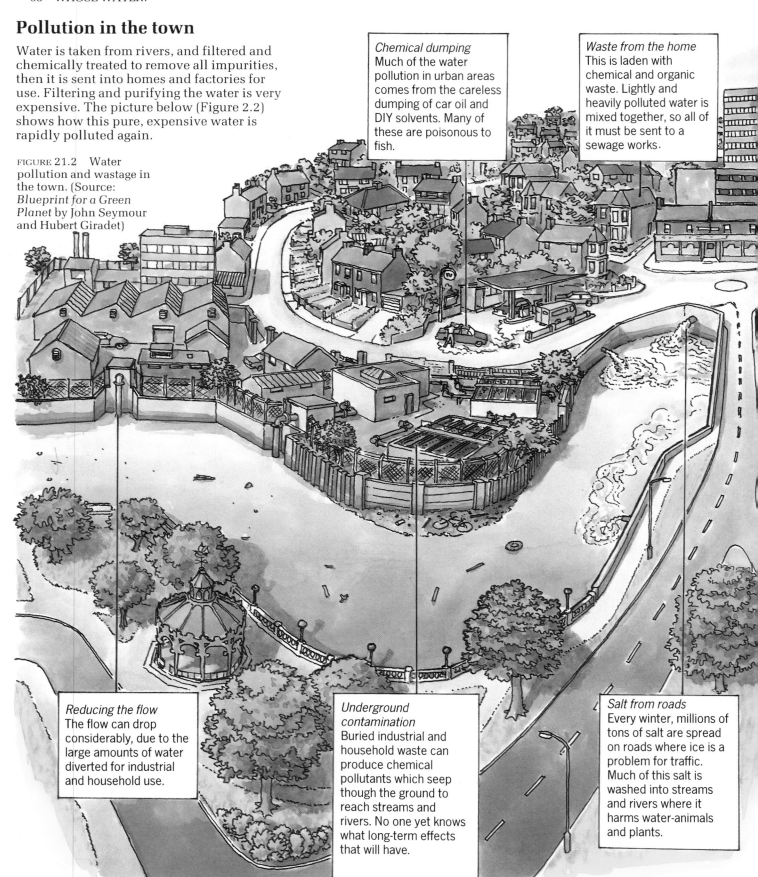

Chemical dumping
Much of the water pollution in urban areas comes from the careless dumping of car oil and DIY solvents. Many of these are poisonous to fish.

Waste from the home
This is laden with chemical and organic waste. Lightly and heavily polluted water is mixed together, so all of it must be sent to a sewage works.

Reducing the flow
The flow can drop considerably, due to the large amounts of water diverted for industrial and household use.

Underground contamination
Buried industrial and household waste can produce chemical pollutants which seep though the ground to reach streams and rivers. No one yet knows what long-term effects that will have.

Salt from roads
Every winter, millions of tons of salt are spread on roads where ice is a problem for traffic. Much of this salt is washed into streams and rivers where it harms water-animals and plants.

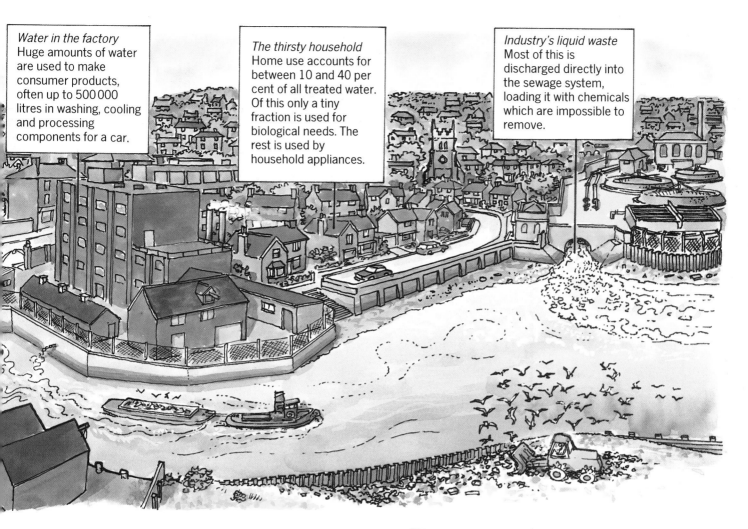

Water in the factory
Huge amounts of water are used to make consumer products, often up to 500 000 litres in washing, cooling and processing components for a car.

The thirsty household
Home use accounts for between 10 and 40 per cent of all treated water. Of this only a tiny fraction is used for biological needs. The rest is used by household appliances.

Industry's liquid waste
Most of this is discharged directly into the sewage system, loading it with chemicals which are impossible to remove.

Most households use between 150 and 500 litres of water each day. Of this only 100 litres need to be very pure for drinking and cooking. All the rest, such as water for flushing the toilet, washing the car or watering the lawn, does not need to be so pure.

Perhaps the answer is for homes to have a dual water system (see Figure 21.3), that is *two* sets of pipes, one thin system bringing pure drinking water, the other larger system bringing less pure water for other uses. Although it would be expensive to install two sets of pipes, the system would soon pay for itself through reduced running costs. All houses would have water meters, and payment would be according to how much water people used.

③ Prepare a special report for a TV programme on the environment, which sets out the advantages and disadvantages of persuading people to switch to a dual water system. Emphasise the costs and benefits to (i) individual homes and (ii) the nation.

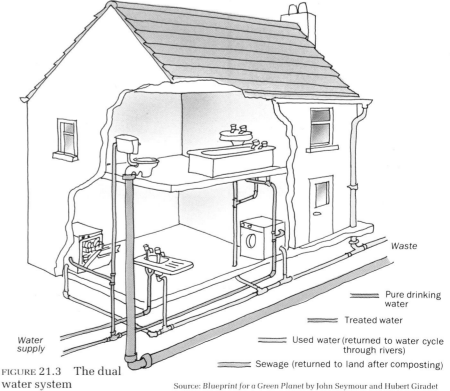

Waste

Water supply

Pure drinking water

Treated water

Used water (returned to water cycle through rivers)

Sewage (returned to land after composting)

FIGURE 21.3   The dual water system

Source: *Blueprint for a Green Planet* by John Seymour and Hubert Giradet

FIGURE 21.4   Britain's coastal pollution

Pollution in the sea

For too long people have regarded rivers, lakes and seas as dumping grounds for their waste. In many places, partially treated sewage is still pumped into the sea, polluting both the water and nearby beaches. The sea and estuaries are also dumping grounds for poisonous materials such as mercury and lead produced by factories. These poisons kill all life in the area as the newspaper extract (Figure 21.4) points out. Worse still, cylinders of radioactive nuclear waste have been dumped around Britain's coasts, yet no one is sure of the long-term effects this may have.

The map on this page shows that oil pollution is still common around our coasts, especially as some oil tankers continue washing out their tanks at sea. Oil slicks kill fish, seaweed and birds. You can see from the map (Figure 21.6) that some parts of Britain's coastline are more vulnerable than others.

FIGURE 21.5

Toxic waste danger increasing

SEWAGE sludge containing toxic waste being dumped in Liverpool Bay is contaminating fish catches so badly that they may have to be condemned as unfit for human consumption.

According to ministry figures in 1986, mercury is the most critical, and levels in fish have now reached 0.29 milligrams per kilogram. The EEC limit for contamination is 0.3mg, at which fish sales must be banned.

Liverpool Bay supports a fishing industry with landings worth £1.5 million a year, plus a large band of fishermen who supplement their dole by group-ownership of boats.

The North West Water Authority dumps 1.6 to 1.8 million tonnes of contaminated sludge in the bay a year. Another 50,000 tonnes of industrial waste is dumped by private companies and up to 5 million tonnes of dredged soil from the Port of Liverpool.

Doctor Cecil Jones, tutor in charge of marine studies of University College of North Wales in Bangor, believes that shellfish in the area could become choked by the sludge.

Mr Eric Barker, principal for river protection for the water authority, said the priority for the authority was to clean up the Mersey. Recently, the Government had asked for a diversion of £35 million resources to clean up Blackpool to comply with EEC directives on bathing beaches.

4. Study Figure 21.6 then answer the following:
   a Which section of coast had most oil slicks between 1980 and 1984?
   b Which were the next two worst areas between 1980 and 1984? Why do you think these areas had so many oil slicks?
   c Which Water Authority has 15–20 per cent of its rivers classified as poor quality?
   d Which Water Authorities have only 0–5 per cent of their rivers classified as poor quality?

5. Study Figure 21.7 below. If pollution of coasts and estuaries was halted and conditions began to improve, which creatures would benefit? Which group of people would benefit?

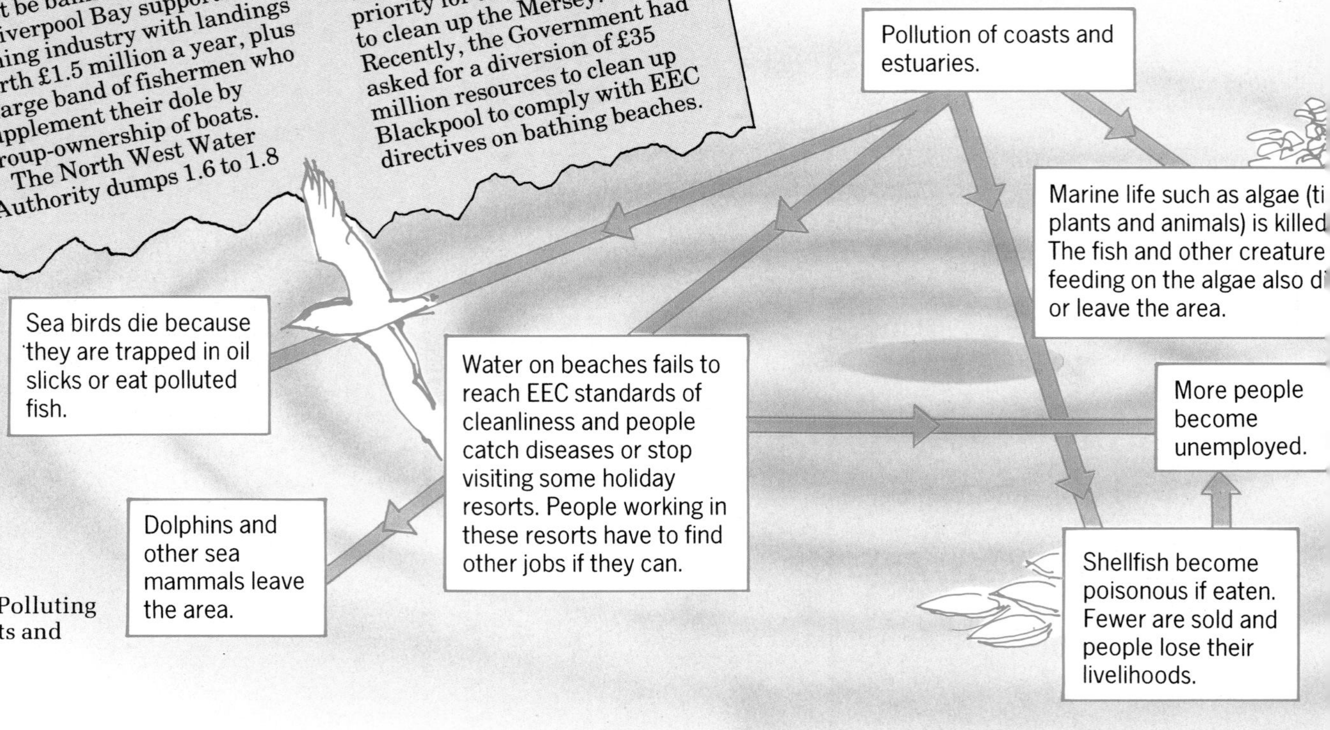

Pollution of coasts and estuaries.

Marine life such as algae (ti plants and animals) is killed The fish and other creature feeding on the algae also d or leave the area.

Sea birds die because they are trapped in oil slicks or eat polluted fish.

Water on beaches fails to reach EEC standards of cleanliness and people catch diseases or stop visiting some holiday resorts. People working in these resorts have to find other jobs if they can.

More people become unemployed.

Dolphins and other sea mammals leave the area.

Shellfish become poisonous if eaten. Fewer are sold and people lose their livelihoods.

FIGURE 21.7   Polluting Britain's coasts and estuaries

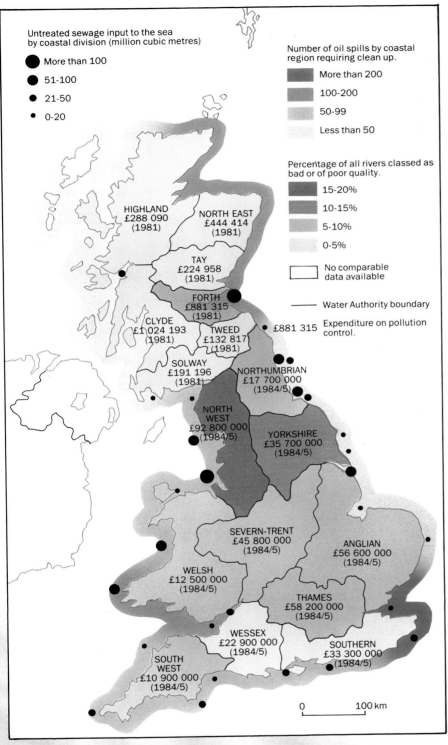

FIGURE 21.6 Pollution in Britain

Map legend:

Untreated sewage input to the sea by coastal division (million cubic metres)
- ● More than 100
- ● 51-100
- ● 21-50
- • 0-20

Number of oil spills by coastal region requiring clean up.
- More than 200
- 100-200
- 50-99
- Less than 50

Percentage of all rivers classed as bad or of poor quality.
- 15-20%
- 10-15%
- 5-10%
- 0-5%
- No comparable data available
- Water Authority boundary

£881 315 Expenditure on pollution control.

Map labels:
- HIGHLAND £288 090 (1981)
- NORTH EAST £444 414 (1981)
- TAY £224 958 (1981)
- FORTH £881 315 (1981)
- CLYDE £1 024 193 (1981)
- TWEED £132 817 (1981)
- £881 315
- SOLWAY £191 196 (1981)
- NORTHUMBRIAN £17 700 000 (1984/5)
- NORTH WEST £92 800 000 (1984/5)
- YORKSHIRE £35 700 000 (1984/5)
- SEVERN-TRENT £45 800 000 (1984/5)
- ANGLIAN £56 600 000 (1984/5)
- WELSH £12 500 000 (1984/5)
- THAMES £58 200 000 (1984/5)
- WESSEX £22 900 000 (1984/5)
- SOUTHERN £33 300 000 (1984/5)
- SOUTH WEST £10 900 000 (1984/5)

0   100 km

Fish (especially flat fish such as plaice) develop cancers and become poisonous if eaten. Shoals of fish leave the area and fishermen have to look elsewhere for a catch or try to find another job.

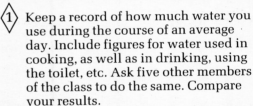

KEY POINTS

- Water is vital to human existence, yet in Britain we tend to take it for granted.

- Demand for water is rising so we have to store it in reservoirs, or use natural stores such as lakes and AQUIFERS.

- Much water is wasted and is frequently POLLUTED by homes, factories, offices and power stations. A dual water system may provide a solution to some of these problems.

- Polluted water affects many types of plants, animals, birds and mammals with which we share the planet.

IDEAS FOR COURSEWORK

1 Keep a record of how much water you use during the course of an average day. Include figures for water used in cooking, as well as in drinking, using the toilet, etc. Ask five other members of the class to do the same. Compare your results.
- Who uses most water? Can you explain this?
- What is most water in the home used for? Write a series of suggestions how we might all save more water, and use them to make up a display poster.

2 Write to your local Water Authority for details of the main water sources for your village, town or city.
- Locate the main sources of supply on a map, and explain how the water gets from its collected point into the domestic system.
- Find out what the Water Authority does to clean up the water, and locate streams or lakes which may still be polluted.
- Try to find the sources of pollution (from factories/farms/towns?) and find out what is being done to clean up the areas.

22 *The demand for energy*

FIGURE 22.1 The city at night. What evidence of power consumption can you see in the picture?

Concern over Britain's energy supplies is constant. There are frequent arguments about the merits of the different power sources, such as coal, oil, natural gas and nuclear energy. There are arguments too, about just how much energy Britain will need in the future. Figure 22.2 below shows how Britain's pattern of energy supplies has changed and Figure 22.3 includes projected figures up to the year 2010. Study Figures 22.2 and 22.3 then answer the questions below.

1. What was Britain's main energy source in 1955?

2. Which source of energy increased rapidly between 1955 and 1970?

3. When did natural gas become an important source of energy?

4. Which form of energy has not changed in importance since 1965?

5. What percentage of Britain's energy comes from nuclear power?

6. **a** Use the statistics to draw pie graphs of energy consumption in 1960, 1985 and 2010.
   b List the main changes shown in your graphs.

FIGURE 22.2 Britain's energy consumption

FIGURE 22.3 Energy: past, present and future (% of total UK energy supplied by each source)

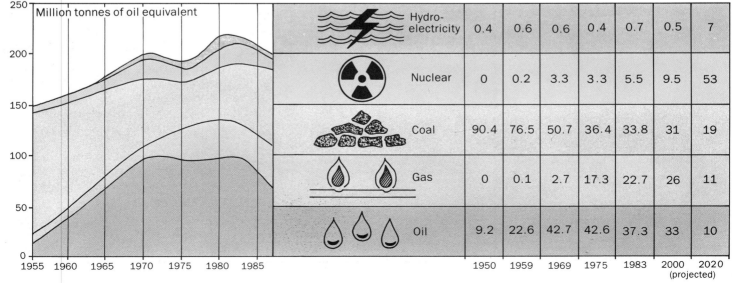

	1950	1959	1969	1975	1983	2000	2020 (projected)
Hydro-electricity	0.4	0.6	0.6	0.4	0.7	0.5	7
Nuclear	0	0.2	3.3	3.3	5.5	9.5	53
Coal	90.4	76.5	50.7	36.4	33.8	31	19
Gas	0	0.1	2.7	17.3	22.7	26	11
Oil	9.2	22.6	42.7	42.6	37.3	33	10

23 Coal: past problems, and now . . . ?

At one time Britain's coalfields provided both the power and many of the raw materials for the industrial revolution. Throughout the nineteenth and early twentieth centuries, coal was a vital growth industry with high exports. Coalfields (see Figure 23.1) in South Wales, Scotland, Yorkshire, Lancashire, the Midlands and the North East became concentrations of industry and of towns. Coal-mining areas were distinguished by rows of terraced houses close to spoil heaps and pithead winding gear. Whole communities grew up dependent on the pit. However, conditions began to change from the 1920s onwards.

① Study Figures 23.2 to 23.7 on this page. They show the changes in British mining since the 1920s. Next, answer the following questions under the title *Coal in Decline*:

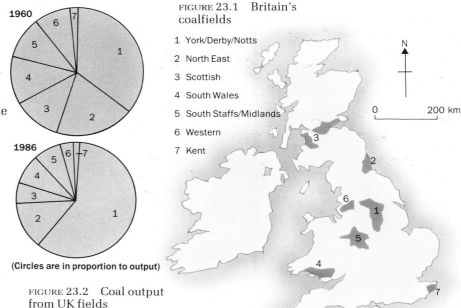

1960

1986

(Circles are in proportion to output)

FIGURE 23.2 Coal output from UK fields

FIGURE 23.1 Britain's coalfields

1 York/Derby/Notts
2 North East
3 Scottish
4 South Wales
5 South Staffs/Midlands
6 Western
7 Kent

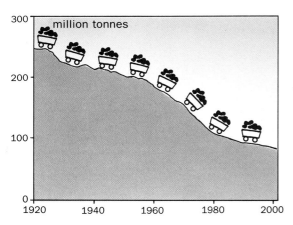

FIGURE 23.3 UK coal production

a By how much has coal output fallen since 1920?

b During which decades has coal output fallen most rapidly?

c How many miners were employed in 1920, in 1960, and in 1987?

d Which markets for coal have expanded since 1920? Which markets have disappeared? Which markets have contracted? Try to explain the changes.

e Which coalfields have increased their proportion of total output since 1950? Which coalfields have declined in importance?

f Describe the changes in output per miner and in the percentage of coal cut by machine since 1940.

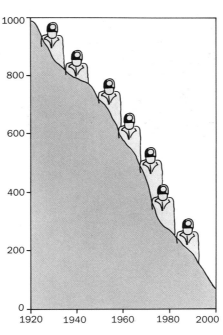

FIGURE 23.4 Number of working miners in UK (thousands)

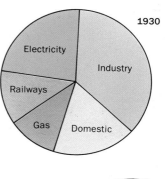

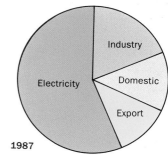

1930

Electricity
Industry
Railways
Gas
Domestic

1987

Industry
Electricity
Domestic
Export

FIGURE 23.5 Main markets for coal

FIGURE 23.6 UK coal output per miner (tonnes per year)

1940	1960	1980	1986
212	310	476	494

FIGURE 23.7 Percentage of coal cut by machines

1940	1960	1980	1986
7	38	94	96

Coal and communities: the Rhondda valley

In many places, such as the Rhondda valley in Wales, pit closure has been devastating for the entire community. In 1910 the Rhondda had 50 collieries producing 10 million tonnes of coal and employing 40 000 people. In 1986 the last pit, Maerdy colliery, finally closed bringing an end to coal-mining in this famous valley.

Coal from the Rhondda was world famous and in the early twentieth century it led to the building of Barry docks to handle exports. Mining was difficult in the narrow, steep-sided valleys so railways and canals were built along the valley floor (see Figure 23.9). Terraced cottages for miners had to cling to steep valley sides, and were often surrounded by huge spoil heaps. Life in the early twentieth century was hard, with up to 15 people crammed into the tiny houses, often with only one cold tap and no bath or toilet. Mining was, and still is, a dirty and dangerous occupation.

In 1801 only 1000 people lived in the Rhondda valley but by 1921 this had risen to 140 000. These mining villages had a strong sense of community. People helped each other in times of hardship such as the economic depression of the 1930s when most men were unemployed. Everyone knew

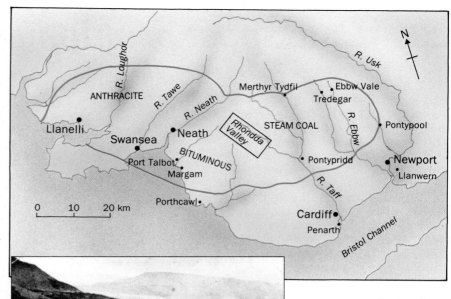

FIGURE 23.8   The South Wales coalfield

FIGURE 23.9   Old Rhondda remembered. Standard Colliery Ynyshir

FIGURE 23.10   Rhondda street sports, 1920s. The whole community took part in events like these

everyone else in these closed communities which were fiercely independent. The people lived, worked and died together. It was normal for sons to follow their fathers down the mines and for daughters to marry miners within the village. Strangers and outsiders were viewed with suspicion. The Rhondda was regarded as a 'militant' area which was often in conflict with colliery owners. In the 1930s Maerdy became known as 'little Moscow'.

By 1945 the most easily worked coal had been removed along the valley and the remaining seams were narrow and faulted. This made mining difficult and expensive. Collieries began to close and there was little investment in new machinery because the National Coal Board was investing in new, deep mines on the Yorkshire coalfields. The loss of export markets, a greater level of mechanisation, and cheaper coal from abroad or other UK fields all forced colliery closures. At the same time people began to leave in search of work, so by 1961 the Rhondda's population was only 100 300. By 1981 it was down to 81 700.

Despite the end of coal-mining, the Rhondda villages and towns retain much of their character. In the 1984/5 miner's strike, there was never a picket line to prevent miners going to work at Maerdy colliery because the community solidly supported the action. There was a strong women's support group who collected and distributed food and clothing for striking miners and their families. The community tradition of self-help and independence is still strong, fuelled by redundancies and pit closures. There is still coal at Maerdy but it is mined by workings from the Tower colliery in the next valley.

Improving the Rhondda

Study Figure 23.12 opposite which represents part of a typical South Wales mining valley such as the Rhondda.
Then answer the questions which follow.

 Copy the outline of Figure 23.12. On it, draw four improvements, chosen from the list below, which could be made to the area. In choosing your four improvements, think about which projects are the most important. Those which improve housing? Those which attract new firms and jobs? Or those which improve the environment?

    Levelling spoil heaps
    Turning the mine into a museum
    Landscaping spoil heaps with trees
    Turning derelict land into dry ski
      slopes
    Building new housing
    Improving terraced houses
    Building new factories on former
      colliery sites or former spoil heaps
    Improving roads to dual carriageway
      standard
    Leisure complex (swimming bath, sauna, fitness centre) on site of former spoil heap

 Write a short paragraph explaining the reasons for your four improvements.

 Now write an advert describing your diagram, as if you were trying to attract new industry to the area. For example, you might mention communications, workforce, local housing, local facilities, local landscape attractions etc.

FIGURE 23.11 Rhondda 1985. Miners' wives sorting provisions for striking miners and their families

 Write a letter to British Coal as if you were a former miner who retired when the local pit closed. Point out the effects of closure on the area, emphasising the social tensions it has created. Outline how things might have been different if the colliery had remained open, or if new industry had been introduced.

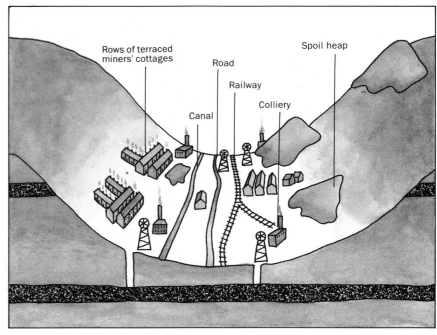

FIGURE 23.12 A South Wales valley (1960s)

British Coal Enterprise

In 1985 British Coal began to try and attract new firms to areas like the Rhondda where collieries were closing. British Coal Enterprise (BCE) was set up to advise redundant miners on ways of establishing new firms, together with providing loans and making contacts with investment banks. Former miners now run steam-cleaning, plastics and engineering firms started with some help from BCE. In 1985 BCE invested £12.9 million, in 1986 this rose to £40 million with the aim of creating 40 000 jobs each year. However, between 1979 and 1986 British Coal cut 87 000 jobs and helped create a mere 8 200 new jobs, so a great employment task remains.

New jobs in coal?

British Coal has started to develop two new coalfields, one at Selby in Yorkshire and the other in the Vale of Belvoir in Leicestershire. These areas have large reserves of coal which can be exploited by large, very modern collieries.

As the newspaper extracts on this page indicate, in 1987 the Central Electricity Generating Board announced the sites for two new coal-fired power stations (see Figure 23.14) and British Coal announced a proposed new mine at Margam in West Glamorgan (see Figure 23.15). These developments may create some new jobs in mining or at least guarantee existing jobs.

FIGURE 23.13   Architect-designed winding tower at one of the five Selby mines which share underground links and centralised coal-handling and despatch. What contrasts do you notice between this picture and Figure 23.9?

Ex-miner Chris Guest has set up his own plastering business with the help of British Coal's 'Job Shop'. Unlike Chris, many miners do not possess skills from other trades, so finding a new occupation is not so easy

British Coal may create 800 jobs

British Coal has offered to create 800 jobs in South Wales.

Sir Robert Haslam gave the go-ahead for the sinking of a £90 million new mine at Margam in West Glamorgan. British Coal envisages the output from the mine, about 1.2 million tonnes a year, going to its national smoke-less fuels subsidiary's coking ovens at Cwm in Dyfed and to the British Steel Corporation's plants at Llanwern and nearby Port Talbot, where it would replace imports.

The Central Electricity Generating Board has chosen West Burton in Nottinghamshire and Fawley near Southampton as the sites for its next coal-fired power stations.

The two stations are expected to cost a total of at least £2 billion. Up to 20,000 jobs will be secured during the six years it takes to build them.

An inquiry is likely at Fawley. The CEGB already has an oil-fired station there, and the local Tory MP, Mr Michael Colvin, complained in the Commons that his constituency was being used as a dumping ground for unwanted developments.

The CEGB is considering ordering up to five coal-fired stations. Investigations are to continue at three other sites: Kingsnorth in Kent, Killingholme on Humberside, and Hams Hall near Birmingham.

Possible sites for CEGB coal-fired power stations

Killingholme
West Burton
Hams Hall
0   km   100
Kingsnorth
Fawley
N

Shortlisted – from eight to five

FIGURE 23.15   Job prospects at new mine (1987)

FIGURE 23.14   New coal-fired power stations (1987)

NCB splits opposition to planned £400m superpit

The Coal Board yesterday drove a wedge through the opposition to its plans for a £400 million superpit when it announced two possible sites for the mine.

Expected production is three million tonnes a year, which would make it by far the most productive single pit in the country.

The proposed sites are at the northern and southern extremities of the area the NCB has been considering – at Hawksmoor Farm, on the outskirts of Coventry, and South Hurst Farm, near Kenilworth

A pit anywhere in the area would give the board access to 165 million tonnes of easily-mined coal. The NCB has said it would take 11 years to build and would eventually employ some 1,800 people.

Consultants would draw up detailed environmental impact assessments of both sites before submitting a planning application for one of them.

Hawksmoor Farm is close to an already industrialised district, but is on high ground. Pit buildings would

be clearly visible, although not from the nearby conservation village of Berkswell.

South Hurst Farm is in a rural setting but has the advantage of being shielded by trees. The tops of the colliery winder towers would be visible from Warwick University and Kenilworth Castle, but not from Crackley Wood, a popular recreation area. The pit buildings and facilities would cover a medieval site which, the NCB say, would be excavated by Warwick Museum before work started.

A further complication will be the transport links. Both would require the re-opening of a disused branch rail line.

South Hurst Farm stands close to it, whereas Hawksmoor Farm would need to be connected by a new stretch of track almost three miles long, which would cross the main London/Birmingham railway route – a task involving sizeable engineering work. A direct link to the main line is "impracticable," say the NCB.

FIGURE 23.16   Superpit proposals (1985)

In 1986 British Coal also announced its decision to build a 'superpit' on one of two possible sites in the Midlands costing £400 million. Study Figure 23.16 which considers the two possible sites, then answer the question which follows.

6 **a** Carry out an *environmental impact assessment* for each of the two proposed sites for the new colliery. Use the information from the newspaper article to complete a copy of the table in Figure 23.16 to help you. When you have completed the table you must give a weighting to each of the factors. The weightings are 40, 30, 20 and 10. Give the highest weighting (40) to the factor you feel is the most important (for example, height of colliery). Then give a weighting to the other factors.

Factors	Hawkhurst Moor	South Hurst Farm	Weighting
1 New transport links necessary			
2 Surrounding land use			
3 Height of colliery and its visual impact			
4 Effect on agricultural land and sites of historic interest			

b On the basis of your assessment, write a short account of your reasons for preferring one of the two sites.

24   *Oil and gas: at what price?*

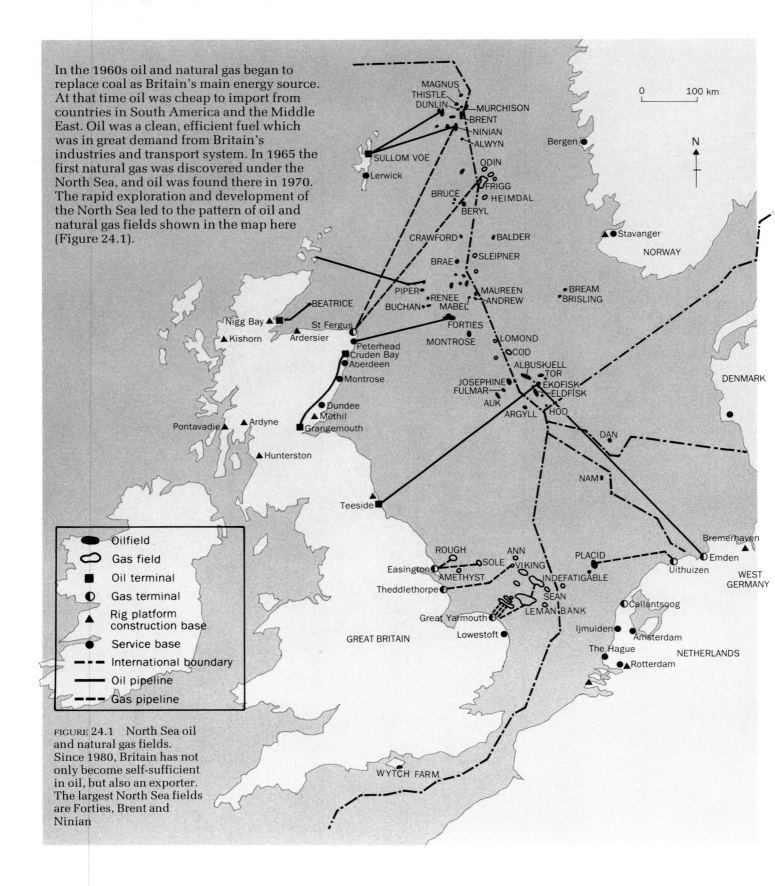

In the 1960s oil and natural gas began to replace coal as Britain's main energy source. At that time oil was cheap to import from countries in South America and the Middle East. Oil was a clean, efficient fuel which was in great demand from Britain's industries and transport system. In 1965 the first natural gas was discovered under the North Sea, and oil was found there in 1970. The rapid exploration and development of the North Sea led to the pattern of oil and natural gas fields shown in the map here (Figure 24.1).

0   100 km

N

Legend:
- ⬭ Oilfield
- ⬯ Gas field
- ■ Oil terminal
- ◑ Gas terminal
- ▲ Rig platform construction base
- ● Service base
- –·– International boundary
- —— Oil pipeline
- – – – Gas pipeline

FIGURE 24.1   North Sea oil and natural gas fields. Since 1980, Britain has not only become self-sufficient in oil, but also an exporter. The largest North Sea fields are Forties, Brent and Ninian

Map labels:
MAGNUS, THISTLE, DUNLIN, MURCHISON, BRENT, NINIAN, ALWYN, ODIN, FRIGG, HEIMDAL, BRUCE, BERYL, CRAWFORD, BALDER, SLEIPNER, BRAE, PIPER, RENEE, MABEL, BUCHAN, MAUREEN, ANDREW, BREAM, BRISLING, FORTIES, MONTROSE, LOMOND, COD, ALBUSKJELL, TOR, JOSEPHINE, FULMAR, EKOFISK, ELDFISK, AUK, ARGYLL, HOD, DAN, NAM, ROUGH, ANN, PLACID, SOLE, VIKING, AMETHYST, INDEFATIGABLE, SEAN, LEMAN BANK, WYTCH FARM

Bergen, Lerwick, SULLOM VOE, Stavanger, NORWAY, BEATRICE, Nigg Bay, St Fergus, Kishorn, Ardersier, Peterhead, Cruden Bay, Aberdeen, Montrose, Dundee, Methil, Pontavadie, Ardyne, Grangemouth, Hunterston, Teeside, DENMARK, Bremerhaven, Emden, Uithuizen, WEST GERMANY, Easington, Theddlethorpe, Great Yarmouth, Lowestoft, GREAT BRITAIN, Callantsoog, Ijmuiden, Amsterdam, The Hague, NETHERLANDS, Rotterdam

The financial costs of developing the North Sea were huge, but so were the profits as the pie graphs on this page illustrate (Figure 24.2). Large MULTINATIONAL firms such as Shell, Esso, BP and Texaco bore the costs of development and so felt entitled to take the profits. Some people argue that Britain has been treated badly by these multinational companies, whose foreign shareholders have taken much of the profit from Britain's oil. The profits from North Sea operations are now double the companies' first investment, even after tax payable to the British government.

There have also been human costs in developing the North Sea in deaths and injuries amongst oil workers. From 1974 to 1987 there were 175 deaths and over 1000 serious injuries. The following comments (Figure 24.3) summarise many people's view of North Sea oil and gas development.

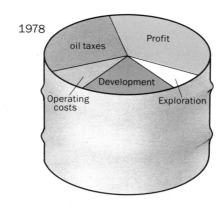

FIGURE 24.2   Costs of developing North Sea oil and gas

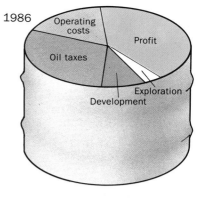

FIGURE 24.3   North Sea oil and gas: what the people think

D I was unemployed and then got a job building oil rigs, but now I am on the dole again because no more oil rigs are needed.

H Many of the newcomers to Scotland did not fit in with the locals. They introduced new, different social values and changed many small communities.

A Oil is a *non-renewable* resource. It will never be replaced. We should not have sold it to foreigners, but saved it for ourselves.

E Many seabirds have died from oil pollution around the Shetland and Orkney islands, despite all the talk about conservation, and there is the constant threat of explosion or more pollution.

I New shops, schools and health clinics have been built in parts of Scotland with the money from oil and gas.

B I live in Aberdeen, which became a centre for the oil and gas industry. My house increased in value five times between 1970 and 1985. But when the boom ended I could not sell my house when I had to move.

F Our traditional Scottish industries such as fishing and textiles have declined as people left for better paid jobs in the oil industry.

J North Sea oil and gas has saved Britain millions of pounds on the import bill. We have also made money from exporting oil.

G New airports have been built which now link up remote areas with the rest of Britain.

C I was an unemployed welder but then I got a job building pipelines. My wife works on the helicopters which take men to and from the rigs.

K We do not have to depend on the goodwill of countries in the Middle East or South America for our vital oil supplies.

 Study each of the comments. Then, under the title *Costs and Benefits of North Sea Oil and Gas*, complete the table below, which has been started for you. For each statement, decide whether you think it reflects economic, environmental or social gain/loss. Enter your reason under the appropriate column heading.

Economic gain	Economic loss	Environmental gain	Environmental loss	Social gain	Social loss

Deciding the future

Britain's oil production reached its peak of 2.59 million barrels per day in 1986. Since then output has begun to decline (see Figure 24.4) and it looks as if this decline will continue. The giant Forties oilfield, discovered in the 1970s, is now well over half empty. Small finds of oil and gas are still being made in the North Sea, but no major ones.

Britain has several important choices to make regarding the future of oil and gas:

- Should efforts be concentrated on trying to find new oil and gas fields north-west of Scotland and off the coast of Ireland? The water here is deep and the costs and dangers great.
- Should Britain continue to try and reduce its use of oil? Between 1980 and 1987 oil consumption in Britain fell by 20 per cent as a result of factory closures, better insulation in homes and factories, and the use of more efficient machines, especially car and aeroplane engines. There is still scope to make better use of the oil we have.

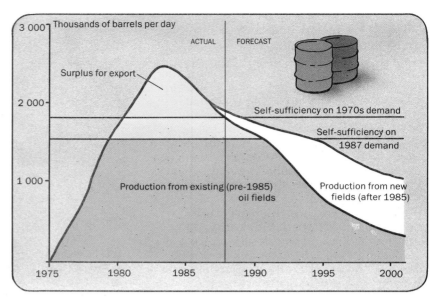

FIGURE 24.4   North Sea oil production (1975 – 2000 projected)

- Should we concentrate on other forms of energy such as coal, nuclear, wind, solar or wave power? These could replace oil if demand exceeds supply.
- Should the research for oil continue on land? This can create environmental problems as the case of Wytch Farm in Dorset illustrates.

FIGURE 24.5 This giant North Sea rig is being battered by 20 metre waves and gale force winds. What will happen to it when the oil runs out?

FIGURE 24.6   British Airways new Airbus has been developed to outstrip its rivals in fuel economy. Its ultra-modern engines should reduce noise levels. But with more passengers taking to the air each year, who will benefit?

Oil on the Dorset coast

The Wytch Farm oilfield in Dorset began as a single exploratory well near Corfe Castle in 1973. It proved to be a spectacular find, producing a million tonnes by 1985. This has led to a mass of drilling rigs, an oil gathering station, a railhead and a pipeline. Unfortunately all these developments have taken place in an area of extremely beautiful and sensitive countryside. For example, the exploratory wells on the Arne peninsula are in an area officially designated a Site of Special Scientific Interest (SSSI). So is the pipeline at Cleaval Point, and the railhead terminal at Stoborough Heath. The well at Kimmeridge is near an important marine nature reserve. Figure 24.7 summarises some people's views of the Wytch Farm development.

I was able to sell some land for the railhead terminal and so made money to invest in the farm.

Our holiday caravan site has suffered. People did not want the noise, dust and dirt of the oil drilling so they moved on.

It has created very few jobs for local people. Most of the work is done by machines and the oil drillers come from all over the world.

FIGURE 24.7   Wytch Farm. What people think

It is not right to create a site of special scientific interest which has rare plants, birds and wildlife, and then to allow oil drilling in the area. The noise and disturbance may spoil the area for ever.

We at BP are proud of our record at preventing oil spills and for safeguarding the environment. Britain needs the oil and we are getting it as carefully as possible.

2 The newspaper extract shown here (Figure 24.8) illustrates a similar problem over drilling on Furzey Island in Poole Harbour. Study it alongside Figure 24.7. What do you think the following people would say about the development on Furzey Island?
a The owner of a boating marina near Furzey Island.
b People with a holiday cottage on the island.
c The Nature Conservancy Council.
d A Dorset firm supplying steel drilling pipes.
e Holidaymakers to Dorset.

3 Which views do you agree with? List the arguments you would use to support your views.

Black gold rush for paradise isle

Under Furzey Island, in Poole harbour, Dorset, is believed to be the biggest onshore oilfield yet discovered in Western Europe.

It was once owned by oil tycoon Algy Cluff, who used it as a holiday retreat. He sold it to BP, who now want to drill through his old tennis court.

Conservation bodies, including the Countryside Commission and the Nature Conservancy Council are pressing the Government to intervene, and on Tuesday the National Trust will call for a public inquiry when it launches a new campaign to save Britain's coast.

In theory Furzey Island should be well protected; it is in the heart of one of the most valuable Sites of Special Scientific Interest and in an Area of Outstanding Natural Beauty.

It is part of Dorset's Heritage Coast, which last year was awarded the Council of Europe's diploma.

Any one of these distinctions should be enough to guarantee an assurance against development for oil. Dorset County Council were swayed by two considerations in allowing drilling – the richness of the oilfield and BP's excellent reputation and proposals for safeguarding the environment.

The oilfield, known as the Sherwood reservoir, lies beneath Britain's biggest existing producing field, at Wytch Farm. It could produce about 40,000 barrels of oil a day, more than many North Sea fields. It qualifies as a 'giant' even by United States onshore standards.

FIGURE 24.8

25 *The nuclear age?*

These are the three most common questions asked about nuclear power. The answers vary, as this unit shows.

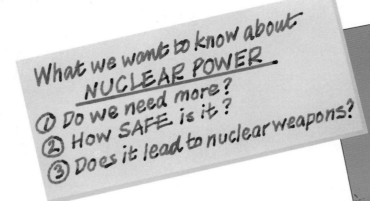

What we want to know about
NUCLEAR POWER.
① Do we need more?
② How SAFE is it?
③ Does it lead to nuclear weapons?

The case for more nuclear power

- The function of the Central Electricity Generating Board (CEGB) is to ensure that Britain has a safe, secure, reliable supply of electricity, *at the lowest possible cost*. The CEGB views nuclear energy as a vital part of Britain's future electricity supply as the pie graphs on this page indicate (see Figure 25.1).
- The Board argues that without more nuclear power, Britain will not be able to produce enough electricity to meet the estimated demand by the year 2000. There could, therefore, be an ENERGY GAP which would mean fewer jobs and lower living standards. Imports would be expensive and too dependent on the goodwill of foreign suppliers.

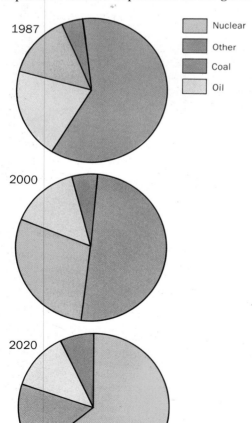

Nuclear
Other
Coal
Oil

1987

2000

2020

- By the year 2000 coal-fired power stations will be very expensive because of the need to install special equipment to prevent air pollution. Nuclear energy is therefore a cheaper, cleaner alternative. The nuclear industry is the only one to fully containerise all its solid waste and seal it off from the environment.
- In its pamphlet *The Facts about Nuclear Energy* the CEGB argues that nuclear power will be the *cheapest* form of electricity to meet the expected demand. 'A UK pressurised water reactor (PWR) would be expected to produce electricity . . . at about two-thirds the cost of a contemporary coal-fired power station.' One of the reasons that electricity from nuclear stations is so cheap is that only small amounts of fuel (uranium) are needed. One tonne of uranium can produce as much electricity as 25 000 tonnes of coal or 15 000 tonnes of oil.
- Nuclear power stations produce only small amounts of highly radioactive waste, which can be stored on site, underground.
- Much money has already been spent on research into nuclear power and large firms and government departments support the nuclear industry, but electricity from so-called 'alternative' or 'renewable' sources, such as solar, wind or wave power will take many years to perfect and may still be too expensive.
- The nuclear power industry employs many people throughout the country. The growth of nuclear power will help to provide stable jobs in areas like Cumbria where there are few alternative sources of employment.

FIGURE 25.1   Electricity for the future. According to the statistics, which will be the most important power source for electricity by the year 2000? and by 2020?

FIGURE 25.2 Sizewell A power station, on the Suffolk coast

The power seekers

Young Guardian recently took a party of youngsters – aged from 14-17 – on a visit to the CEGB nuclear power station at Sizewell. This is their report.

Katie Nibbs (14) said: "The day began with a highly simplified explanation of how nuclear power operates – descriptions like 'glorified kettle' and 'the object of all this controversy is boiling water' were perhaps meant to set our minds at rest."

Kala Subbuswany (14) added: "The power station was clean and the people friendly but I couldn't help feeling like a customer who had been subjected to a lengthy sales talk, the salesman – the CEGB, the product – nuclear power."

The three boys were more certain that nuclear power was safe and necessary. "I left Billericay with an open mind," said 14-year-old Ian Hammond. "I came away feeling I was for nuclear energy."

Zafar Sarfraz (17) agreed. "I must admit Sizewell 'A' impressed me greatly. We took around a device to measure radiation – all the levels were harmless. I still believe, though, the major problem is the handling and disposal of radioactive waste."

David Thomas said he too had been dubious about safety before he went but "the managers we talked to thought the most dangerous part of their jobs was driving to and from work. I think public concern stems from lack of knowledge."

The group were able to tour the plant, including the reactor building and later closely questioned Sizewell staff about all the aspects of safety and radioactive waste – the two main issues that bothered them.

Collette Gilmore (16), while impressed by the replies, was still worried: "I was dubious about safety and in the end I was not convinced of the need for nuclear power. In about ten years Sizewell will have to be shut down at great cost – the waste disposal question is unanswered."

Katie continued: "The nuclear inspecto-rate (who look after safety matters in the public's name) are not present at every stage of construction and operation. Accidents that theoretically cannot happen in practice do."

FIGURE 25.3

The case against more nuclear power

○ Some experts claim that there will not be an energy-gap in the year 2000 or beyond. They argue that demand for electricity fell in the early 1980s because (i) many factories closed, (ii) better insulation in homes ensured less electricity was needed (iii) low energy household appliances such as washing machines became more widespread (iv) new industries such as micro-electronics use less electricity. Hence predictions about future electricity demand may be wrong.

○ Coal-fired power stations may not be as expensive as the CEGB argue. Increased mechanisation may reduce coal costs, and using coal would avoid the dangers and costs of having to rely on imported fuel. Also anti-pollution equipment on coal-fired power stations after 1986 proved less expensive than forecast.

○ RENEWABLE ENERGY forms using wind power are already being tried by the CEGB and may be cheaper than forecast (see Unit 26).

○ Renewable energy and coal-fired power stations could provide nearly as many jobs as the nuclear industry, though not in the same parts of the country.

○ Although nuclear power stations produce little waste, it is highly dangerous and requires very careful handling. Many environmental and conservation groups are very worried about waste disposal.

○ Since the 1986 explosion at a Soviet nuclear power station in Chernobyl when radioactivity spread to many countries, fears of a similar danger remain.

 a Study the two arguments presented here and the newspaper extract (Figure 25.3) above which summarises the reactions of a group of young people after visiting Sizewell nuclear power station. Then complete a copy of the table below by writing a series of short sentences, summarising each argument for and against more nuclear power.

FOR more nuclear power	AGAINST more nuclear power
1) By the year 2000 Britain may have an energy gap	1) There may be no energy gap by the year 2000 or even after

b Now write a short paragraph putting forward your own views and explaining the reasons behind them.

What are the dangers?

1 Transporting nuclear material

At the heart of a nuclear power station is the reactor, where uranium atoms are split to create intense heat. This process of splitting atoms is called nuclear fission. The heat generated by the process is used to convert water into steam which is then used to turn turbines and generate electricity.

The fuel rods used in the reactor have to be replaced every seven years. The spent fuel rods are taken by train or lorry to the Sellafield plant in Cumbria, where they are processed for future use. The rods are carried by rail or road in massive 50 tonne steel flasks, which are designed to survive accidents or fire (see Figure 25.5 below).

However, many people oppose transporting dangerous nuclear waste through built-up areas such as London. The diagram opposite (Figure 25.4) shows what might happen if there was a spillage of nuclear waste at Camden Town on the North London rail line (used to carry nuclear waste).

 Write a short article as if for a newspaper, to accompany Figure 25.4 entitled *The Dangers of Transporting Nuclear Waste*. In your article point out what might happen in densely populated areas like those shown on the map immediately after the accident (for example, evacuation of certain areas first, dangers of panic on roads and on public transport, role of police, army, fire and ambulance services).

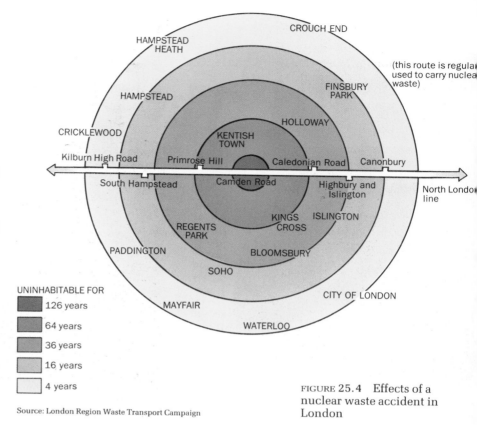

UNINHABITABLE FOR
- 126 years
- 64 years
- 36 years
- 16 years
- 4 years

Source: London Region Waste Transport Campaign

FIGURE 25.4 Effects of a nuclear waste accident in London

FIGURE 25.5 Nuclear flask train crash demonstration, 1984, organised by the CEGB. The nuclear fuel flask can be seen on the right, still intact

2 Reprocessing nuclear fuel

The Sellafield factory on the coast of Cumbria, run by British Nuclear Fuels, is able to reprocess spent fuel and even create new fuel (plutonium). This reduces the need to import uranium or other raw materials and by reprocessing fuel from other countries earns export income for Britain. This large factory provides employment for over 3000 people and many workers are satisfied with the safety provisions designed to prevent the escape of radioactivity.

However, groups such as Greenpeace and Friends of the Earth are very critical of reprocessing nuclear fuel at Sellafield. They argue that deaths from leukaemia (cancer of the blood) near the factory are much higher than the national average. They link these deaths to leaks of radioactivity from Sellafield. They claim that since the plant opened in the 1950s the Sellafield complex has released 250 kilograms of plutonium – the most lethal of all human produced poisons – into the air or into the sea. Greenpeace also claim that the local beaches are often so radioactive that they have to be closed to the public.

Feelings about the Sellafield factory run high. A widow whose husband died of cancer after working at Sellafield indicated this when she said, 'I never knew much about his job and I did not realise just how dangerous it was. He was only fifty when he died, and he blamed the factory.'

 Now write what you think each of the following people might say about Sellafield:
a A public relations spokesperson for British Nuclear Fuels, keen to stress its safety.
b A local man aged 35, unemployed for four years and now with a job at Sellafield.
c A mother with young children who lives near the factory.
d The owner of an hotel he wishes to sell on the Cumbria coast and who cannot find a buyer.

3 Nuclear waste disposal

Part of the spent uranium fuel from nuclear power stations is converted into a liquid and stored. There are different levels of RADIOACTIVITY in nuclear waste, and it is therefore disposed of in different ways:

- In the past, low level radioactive waste was encased in concrete within large steel drums and dumped in deep parts of the sea. The British Union of Seamen voted against continued involvement in deep sea dumping, and conservation groups also contributed to halting dumping at sea after direct action like that shown in Figure 25.6.
- Low level waste is also buried in trenches dug in the ground of geologically stable areas such as Drigg, a site next to the Sellafield reprocessing plant. However, plans for new nuclear waste dumps at Killingholme on Humberside, Fulbeck in Lincolnshire, and Elstow and Bradwell in Essex produced strong protest from local people and were later abandoned.
- High level waste is stored in special tanks at the Sellafield reprocessing plant.
- Some effluent with low levels of radioactivity is discharged into the seas around Britain.

 Imagine that you live in a rural area where British Nuclear Fuels is planning a nuclear waste site. Draw up a list of questions you would ask British Nuclear Fuels at a public meeting being held to discuss the plans.

FIGURE 25.6   Greenpeace dinghy protest against nuclear dumping. Notice the cargo ready for ditching. What else is happening? Why?

FIGURE 25.7   Transporting nuclear waste for storage, Drigg (right)

Does nuclear power lead to nuclear weapons?

Britain's first nuclear power stations were built partly to produce plutonium. One use of plutonium is to make nuclear bombs. Britain carried out various tests using these bombs in the 1950s, but stopped tests in the atmosphere in 1963, after public protest. Today, plutonium is used to fuel certain types of nuclear power installations (see page 84) and so has an important peaceful use. The fact that Britain uses nuclear power to generate electricity does not mean that the country has to have nuclear weapons. However, many critics of nuclear power feel that there is always a danger, so long as nuclear technology can be applied to either purpose. It is important for the government and the people of Britain to decide how nuclear energy is used.

The situation is further complicated by Britain's role as the second largest nuclear waste reprocessing centre in the world. Britain is now in a position to re-export plutonium produced from other countries' reprocessed nuclear waste. There can be no absolute guarantee on the final use of this deadly export cargo, or on its safety when in transit.

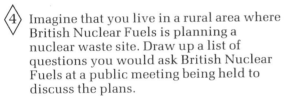 Make a list of questions you would like to ask the Minister for Defence about the control of nuclear technology for military purposes. (Think about security at power stations, agreements between countries, the spread of nuclear technology to more countries in the world.)

Future power stations

Figure 25.8 opposite shows the distribution of nuclear power stations in 1987. Because the nuclear stations need large amounts of water and because of public fear of radioactive leaks, remote coastal sites were favoured as locations. The need for large areas of geologically stable, cheap, flat land was also important. Some of the early nuclear stations such as Bradwell in Essex were built in 1962 and were only designed to last twenty years. The CEGB wants to prolong their life to 1992 but safety experts are worried about possible accidents from such old stations.

There are three main types of nuclear stations competing for future use.

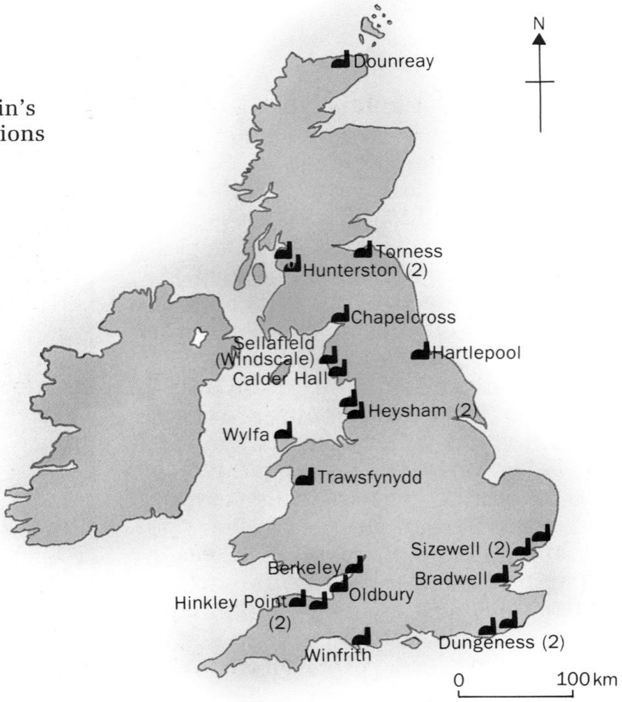

FIGURE 25.8   Britain's nuclear power stations

Advanced gas cooled reactors (AGRs) like those at Heysham near Morecambe which use gas to cool the reactor. They have proved very expensive and difficult to build.

Pressurised water reactors (PWRs) which use water under great pressure for cooling. This American-designed system is cheaper and simpler to build. In 1987 the government gave permission to build a PWR at Sizewell on the Suffolk coast, and other PWRs are likely to follow.

Fast-breeder reactors which use plutonium, a material created from uranium, as a fuel. These reactors create as much fuel as they use so they may be extremely efficient. In 1987 there were two fast-breeder reactors at Dounreay in northern Scotland, but they were still experimental.

⑥ The extract below (Figure 25.10) illustrates an alternative to further nuclear power development using electricity imported from Iceland. Imagine you are employed by the CEGB. Write a memo to the Energy Minister pointing out the *disadvantages* of adopting the Icelandic scheme. (Think of points such as cost, reliance on foreign governments, jobs in the UK etc.)

FIGURE 25.9   What serious point is the cartoonist making?

"GORDON IS DETERMINED NOT TO MOVE"

SIZEWELL DESIGNATED SITE FOR NEW NUCLEAR POWER STATION

Iceland link-up could heat up Britain

ICELAND plans to take power to – if not in – Britain. The electricity chiefs want to build a £1 billion submarine cable link to transmit cut-price energy to the UK.

At present, Iceland only uses 13 per cent of its hydro-electric power capacity and a tiny fraction of the geothermal energy that it gets from hot springs and underground rocks.

That is a waste – especially at a time when there are so many worries about pollution from oil, coal and in particular nuclear power generation.

The new Icelandic plan – outlined in a feasibility study that National Power Council engineers will complete later this year – calls for the construction of a £500 million hydro-electric plant to provide the power and a £500 million cable to carry the electricity to north Scotland.

For Britain there would also be advantages, says the NPC. The country would be provided with a source of power that would not cause acid rain or the release of nuclear radiation, nor use up valuable resources.

FIGURE 25.10

26   *Power from water*

1 Hydro-electric power

The force of falling water can be used to drive turbines which generate electricity. Sites for such hydro-electric power stations in Britain are few, as Figure 26.1 illustrates. This is because hydro-electric stations need these very special conditions:

- A regular supply of fast flowing water.
- Lakes (if possible) to even out the flow of water during the year.
- Deep, high sided valleys where it is easy to build a dam.
- Impermeable rocks to prevent the water seeping away.
- A nearby town or factory to use the electricity.

In Britain a dam is usually built which creates a lake at a higher level upstream. The lake stores the water and also provides the power of falling water. Hydro-electricity has many advantages but it is not popular with everyone.

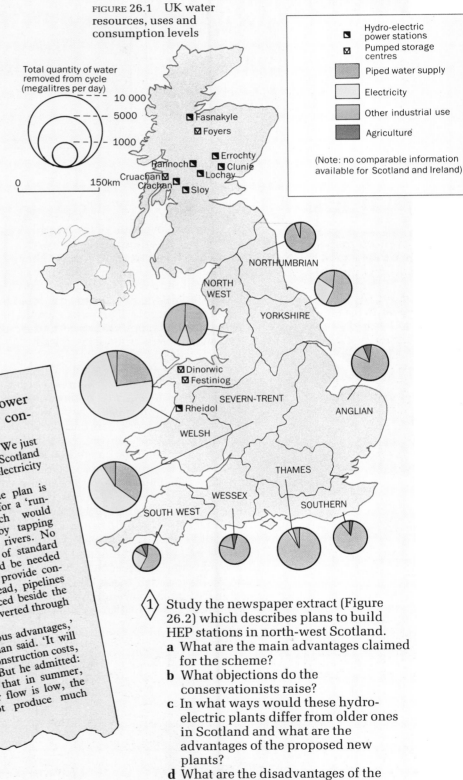

FIGURE 26.1   UK water resources, uses and consumption levels

Total quantity of water removed from cycle (megalitres per day)

10 000
5000
1000

0   150km

- Fasnakyle
- Foyers
- Errochty
- Clunie
- Rannoch
- Lochay
- Cruachan
- Crachan
- Sloy

NORTHUMBRIAN
NORTH WEST
YORKSHIRE

- Dinorwic
- Festiniog
SEVERN-TRENT
- Rheidol
WELSH
ANGLIAN

THAMES
WESSEX
SOUTHERN
SOUTH WEST

Hydro-electric power stations
Pumped storage centres
Piped water supply
Electricity
Other industrial use
Agriculture

(Note: no comparable information available for Scotland and Ireland)

FIGURE 26.2

PLANS to revive construction of hydro-electric power plants have been stalled because of growing controversy.

The scheme is intended for the two rivers, Talladale and Grudie near Loch Maree in north-west Scotland.

The £8.5 million project was thought originally to be an ecologically sound way to generate power. It is relatively small, uses an inexhaustible fuel – running water – and would produce no waste. Its construction would also provide 60 jobs in an area of high unemployment.

But conservationists say the scheme is a menace. Local groups allege the 10-megawatt power station would disrupt salmon and trout fishing and damage a remote, unspoilt area already designated a Site of Special Scientific Interest.

'This is magnificent countryside,' said Mr Roger Smith, chairman of the Scottish Wild Land Group. 'Building power plants on the Grudie and Talla-

dale rivers would ruin it. We just don't need this plant. Scotland already produces more electricity than it needs.'

The Talladale-Grudie plan is unusual because it is for a 'run-of-river' plant which would generate electricity by tapping the flow of existing rivers. No large dams, typical of standard HEP stations, would be needed to store water and provide controlled flows. Instead, pipelines will simply be placed beside the rivers and water diverted through them.

'This has obvious advantages,' a board spokesman said. 'It will greatly reduce construction costs, for one thing.' But he admitted: 'It also means that in summer, when the river flow is low, the plant will not produce much electricity.'

1 ⬦ Study the newspaper extract (Figure 26.2) which describes plans to build HEP stations in north-west Scotland.
  a What are the main advantages claimed for the scheme?
  b What objections do the conservationists raise?
  c In what ways would these hydro-electric plants differ from older ones in Scotland and what are the advantages of the proposed new plants?
  d What are the disadvantages of the proposed new plants?

2 Tidal power: the Mersey barrage

Another method of using water to generate electricity involves tidal power. Twice every day the tide surges into the Mersey estuary. There is a plan to build a barrage across the estuary to retain the high water. On the ebb tide, the head of water would drive turbines built into the barrage (see Figure 26.4), and so generate clean, pollution-free electricity. The barrage would cost £500 million, take seven years to build and create a lake 22 kilometres in length. However, like the hydro-electric plants, this scheme has aroused fierce arguments for and against.

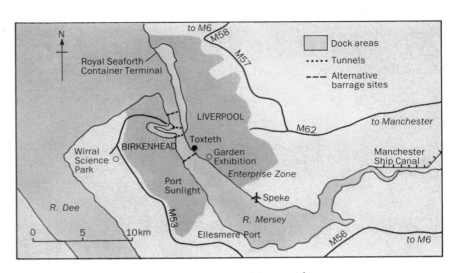

FIGURE 26.3   Merseyside

The case in favour

Supporters of the scheme include industrialists, engineers, the Merseyside Development Corporation, the North West Water Authority and even the Roman Catholic Archbishop of Liverpool. They argue that the Mersey estuary has one of the highest tidal ranges (difference between high and low tide) in the world and so is ideal for generating electricity. The power would be cheap, renewable, pollution free, and would have none of the risks associated with nuclear power generation.

Merseyside is an area of high unemployment which saw many factories, offices, shipyards and docks close in the 1970s and 80s. Some people have moved away in search of work. The barrage would create up to 7000 jobs during construction and other jobs would be created by leisure and tourist developments around the shores of the lake. The £500 million is seen as a vote of confidence in an area with many problems, which would help to revive inner areas of Liverpool and Birkenhead. The new lake would create the best watersports facilities in north-west England in safe, protected water. At present the Mersey has violent, unpredictable seas and the coastguards make many rescues.

The Mersey has always been an industrial river and the barrage, if built on line A (see Figure 26.3), would have double locks 360 metres in length to allow 200-metre vessels in and out of the estuary to supply crude oil for the Stanlow Refinery, and to reach the docks and the Manchester Ship Canal. The Albert Dock Development in Liverpool shows that there are signs of growth in the region. These old docks have been redeveloped and now contain shops, offices and a maritime museum. The barrage would speed the process of growth and be a symbol of hope and pride for the people.

It is possible that reed beds would grow around the edges of the new lake. This would attract interesting new wildlife to the area such as the bittern and the marsh harrier. Although the Mersey is currently badly polluted, the North West Water Authority is building treatment plants to cleanse the river. By the time the barrage is built the water behind it should be relatively pure.

Up to 15 per cent of the demand for electricity in England and Wales could be provided by tidal power, and the Mersey barrage could be a model for other estuary barrages; the Severn Estuary for example might produce 10 times the power obtained from the Mersey.

FIGURE 26.4   Planners' model of Mersey barrage

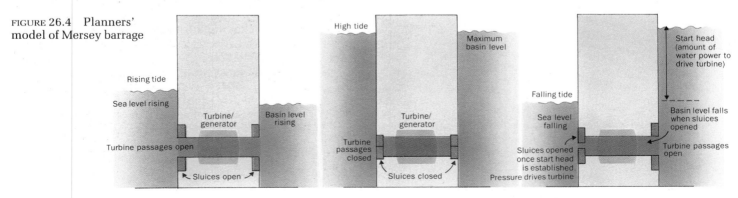

The case against

Opponents of the scheme include the Merseyside Naturalists Association, the RSPB and local conservationists. They argue that the Mersey estuary is a unique and vital area of habitat for birds from Britain and Europe. The estuary has 1 per cent of the world's total breeding population of wildfowl and wading birds such as shelldrake, teal and widgeon. As such, part of it is a Grade 1 Site of Special Scientific Interest (SSSI). In December as many as 50 000 ducks may be found feeding on the mud flats exposed by the falling tide. They argue that water behind the barrage will cover some mud flats permanently and so create an ecological disaster. Many birds would have to find alternative feeding grounds or die.

The problem is that it is difficult to put a value on wildlife sites. In contrast it is easy to put a value on, say, a painting. Opponents argue that the estuary is far more valuable than the most expensive painting.

Opponents also argue that the barrage would reduce the scouring action of the tides and so expensive dredging would be necessary to keep open a channel for ships. Shipping would also be delayed by having to go through the lock system.

Water is classified in four ways:
- fit to drink
- contaminated but suitable for leisure and sports
- severely polluted
- dead

The Mersey for most of its length is categorised as dead. The barrage would reduce the flushing action of the tides, so could cause increasing levels of industrial and domestic pollution in the slower moving water upstream.

The barrage would only generate 0.5 per cent of the electricity needed in England and Wales in the 1990s – a tiny proportion of the total needed. Furthermore, production would not be continuous as the barrage would produce electricity in two six-hour periods out of every 24 hours, in line with falling tides.

Merseyside Fact Sheet

Population
1961	1.7 million
1971	1.6 million
1981	1.5 million
1987	1.4 million

2 Liverpool is the centre of the Merseyside region where industrial decline during the 1970s and 80s has been particularly severe. Major changes include:

a Rapid decline of the *Port of Liverpool*. Most trade is now handled by the Royal Seaforth Dock (especially grain, timber and containers). Ferries no longer operate to the Isle of Man or Ireland. The trans-Atlantic passenger liners have ceased. In 1965 Liverpool had 10 per cent of UK trade, by 1980 it was 3 per cent. Port employment fell from 14 000 in 1965 to 1800 in 1986.

b *Port industries* such as sugar refining, flour milling, paper and paint making have declined and factories closed, (e.g. Tate and Lyle factory closed with the loss of 10 000 jobs). Forty per cent of all jobs in manufacturing were lost between 1960 and 1981.

c *Related industries* such as shipbuilding at Birkenhead (on the other side of the estuary) and engineering have also declined. For example the British Leyland factory at Speke closed in 1978 with the loss of 6000 jobs.

3 Inner city areas such as Toxteth have rates of unemployment up to 50 per cent of the adult population, together with decaying buidlings and a desolate industrial landscape.

4 The Enterprise Zone at Speke has attracted light industry as has the Wirral Science Park, which also has some high-tech firms. However these do not offer mass employment.

 You have been asked by the government to advise on the Mersey Barrage scheme. You must study the arguments for and against the project, and the data in the fact sheet. You should then write a report with the following broad sections:

Background to the project

a A brief description of the area – the estuary itself, main towns, motorways, road tunnels, and Enterprise Zone.

b Liverpool and Merseyside's problems – population trends (1961-87), unemployment (1970-87), industrial structure and likely areas of future industrial growth.

c (Summary) Is Merseyside likely to have a prosperous industrial future? Which industries could grow? Where could growth occur? Is the domestic and industrial demand for electricity likely to rise up to the year 2000?

The barrage

a Summary of main points for and against the scheme, including your own view on those arguments. Try to say which arguments you feel are the most important ones and which you feel are either correct, incorrect or biased.

b Likely national demand for electricity from the barrage.

Recommendations

On the basis of your analysis of the needs of Britain (refer to Unit 22, page 72) and of Merseyside, suggest what action the government should take over the barrage.

27 Renewable energy: the answer?

Britain's major sources of energy are non-renewable fuels such as coal, oil, gas and uranium. Increasing attention is being paid to the 'renewable' or alternative sources such as water (see Unit 26), the sun, wind and even organic waste. These sources of power not only require no 'fuel' but do not pollute the environment. They are expensive and difficult forms of energy to tap, but recently much progress has been made.

Wind power

Britain has made small wind turbine generators producing electricity for many years. These are mostly exported to places where wind power is cheaper than diesel engines. More recently huge wind turbine generators have been built, such as the one shown in Figure 27.1. They are over 30 metres high. Two are in service at Orkney and in Wales feeding power to the national grid. However, it would need 1600 of these massive turbines to generate as much electricity as the new PWR nuclear power station at Sizewell. British firms employing 200 people produce WTGs for export to 'windfarms' in California, and although there are some problems with the huge rotor blades, research is making considerable advances.

FIGURE 27.1 Windmills for the year 2000? Experimental wind turbine at Camarthen Bay, South Wales. This most advanced model in the world consists of huge blades turning on a 26 tonne rotor. If successful, it could lead to a multi-megawatt machine four times as large

Geothermal power

Research in Cornwall has shown that power might be generated from very hot rocks deep underground. The very hard rocks found in areas like south-western England, the Lake District and the eastern Highlands of Scotland are extremely hot. This heat could be used to turn water into steam, which in turn could generate electricity. There would be some loss of wildlife habitat during construction, but little afterwards.

Biogas energy

Over 20 million tonnes of organic waste is disposed of each year in the UK. Much of this is used to fill holes in the landscape left by mining and quarrying. There are 300 potential sites where the gases produced by decaying organic waste can be used either to generate electricity or to supply methane gas to brickmaking, paper and food industries. At present only 10 per cent of these sites are in use, but BIOGAS looks likely to become a more important source of renewable energy in the future.

Biogas, or landfill gas as it is also known, has been traditionally considered a hazard at waste disposal sites. Turning it to controlled use still leaves some critics concerned about dangers to health, or possible gas explosions.

FIGURE 27.2 Geothermal power plant, Iceland

FIGURE 27.3 Systematic production of biogas: how it works

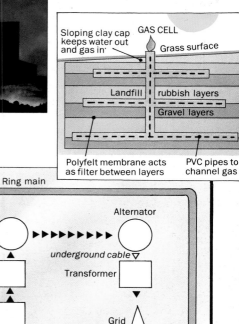

Sloping clay cap keeps water out and gas in · GAS CELL · Grass surface

Landfill · rubbish layers · Gravel layers

Polyfelt membrane acts as filter between layers · PVC pipes to channel gas

Gas from cells · Ring main

Flowmeter · Turbine · Alternator

Monitor O_2 CO_2 CH_4 · Receiver · *underground cable* ▽ · Transformer

Blower · Heater to vaporise remaining impurities · Grid

1st stage compression · 2nd · 3rd · Filter to remove particles · Power to the home

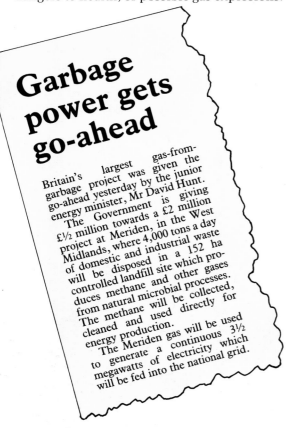

Garbage power gets go-ahead

Britain's largest gas-from-garbage project was given the go-ahead yesterday by the junior energy minister, Mr David Hunt.

The Government is giving £½ million towards a £2 million project at Meriden, in the West Midlands, where 4,000 tons a day of domestic and industrial waste will be disposed in a 152 ha controlled landfill site which produces methane and other gases from natural microbial processes. The methane will be collected, cleaned and used directly for energy production.

The Meriden gas will be used to generate a continuous 3½ megawatts of electricity which will be fed into the national grid.

FIGURE 27.4 Launch for biogas project, 29.10.1986

Wave power

The energy from waves might provide 20-30 per cent of Britain's needs. The problem is to design machinery which can withstand storms. Peak electricity demand is in winter just when waves tend to be at their highest. So waves are capable of generating power when it is most needed.

In 1982 the government reduced funds for research into wave power because it argued that the projected cost of electricity would be too expensive. However, in 1987 the first British 'shoreline' wave power station was authorised on the Island of Islay in the Inner Hebrides.

Solar power

The sun produces energy in the form of heat and light. Solar collectors are glass-covered panels which allow heat from the sun to pass through, then trap the energy inside a box-like apparatus. In Britain, these are at present mainly used to provide heat and light for people's homes.

Solar farms are huge reflectors laid out to concentrate sunlight on pipes containing gases which become heated. These heated gases can then be used to generate electricity. Such farms have been criticised for destroying wildlife habitat and for being a blot on the landscape.

 1 Re-read Unit 26. What two renewable methods of producing energy can you find to add to those given in this Unit?

THE HIDDEN COSTS OF PRODUCING ENERGY

Producing energy always has a hidden cost: all of the established methods of energy production result in hazards to the environment, to wildlife and to human health. With the exception of hydro-electric power, which is only workable in certain countries, all current large-scale methods have drawbacks – yet it is often the most dangerous of them which are used to produce the most power.

Method		Environmental hazards	Wildlife hazards	Health hazards
Nuclear		Danger of release of radioactivity into air, water and soil. Unknown future risks from waste storage and old power stations.	Destructive effect of accidental radiation releases. Long-term hazard posed by the disposal of nuclear waste.	Unpredictable dangers from major accidents. Risk of cancer to people exposed to low-level radiation from nuclear waste.
Oil-fired		Pollution from accidental oil spillages. Atmospheric pollution and acidification by waste gases from furnaces. Causes overheating in the atmosphere.	Mass destruction of marine life, from plankton to fish and birds, caused by oil spillages.	Risk of explosions from stored oil; possible risk from atmospheric pollution.
Coal-fired		Dereliction of land by mining, especially with surface mines. Severe atmospheric pollution and acidification from impurities. Causes overheating in the atmosphere.	Poisoning of plants by mining waste; some risk to water life through waterborne pollution.	Indirect health hazard through atmospheric pollution, especially from sulphur dioxide. Considerable health hazards during mining.
Gas-fired		Small amount of air pollution as a result of burning.	Some destruction of habitats by pipelines, otherwise marginal effect.	Risk of explosions, otherwise little direct effect.
Hydro-electric		No pollution hazards. Loss of land through flooding; minor risk of landslides.	Destruction of habitats through flooding. Disturbance of river life through altered water flow.	Safe, apart from danger of dam bursts.

FIGURE 27.5   Source: *Blueprint for a Green Planet* by John Seymour and Hubert Giradet

The greenhouse effect

The table above indicates how some sources of power heat up the Earth's atmosphere and contribute to what is known as the GREENHOUSE EFFECT. The amount of carbon dioxide (CO_2) in the atmosphere has increased rapidly in the twentieth century. This is partly the result of burning fossil fuels (coal, and oil, for example) and partly from clearing forests, for timber or farmland. Figure 27.6 shows how Britain contributes to the greenhouse effect, and some of the changes this continued overheating could cause. What might be the effects on Britain?

 Study Figure 27.5, above. Now produce a similar table for wind, wave, biogas, solar and tidal power using the data in this unit, and in Unit 26, Use these column headings to help you.

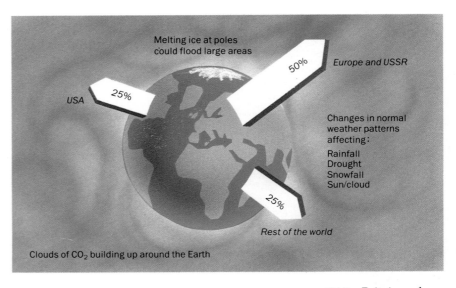

Melting ice at poles could flood large areas

50% Europe and USSR

25% USA

Changes in normal weather patterns affecting:

Rainfall
Drought
Snowfall
Sun/cloud

25% Rest of the world

Clouds of CO_2 building up around the Earth

FIGURE 27.6   Britain and the greenhouse effect

Form of energy	Effect on environment	Effect on wildlife	Risk element

KEY POINTS

- The demand for energy from people and industries in Britain is likely to continue rising.
- Opinions differ on the best method of generating the maximum amount of energy at the lowest cost.
- The coal industry has been one of the most important sources of energy for many years. Britain still has large, untapped reserves of coal, but they will be expensive to exploit.
- Oil and natural gas have become important power sources in the last twenty years. Despite some fears over pollution, the search for new deposits continues both on land and in the Celtic Sea (between Scotland and Ireland).
- Nuclear power creates much controversy. Some people believe it will provide abundant cheap power for the future. Others argue that dealing with radioactive material provides an unacceptable threat to people and the environment.
- Energy from hydro-electric or tidal sources is not free. There are the construction and operating costs of such projects, together with the environmental costs such as the loss of wetland habitat which are much more difficult to calculate.
- Money for research into non-polluting, renewable sources of energy varies with government interest. Currently researchers are concentrating on the potential of wind and tidal power as being the most likely to yield profitable results.

IDEAS FOR COURSEWORK

 You may live near a coalfield, or visit a mining museum. Try to find a place where coal-mining has ceased.
- What is British Coal or the local council doing to improve the area? For example, are old spoil heaps being levelled? Are trees being planted? Are holes being filled in? Is grass being sown? Are playing fields being created?
  Map the location of these in relation to the old coal mines and pit heaps (old maps of the area will show this).
- What else is being done to improve the area? (new houses/roads/ industrial estates/dry ski slopes?)

 Make a study of a development linked to power production in your area. This might be the building of a new power station (nuclear-powered, or coal-fired, or an HEP station) or the development of a resource such as oil or natural gas, or the construction of a tidal barrage.
- Find out the main reasons why the power development is needed. Will it create new jobs? How much power will it generate? Is there a demand for power?
- Use a questionnaire to ask local people for their opinion on the development – do they think it is a good idea? If so, why? If not, why not?

 Find as many different examples as possible of the use of renewable energy near you.
- Find out if your rubbish is burned to generate power or if landfill sites are being used to produce methane.
- Is solar power in use – if so where?
- Is wave, or wind power a possibility in your area?

Managing industrial environments

Industrial change

Industrial enterprise

Industry, environment and the future

Steelmaking is just one of Britain's older industries that has made massive changes to survive in an increasingly competitive world market. The workforce has been drastically reduced, and a number of smaller steelworks have been closed down (like the one shown here in Ebbw Vale). In 1988 British Steel was sold by the government to private investors. Can you think of some effects of all these changes?

28 Tradition and change

A country's EMPLOYMENT STRUCTURE is the way in which the working population is divided among the different industrial groups. In Britain the main industrial groups are:

PRIMARY INDUSTRIES These obtain food and raw materials from the land and sea. Agriculture, forestry, fishing, mining and quarrying are in this group.

SECONDARY INDUSTRIES These change the raw materials into finished products. This group includes most manufacturing industries such as engineering, textiles, steel-making.

TERTIARY INDUSTRIES These provide services. Transport, warehousing, retailing, nursing and entertainment are part of this group.

QUARTERNARY INDUSTRIES These provide specialist infomation and expertise. Research and development, accountancy, banking are examples of this group.

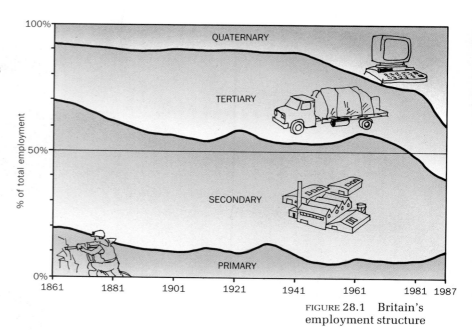

FIGURE 28.1   Britain's employment structure

FIGURE 28.3   Britain's regional employment structure

FIGURE 28.2   Changing employment in selected British industries

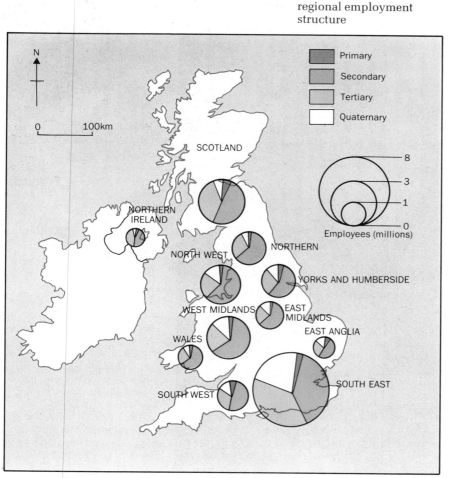

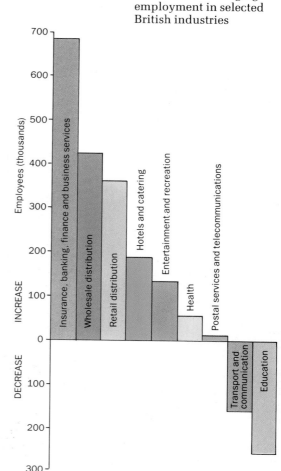

1 Figure 28.1 shows how Britain's employment structure changed between 1861 and 1987. Study the data and then answer the following:
   a What percentage of the working population were employed in primary industries in 1861, 1921, 1987?
   b What percentage of the working population were employed in secondary industries in 1881, 1938, 1960, 1985?
   c What percentage of the working population were employed in tertiary industries in 1871, 1901, 1960, 1985?
   d What percentage of the working population were employed in quaternary industries in 1861, 1901, 1970, 1985?
   e Briefly summarise Britain's employment structure by giving the percentage of people employed in each industrial sector in 1891, 1938, 1985.

2 Study Figures 28.2 and 28.3. They show the changing numbers of people employed in key industries between 1978 and 1986, together with the employment structure for each region. Now answer the following:
   a Were the industries which suffered a decline in employment between 1978 and 1986 in the secondary or tertiary group?
   b Which groups (secondary, tertiary, quaternary) showed an increase in employment between 1978 and 1986?
   c List the regions of Britain in order according to the total number of people employed (use the size of circles as a guide).
   d Which regions have over half their employees in secondary industries?
   e Which regions have half or more of their employees in tertiary industries?
   f Which three regions have significant percentages of employees in quaternary industries?
   g Which region has the largest percentage of workers in the primary sector?

FIGURE 28.4 Three changing faces of industry. This Rochdale cotton mill (*left*) is being converted to house small business units. The steelworks at Consett (*below*) had an annual output of one million tonnes before it was closed down in 1980 as part of British Steel's restructuring programme. The nineteenth-century foundry (*bottom*) shows what working conditions were like in the older industries. What differences would you expect to find today?

'The de-industrialisation of Britain'

The rapid decline of secondary (manufacturing) industries over the last ten years has been called 'the DE-INDUSTRIALISATION of Britain'. Traditional, nineteenth-century industries suffered a rapid decline. Mines, steelworks, shipyards and factories closed across the country and unemployment rose rapidly.

Some of the common characteristics of the declining industries are:
- They are heavy industries producing bulky goods such as steel, ships.
- The factories employed mostly men (except textiles).
- Many factories are in inner city areas.
- Factories are on canals, coalfields, ports or raw material sites.
- They date from the nineteenth century.
- They often polluted the local environment.
- They are surrounded by little open green space.

Industrial decline: who suffers?

Most of the statistics concerning industrial decline deal with the number of factories closed and jobs lost. It is easy to lose sight of the human costs involved.

Don Nixon used to work in the production control department of British Steel's Cleveland works. In 1981 he was made redundant, as the company's workforce fell from 29 000 in 1973 to a mere 8000 in 1981. At 42, he found it impossible to get another job. Don has a wife and two daughters, aged 14 and 10.

His wife, Mary, was already working as a secretary in Darlington, but her income alone could not pay for their house in Durham and their two cars. Eventually Don did find a job, but it is at a steelworks in South Africa! Don leaves home for six months at a time to live and work near Durban, after which he can return to Durham for three weeks before his next six-month spell of duty.

Don and Mary have been able to keep their home, but at a price. Their family life suffers. Mary says, 'He is missing the excitement of seeing our children grow up. It also means I have to be alone as head of the family, and at first I found that quite hard.' Don adds, 'I enjoy the letters and the photographs from home, but it is still not the same as seeing them.'

 3 Imagine you are Don's elder daughter. Write a letter to him in South Africa. You could include the following topics in your letter:
a how you and the family feel without him.
b How you feel about him working so far away, and in South Africa.
c What are your hopes for the family in the future?

Industrial decline: what are the causes?

Some of the commonest reasons given for factory closures and general industrial decline are:
- Fierce competition from foreign companies.
- Competition from cheaper imported goods, often from the Third World.
- Inefficient management.
- Failure to introduce new methods and new technology.
- A fall in the demand for certain products.
- Large foreign-owned companies deciding to concentrate production in other countries.
- Lack of sufficient investment.
- Lack of government support such as insufficient finance or failure to protect industry from foreign imports.

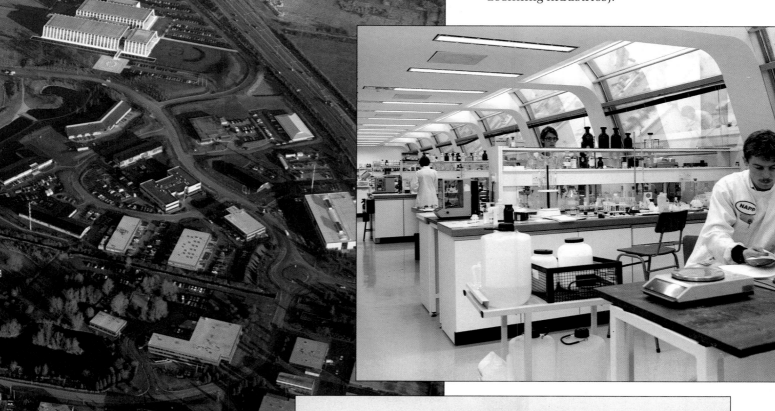

A time of change

In contrast to traditional industries, the new GROWTH INDUSTRIES look rather different as these pictures of Cambridge Science Park (Figure 28.5) show.

 Study Figure 28.5, then summarise the common characteristics of the growh industries (often the opposite of the declining industries).

FIGURE 28.5   View of Cambridge Science Park (*above*). The main emphasis here is on research and development. The work is often carried out in partnership with nearby Cambridge University. There are fewer employees than in the traditional industries, and most are highly skilled, like those shown in the test laboratory (*above right*). Only a few of the businesses here manufacture goods. Most concentrate on producing and marketing expertise and research information.
(*Right*) The girl is using a computer to identify raw materials being used in drug products. The use of electronics in research and industry has made it much quicker to organise, store and communicate information. What effects do you think this might have?

29   *Help for declining industries?*

A case study: shipbuilding

In the 1950s Britain was the world's most important shipbuilding nation. British yards produced one third of the world's shipping total. Since 1956, however, Japan, South Korea and many other countries have overtaken Britain which now ranks as only the world's fifteenth shipbuilding nation.

1 Figures 29.1 to 29.5 chart the decline of shipbuilding in terms of employment and output. Use the data in each to prepare your own fact sheet.

a Draw bar graphs, showing Britain's declining share of world shipbuilding. (See Figure 29.1.)
b Draw line graphs of declining employment and output in shipbuilding. (See Figures 29.4 and 29.5.)
c List the three main shipbuilding regions in 1985. (See Figure 29.2.)
d On a copy of the UK map (Figure 29.6) draw *located* bar graphs to represent percentage of total output in 1986 for Clydeside, Wearside, Tyneside, Belfast, Teesside, Birkenhead, Appledore and Barrow. (See Figure 29.2.)

FIGURE 29.2   Ship launchings by UK yard (1986)

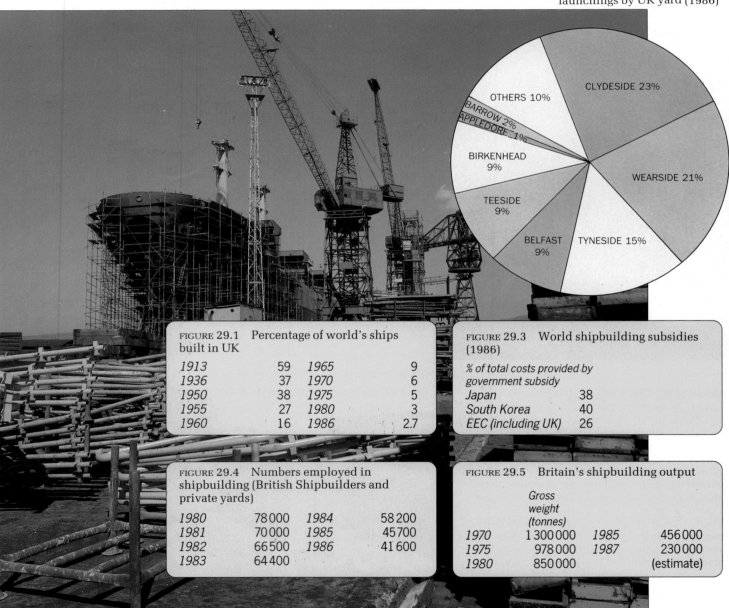

Pie chart: CLYDESIDE 23%, WEARSIDE 21%, TYNESIDE 15%, BELFAST 9%, TEESIDE 9%, BIRKENHEAD 9%, APPLEDORE 1%, BARROW 2%, OTHERS 10%

FIGURE 29.1   Percentage of world's ships built in UK

1913	59	1965	9
1936	37	1970	6
1950	38	1975	5
1955	27	1980	3
1960	16	1986	2.7

FIGURE 29.3   World shipbuilding subsidies (1986)

% of total costs provided by government subsidy

Japan	38
South Korea	40
EEC (including UK)	26

FIGURE 29.4   Numbers employed in shipbuilding (British Shipbuilders and private yards)

1980	78 000	1984	58 200
1981	70 000	1985	45 700
1982	66 500	1986	41 600
1983	64 400		

FIGURE 29.5   Britain's shipbuilding output

	Gross weight (tonnes)		
1970	1 300 000	1985	456 000
1975	978 000	1987	230 000
1980	850 000		(estimate)

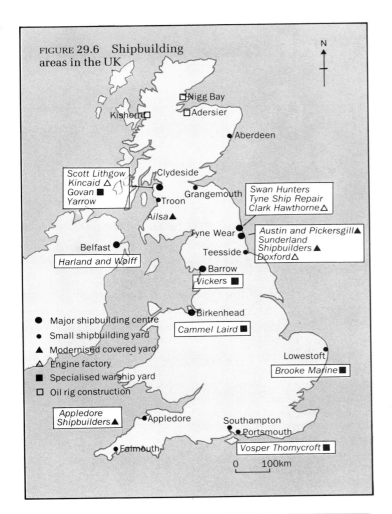

FIGURE 29.6 Shipbuilding areas in the UK

N

Nigg Bay
Kishorn
Adersier
Aberdeen
Scott Lithgow
Kincaid △
Govan ■
Yarrow
Clydeside
Grangemouth
Troon
Ailsa ▲
Swan Hunters
Tyne Ship Repair
Clark Hawthorne △
Tyne Wear
Austin and Pickersgill ▲
Sunderland
Shipbuilders ▲
Doxford △
Teesside
Belfast
Harland and Wolff
Barrow
Vickers ■
Birkenhead
Cammel Laird ■
Lowestoft
Brooke Marine ■
Appledore
Shipbuilders ▲
Appledore
Southampton
Portsmouth
Falmouth
Vosper Thornycroft ■

● Major shipbuilding centre
· Small shipbuilding yard
▲ Modernised covered yard
△ Engine factory
■ Specialised warship yard
□ Oil rig construction

0   100km

Some shipbuilding yards such as Swan Hunter on Tyneside and Vosper Thorneycroft at Southampton have been PRIVATISED; in other words the government sold them so they are now owned by shareholders. However, most shipbuilding yards are still owned by British Shipbuilders which is a state-owned concern.

British Shipbuilders point to statistics such as those shown in Figures 29.3 and 29.7 to show that this decline is not just a British problem. Shipbuilding yards throughout the world are closing because demand for ships has fallen. In countries such as South Korea and Japan the government subsidises 40 per cent of the cost of new ships to help the industry. In Britain and the EEC the subsidy is only 26 per cent. So Japan and South Korea can produce cheaper ships thanks to higher government subsidies.

Other reasons given for the decline of British shipbuilding are:
- Little investment in new, larger, covered yards.
- The slow pace of modernisation and adapting to changes in demand.
- Failure (in some cases) to deliver on time.
- Lack of forward planning.
- Decreasing demand for ships due to competition from airlines and railways.

 In South Tyneside unemployment in 1987 affected 26 per cent of the working population. Sixty-seven per cent of all workers in the area are employed in shipbuilding or related industries. Imagine you work in a South Tyneside shipyard. Write a letter to the government, explaining why you think they should give more support to the shipbuilding industry. You might include points such as world trends, subsidies in competing countries, the importance of shipbuilding locally, alternative job opportunities in the area, and reasons why you think Britain should continue to build ships.

 People disagree over the issue of government help to declining industries. Some of the arguments for and against government aid are given in Figure 29.8 below. Study these, then write a paragraph setting out your own views. Compare your views with others in the class. Do they differ? If so, how and why?

FIGURE 29.8 Declining industries: should the government help?

In favour of government help

'The government must help declining industries otherwise unemployment will be even higher. It is unfair to make people redundant with no government help.'

'It is hard for areas of declining industry to attract new industries without government help.'

'Declining industries in other countries get help.'

'Some strategically important industries such as shipbuilding must remain in Britain even if it is expensive.'

'Some industries may need government help for a short time to overcome difficulties but will be successful later.'

FIGURE 29.7 World shipbuilding output

Gross weight (million tonnes)	
1975	72
1980	48
1985	25

Against government help

'If our industries cannot compete in the world they should close down.'

'Britain should buy the cheapest cars, machines, clothes, no matter which country produces them.'

'Competition forces industries to modernise in order to keep costs down. Government help may prevent this happening.'

'Areas of declining industries should persuade private companies to invest. This in turn will attract other industries.'

'Unemployed people should be prepared to travel longer distances to work or to retrain, or to start new businesses of their own.'

30   *Whose car industry?*

In 1972, 76 per cent of the 1.6 million new cars registered in Britain were British made. By 1985 only 42 per cent of 1.8 million new cars were 'British'. Even this percentage is probably an exaggeration, because some parts of British cars such as headlights, seats, brakes or tyres were made abroad. In 1972, British Leyland (as it was called) employed 180 000 people, but by 1986 the Rover Group (its new name) employed only 85 000.

Figure 30.1 shows the changes in car production since 1971, and Figure 30.2 illustrates the small size of the Rover Group compared to some of its rivals.

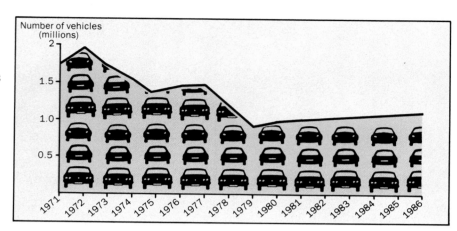

FIGURE 30.1   UK car production (1971–86)

Boom, decline and readjustment

The British car industry grew up in the early 1900s in the West Midlands and later in south-east England. There were many firms in these areas with people who already had engineering skills from making bicycles or horse-drawn carriages. The West Midlands also had many metalworking industries which supplied components for the early factories. In 1930, 90 per cent of the jobs in the car industry were either in the West Midlands or the South East.

During the boom of the 1960s, manufacturers who wanted to expand were encouraged to build new factories in the ASSISTED AREAS to reduce unemployment. Ford, General Motors (Opel/Vauxhall), Talbot and the Rover Group built new factories on Merseyside or in Scotland. However, during the 1970s when imported cars began to take more of the market, many of these 1960s factories closed (see Figure 30.3). British car producers were accused of being overmanned, slow to introduce new technology and achieving low output per worker. Certainly in 1978 a Japanese car worker would produce 30 cars per year, whilst in Britain the figure for each car worker was only 7 cars per year.

FIGURE 30.2   UK and foreign car production

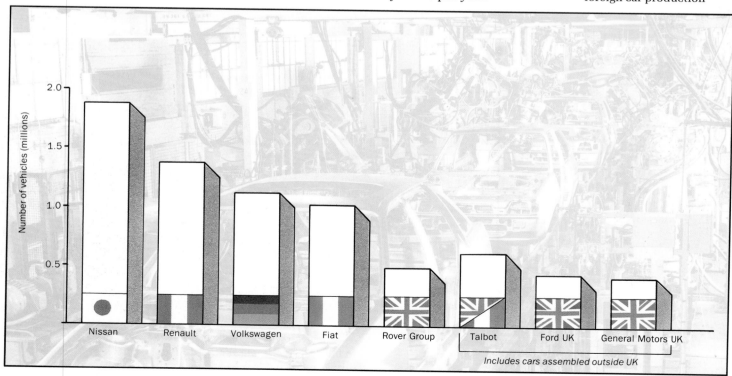

Nissan   Renault   Volkswagen   Fiat   Rover Group   Talbot   Ford UK   General Motors UK

Includes cars assembled outside UK

British Leyland ◇

Ford ◆

Chrysler ○

Vauxhall ●

Plants closed 1978-86

British Leyland ▼

Chrysler □

Bathgate
Linwood

(Liverpool) ◇ Leyland
Halewood ◆▼ Speke
Ellesmere Port ●
(Birmingham)
Solihull ▼
Longbridge ◇ (Coventry)
Browns Lane ▼ Canley
○ Ryton
(Oxford) ● Luton
Abingdon ▼ ◇
Cowley ◆ Dagenham

0   100km

In the 1980s British manufacturers fought back by introducing new products and new technology. However only the Rover Group, Jaguar, Rolls Royce and some specialist firms such as Lotus remain British-owned. In order to survive, the Rover Group received over £1 200 million help from the government between 1975 and 1985.

Other British car makers such as Hillman and Vauxhall were taken over by foreign rivals – Chrysler/Talbot and General Motors respectively. Now car production is dominated by TRANSNATIONALS, that is companies with headquarters in one country, and factories in many others. So British car workers are now employed by foreign-run companies such as Ford (USA), Peugeot/Talbot (France), Fiat (Italy) and Nissan (Japan).

One important aspect of these transnational companies is that they are controlled from outside Britain; so decisions about factory closures or redundancies may be made thousands of miles away, with little thought for the effects on the local British economy. People may lose their jobs as a result of decisions taken in Paris or Detroit.

◇1 Using the data in Figures 30.1, 30.2 and 30.3, find out the following:
  a When did British car production decline most rapidly?
  b When did car production fall below one million vehicles?
  c How does the output of Nissan, Renault and Volkswagen compare with the Rover Group?
  d Where did car factories close between 1978 and 1985?

FIGURE 30.3   UK motor vehicle assembly factories

Transnational companies: theory and practice

The Nissan case

The Nissan car factory (see Figure 30.4) at Washington New Town, near Sunderland, is an example of a plant built by a transnational company. Nissan chose the Washington site because there was good financial encouragement from the British goverment, such as freedom from tax. Nissan also wanted a base in an EEC country from which they could produce vehicles for sale in all twelve EEC countries. In this way Nissan would not have to pay high import duties on its cars.

FIGURE 30.4   Nissan car factory at Washington New Town, Sunderland

② Study Figure 30.5 which summarises the arguments put forward by people for and against the Nissan factory. Imagine another Japanese car manufacturer was thinking of building a factory in South Wales. Write a letter to the Welsh Development Agency outlining the important questions they should ask the Japanese firm, such as:

- How many jobs will be created in two years? And in five years?
- What percentage of components will be British made?

FIGURE 30.5 Nissan in Sunderland: for and against

1

Nissan has invested £50 million in Britain.

680 jobs in 1987 rising to 2800 by 1991 isn't much for such a huge investment.

2

40 per cent of the car parts are British made. This is providing jobs for many people.

Even by 1991 only 80 per cent of the components will be British car parts.

3

Over a third of the 100,000 cars will be exported to Europe. Nissan just want a place with cheap labour in the E.E.C.

DAILY CLARION
ANOTHER £300,000,000 IS BEING INVESTED TO EXPAND OUTPUT TO 100,000 CARS BY 1991

4

British workers have been blackmailed into adopting Japanese working methods. The alternative is unemployment.

JOB CENTRE

The wages earned by the car workers will create a demand for more goods and services in the North East. So other new firms will grow up to meet this demand.

5

Nissan has trained the labour force and introduced avanced technology which we would not have otherwise.

But the Japanese not the British control the technology and the main decisions are made in Tokyo.

6

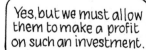

The profits go to the shareholders back in Japan so a lot of money leaves Britain.

Yes, but we must allow them to make a profit on such an investment.

7

Once they have invested so much money in Britain they won't simply close down the factory.

They only came because they pay no tax for ten years. After that they can close the plant and move to Italy or Greece where wages and taxes are even lower.

31   On the scrap heap?

Unemployment

The closure of factories, mines, shipyards and engineering works during the 1970s and early 1980s led to rising unemployment. Figure 31.1 shows the economic planning regions of Britain, and Figure 31.2 lists their unemployment rates in 1972, 1982 and 1987.

 1 On a copy of Figure 31.1 draw located bar graphs to show unemployment in each region in 1972, 1982 and 1987.

 2 Study your map and bar graphs. Then answer these questions:
  a Which four regions had the highest unemployment rates in 1972?
  b Had the four regions with the highest unemployment rates changed by 1982?
  c Which four regions had the highest unemployment rates in 1987?
  d In which regions did unemployment fall between 1982 and 1987?

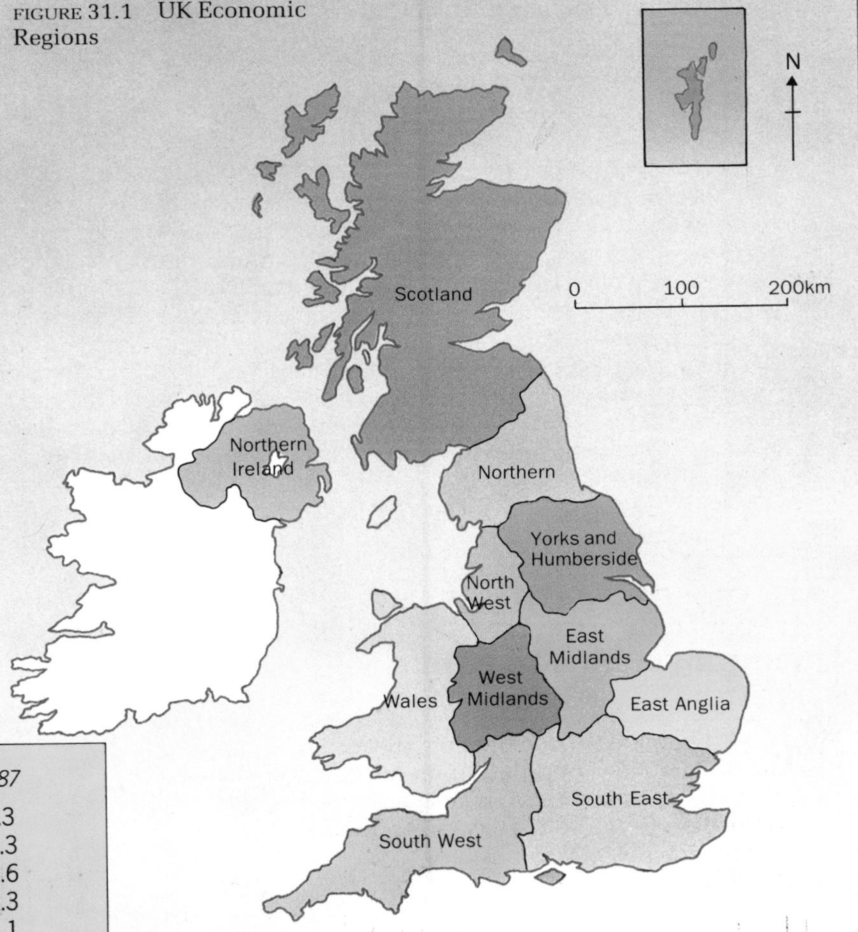

FIGURE 31.1   UK Economic Regions

Region	1972	1982	1987
Northern	6.9	16.0	17.3
Yorks and Humberside	4.8	13.2	13.3
North West	5.0	15.0	14.6
East Midlands	3.6	10.9	11.3
West Midlands	5.0	15.1	14.1
East Anglia	3.6	10.4	8.8
South East	2.4	9.2	8.6
South West	4.2	11.0	10.2
Wales	5.8	16.1	14.0
Scotland	7.1	14.9	14.6
Northern Ireland	8.9	19.0	18.0

FIGURE 31.2   Registered unemployment in Britain (% of total employees)

Unemployment is generally regarded as a problem because it wastes people's skills and talents. Making people redundant may also be expensive, because it can involve redundancy payments and social security benefits for which people qualify. Your map shows that all areas of Britain have been affected by unemployment, but that the problems are particularly severe in Northern Ireland, Scotland, Wales, the North and the North West. It is also important to remember that there is a human side to unemployment, which is hidden by the statistics.

Mike Vernon is 29, married with two children, Louise aged two and Wayne aged five. The family live in Blackburn, Lancashire. Mike has been unemployed since 1985 when the weaving firm he worked for closed down. The firm could trace its history in Blackburn back to 1842 but imports of cheaper cloth made the firm unable to compete. Mike's skills were no longer in demand because so many other weaving firms in the North West had already closed. He describes how he felt.

At first it was not too bad. I thought I would be able to get another job quite quickly. When you see television programmes about unemployed people you always think, well at least I would be able to get a job. But when it happens to you, you are just like everyone else.

I applied for 60 jobs. Some firms never even bothered to reply, others said they wanted people with more experience, whilst some said they only wanted people under 25. It gets very depressing.

After a while you feel it is not worth the trouble of applying. Doreen, my wife, had to find part-time work cleaning offices, just to make ends meet. I feel guilty staying at home while she goes out to earn the money.

I did get a job for six months with an engineering firm, but then they closed down as well. So it was back to square one. We have not had a holiday since 1983, and we have to be very careful with our money.

Mike's story is typical of many people in Blackburn, and in other parts of the country. Blackburn lost half of all its manufacturing jobs between 1978 and 1987. Ten thousand people are unemployed in a city of 175 000. In 1978 the textiles industry employed 6300 people, by 1987 this was down to 2800.

Unemployment and ethnic origin

Mike is still better off than some people in Blackburn. The city's population includes 11.4 per cent of Asian origin, whose parents came to Britain in the 1930s to work in the textile mills. In 1987, 20 per cent of Blackburn's adult male population were unemployed, but 55 per cent of the adult male Asian population were unemployed. They have been amongst those hit hardest by unemployment. On average, unemployed Asian males spend twice as long between jobs as non-Asian males.

The situation amongst unemployed Asians in Blackburn is typical of that amongst other ethnic minority groups in Britain, as Figure 31.3 for 1985 illustrates.

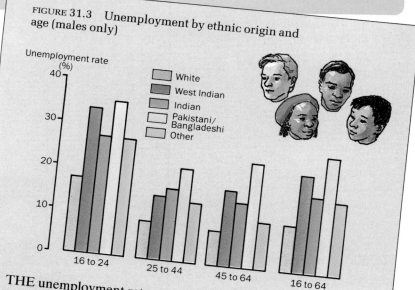

FIGURE 31.3 Unemployment by ethnic origin and age (males only)

Unemployment rate (%)

White
West Indian
Indian
Pakistani/Bangladeshi
Other

16 to 24   25 to 44   45 to 64   16 to 64

THE unemployment rate among ethnic minorities is twice as high as that for the white population, according to a special analysis of the offical Labour Force survey.

The article in the Department of Employment's Gazette also finds that a third of all ethnic minority young people aged between 16 and 24 were out of work, compared with 16 per cent for the white population.

The survey finds that young whites were more likely to be economically active – either working or looking for work – than young people from ethnic minorities, partly because the whites were less likely to continue in full-time education after the age of 16.

The survey was conducted in the spring of 1985.

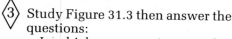

3 Study Figure 31.3 then answer the questions:
  a In which age group is unemployment highest amongst all ethnic groups?
  b Which ethnic group had the highest percentage of its members unemployed in all age groups in 1985?
  c Compare the pattern of unemployment of West Indian and Indian ethnic groups, in the age groups 16–24 and 25–44.
  d What percentage of all ethnic minority groups aged 16–24 were unemployed in 1985? How did this compare with white people of the same age?

The migrant workers

Peter Beckworth is forty and lives in Bradford, West Yorkshire with his wife Pat, daughter Debbie (aged 16) and son Roger (14). Peter is a bricklayer, who after being unemployed for eight months has been forced to find work away from home.

Every Monday Peter leaves home at 4.30 a.m. to travel down to Essex where he will spend the next five days working on a new housing development. Whilst he is away Peter lives in a caravan with three other workers, because hotels and boarding houses are expensive. Peter is one of a growing band of MIGRANT WORKERS, who leave home in search of work, but for whom separation is the result of unemployment.

Pat has to look after the family alone during Peter's absence, and she does not want to leave Bradford where her friends and family still live. Even if Pat wanted to move nearer Essex they could not afford to buy a house, because prices are so much higher in the South East. From all over the regions of high unemployment, skilled workers like Peter face the choice of unemployment or working away from home.

FIGURE 31.4   Monday morning for Peter Beckworth starts with the three-hour commute down the M1. He is on site by 8 a.m.

 ④ Imagine you are Debbie or Roger Beckworth. You have just received a letter from your father in which he tells of a possible new house building project in Bradford, where he could get work and live at home. Unfortunately, the pay would be lower than his current salary and there is no long-term guarantee of work in the area. He wants to know your views about whether to apply for a job. Write one letter pointing out the advantages and disadvantages of the new job, ending with your preference.

Derelict land

Another effect of industrial decline is the mess left behind when factories close. For example, in 1979 the Shelton steelworks closed in Stoke-on-Trent. It left behind a landscape of slag heaps, twisted machinery and giant holes in the ground full of coal slurry and tar. Yet by 1986 this area had been reclaimed (Figure 31.5) to become the site of a National Garden Festival.

One part of the site, the central ridge, was too bad ever to be built on. It was a mixture of steel and colliery waste. The engineers covered it with a mixture of clay and peat on which 220000 trees were planted. This central ridge has stayed public parkland, surrounded by a U-shaped area of 40 hectares with land for industry, commerce, housing and sport.

FIGURE 31.5   How the residue of Shelton steelworks (*above left*) formed the foundations of the Stoke Garden Festival site

⑤ How high was the central ridge of the Stoke-on-Trent festival site? What did the ridge consist of?

⑥ How did the landscape developers prevent weeds growing on the ridge?

Stoke Garden Festival's central ridge: steel and colliery waste, slurry lagoons and the remains of blast furnaces stand 35 metres high. Ridge covered by clay to seal the dumped waste and covered with peat to prevent weeds growing and to encourage 220000 trees to flourish.

32 *A divided nation?*

Ninety-four per cent of all jobs lost by industrial decline in Britain between 1978 and 1987 were in areas north and west of Birmingham. The South East, South West and East Anglia lost only 6 per cent of the total. This remarkable difference between the two parts of Britain has led some people to talk of a 'North-South divide'. People saw the South East as an area of prosperity with many job opportunities, and the rest of the country as a grim, grey area with high unemployment and crumbling empty factories. *But is there really such a 'North–South divide'?*

1 From Figure 31.1 on page 105 trace five outlines of the UK economic regions. Use the data in Figure 32.1 on this page to complete the five maps by shading them in as follows:

  a *UK average weekly household income.* Shade areas over £200 per week in yellow, areas £190-£199 per week in red, areas £180-£189 per week in green and areas over £170 per week in blue.

  b *UK infant mortality.* Shade areas with over 10 deaths per 1000 live births in blue, areas 9.0 to 9.9 in green and areas 8.0 to 8.9 in yellow.

  c *UK percentage of school leavers going into further education.* Shade areas with over 30 per cent in yellow, areas 25–29 percent in red and 20–24 per cent in blue.

  d *UK percentage of people who own their own home.* Shade areas with over 65 per cent in yellow, areas 60 per cent–64 per cent in red and areas 50 per cent–59 per cent in blue.

  e *UK prices of semi-detached houses.* Shade areas where prices are over £40 000 in yellow, areas £30 000 to £39 000 in red and areas below £29 000 in blue.

2 Now study the maps you have drawn, *together with* Figures 32.2 and 32.3.

  a Which four maps support the idea of a North–South divide?

  b Briefly describe the pattern shown on each of the four maps you have identified and explain how it supports the idea of a North–South divide.

  c Briefly describe the patterns shown on each of the remaining three maps. Explain why these do *not* support the idea of a North–South divide.

Region	Average weekly household income	Infant mortality (under one year old per 1000 live births)	Percentage of school leavers going into further education	Percentage of people who own their home
North	£170	8.4	Not available	55
North West	£183	9.4	21.7	65
Yorkshire & Humberside	£172	10.3	28.3	62
West Midlands	£187	10.5	23.4	63
East Midlands	£203	8.3	27.9	66
East Anglia	£204	9.4	26.2	66
South West	£208	8.5	29.4	69
South East	£248	9.0	33.4	64
Scotland	£198	9.4	30.6	41
Wales	£187	9.8	25.5	67
Northern Ireland	£179	9.6	31.1	61

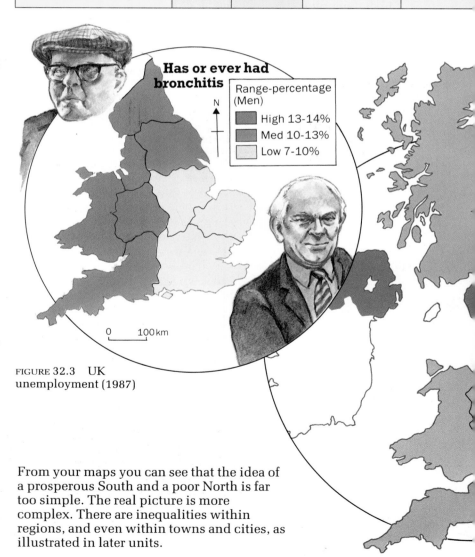

Has or ever had bronchitis

Range-percentage (Men)
- High 13-14%
- Med 10-13%
- Low 7-10%

FIGURE 32.3 UK unemployment (1987)

From your maps you can see that the idea of a prosperous South and a poor North is far too simple. The real picture is more complex. There are inequalities within regions, and even within towns and cities, as illustrated in later units.

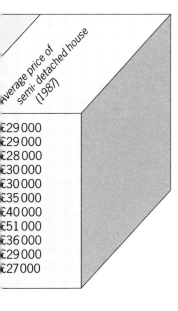

FIGURE 32.1 Regional differences in Britain

Average price of semi-detached house (1987)

£29 000
£29 000
£28 000
£30 000
£30 000
£35 000
£40 000
£51 000
£36 000
£29 000
£27 000

KEY POINTS

- The numbers of people employed in manufacturing industry declined rapidly during the early 1980s, but the numbers employed in the TERTIARY and QUATERNARY sector grew rapidly.

- Government aid to declining industries may prevent some job losses but also may reduce competitiveness.

- More and more British companies are owned and controlled by huge TRANSNATIONAL corporations whose decision-making headquarters are located in other countries.

- Industrial decline may leave behind it decaying empty factories, surrounded by acres of derelict, POLLUTED land. In some places such environments have been renewed to create space for new parks, factories, offices and shops.

- Unemployment is one major human consequence of industrial decline. The waste of skill, initiative and talent amongst unemployed people can create social problems. Some groups, such as people over 45 and ethnic minorities, are worst hit by unemployment.

- The idea of a rich southern Britain and a poor northern one is too simplistic. There are areas of poverty in the South and areas of wealth in the North.

IDEAS FOR COURSEWORK

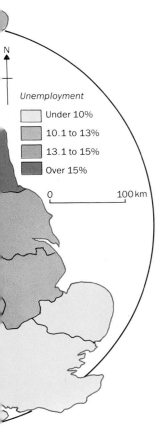

FIGURE 32.2 Cases of bronchitis in England and Wales (1987)

N

Unemployment
- Under 10%
- 10.1 to 13%
- 13.1 to 15%
- Over 15%

0   100 km

 1 Make a study of factory closures in your area over a period of about five years, using sources such as local newspaper archives, local people previously employed in closed factories, the local planning department.
  - How many factories have closed?
  - What were the main products of the various factories?
  - How many people were affected by the closures?
  - What were the main reasons for the closures?
  - What has happened to the sites of the former factories? (Have they been redeveloped for houses/ warehouses/offices etc. or are they simply abandoned and derelict?)
  - How did employees feel about the closure?
  - What percentage of former employees have found alternative jobs?
  - What types of job have people been able to get?

 2 Analyse a manufacturing plant in your area using maps (past and present) together with a questionnaire to establish the main INPUTS, PROCESSES, and OUTPUTS. Use this information to produce a systems diagram for the plant similar to Figure 14.5 (page 46) which is based on a farm. How has the system in your plant changed over the past five to seven years?
  - What inputs have changed?
  - Has the source of inputs changed?
  - Has the destination of outputs changed?
  - Have the processes changed?
Try to explain the changes you highlight.

 3 If there is derelict land in your area, map its location and extent.
  - Is it confined to certain areas?
  - Can you explain the patterns on your map?
Visit the site and ask the local planning department for information on past use of the sites.
  - Why is the land now derelict? (Factory closure/waste disposal area/past mining or quarrying?)
  - What proposals are there for reclaiming the land?
  - Are there alternative proposals? If so, which do you think would be most appropriate, based on your analysis of the site and its surrounding area?

33   *For or against Assisted Areas?*

As traditional industries such as textiles, steel and engineering closed down, unemployment rose, and in the 1980s whole areas began to decline. The government was and is involved because it wishes to reduce unemployment by encouraging companies to locate in areas of decline.

On the one hand, the government has the power to restrict industrial growth in areas like the South East (though it has not done so during the 1980s). On the other hand, it can offer grants, loans and tax concessions to attract firms to areas of high unemployment. The ASSISTED AREAS shown in Figure 33.1 are the places where government help is available.

1　Study Figures 33.2–33.5 which are advertisements from areas trying to attract new companies. Use an atlas and Figure 33.1 to check which of the places is in an Assisted Area. Then make a larger copy of the table below and use the Figures to complete it. This will allow you to compare the attractions of the different places. Put a tick and add further details if the advertisement mentions each attraction, as shown in the example.

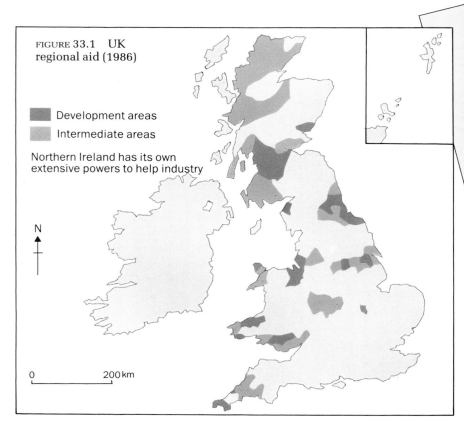

FIGURE 33.1   UK regional aid (1986)

Development areas
Intermediate areas

Northern Ireland has its own extensive powers to help industry

N

0   200 km

Attractions	Mid Glamorgan	Peterborough	North Kent	Washington
1 Assisted Area advantages				
2 Ready-built factories				
3 Cost of factory rents				
4 Labour force				
5 Other companies already attracted				
6 Access to main roads and motorways				
7 Access to seaports and airports	✓M 4	✓A 1	M 25 ✓M2 M20	
8 Rail transport				
9 Travel times				
10 Tax allowances				
11 Freedom from rates				
12 Grants for training and relocation				
13 Local/other attractions				

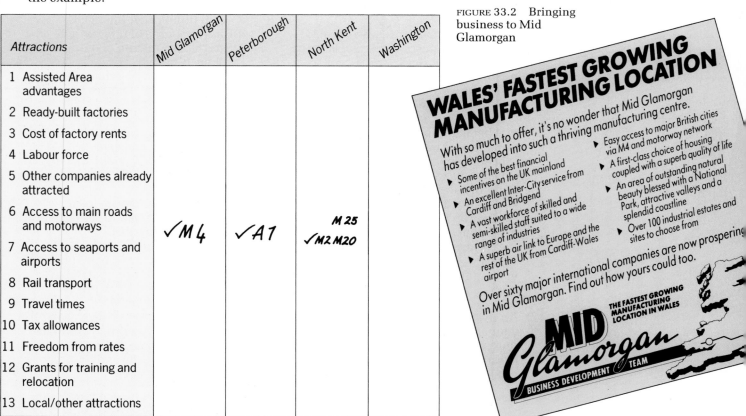

FIGURE 33.2   Bringing business to Mid Glamorgan

WALES' FASTEST GROWING MANUFACTURING LOCATION

With so much to offer, it's no wonder that Mid Glamorgan has developed into such a thriving manufacturing centre.

▶ Some of the best financial incentives on the UK mainland
▶ An excellent Inter-City service from Cardiff and Bridgend
▶ A vast workforce of skilled and semi-skilled staff suited to a wide range of industries
▶ A superb air link to Europe and the rest of the UK from Cardiff-Wales airport

▶ Easy access to major British cities via M4 and motorway network
▶ A first-class choice of housing coupled with a superb quality of life
▶ An area of outstanding natural beauty blessed with a National Park, attractive valleys and a splendid coastline
▶ Over 100 industrial estates and sites to choose from

Over sixty major international companies are now prospering in Mid Glamorgan. Find out how yours could too.

THE FASTEST GROWING MANUFACTURING LOCATION IN WALES

MID Glamorgan
BUSINESS DEVELOPMENT TEAM

FIGURE 33.3 Bringing business to Peterborough

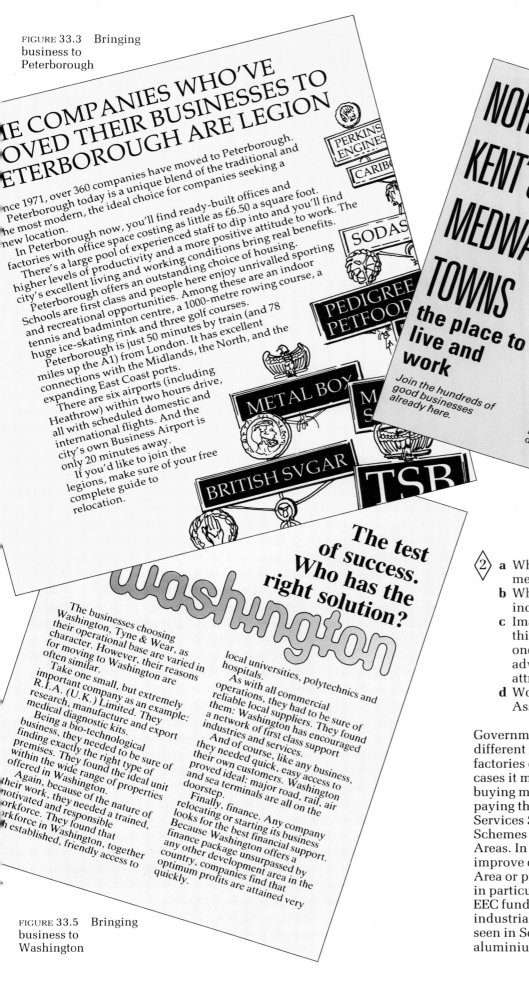

[TH]E COMPANIES WHO'VE [M]OVED THEIR BUSINESSES TO [P]ETERBOROUGH ARE LEGION

[Si]nce 1971, over 360 companies have moved to Peterborough. Peterborough today is a unique blend of the traditional and [t]he most modern, the ideal choice for companies seeking a new location.

In Peterborough now, you'll find ready-built offices and factories with office space costing as little as £6.50 a square foot. There's a large pool of experienced staff to dip into and you'll find higher levels of productivity and a more positive attitude to work. The city's excellent living and working conditions bring real benefits.

Peterborough offers an outstanding choice of housing. Schools are first class and people here enjoy unrivalled sporting and recreational opportunities. Among these are an indoor tennis and badminton centre, a 1000-metre rowing course, a huge ice-skating rink and three golf courses.

Peterborough is just 50 minutes by train (and 78 miles up the A1) from London. It has excellent connections with the Midlands, the North, and the expanding East Coast ports.

There are six airports (including Heathrow) within two hours drive, all with scheduled domestic and international flights. And the city's own Business Airport is only 20 minutes away.

If you'd like to join the legions, make sure of your free complete guide to relocation.

PERKINS ENGINES · *CARIB[...]* · *SODAS[...]* · *PEDIGREE PETFOOD[S]* · *METAL BOX* · *BRITISH SVGAR* · *TSB*

FIGURE 33.4 Bringing business to North Kent

NORTH KENT'S MEDWAY TOWNS
the place to live and work

Join the hundreds of good businesses already here.

★ An excellent location for London, whole of UK and Europe via motorways (M2, M20, M25), rail, local and international air and sea ports, with Channel Tunnel facilities from the mid 1990s.

★ Rapidly expanding Roll-on-Roll-off and Container Services from new Chatham Docks.

★ Lower rates, higher investment potential, attractive land and property prices and rentals.

★ An existing thriving business community with a young, skilled and keen workforce and excellent labour relations throughout the area.

★ An historic setting, beautiful countryside, extensive leisure facilities including sailing, golf and many others.

GRAVESEND ● STROOD
ROCHESTER ● CHATHAM ●
GILLINGHAM

Benefits available now on five prime sites including nil rates until November 1993 and 100% tax allowances on Capital developments.

The test of success. Who has the right solution?

washington

The businesses choosing Washington, Tyne & Wear, as their operational base are varied in character. However, their reasons for moving to Washington are often similar.

Take one small, but extremely important company as an example: R.I.A. (U.K.) Limited. They research, manufacture and export medical diagnostic kits.

Being a bio-technological business, they needed to be sure of finding exactly the right type of premises. They found the ideal unit within the wide range of properties offered in Washington.

Again, because of the nature of their work, they needed a trained, motivated and responsible workforce. They found that in Washington, together with established, friendly access to local universities, polytechnics and hospitals.

As with all commercial operations, they had to be sure of reliable local suppliers. They found a network of first class support industries and services.

And of course, like any business, they needed quick, easy access to their own customers. Washington proved ideal: major road, rail, air and sea terminals are all on the doorstep.

Finally, finance. Any company relocating or starting its business looks for the best financial support. Because Washington offers a finance package unsurpassed by any other development area in the country, companies find that optimum profits are attained very quickly.

FIGURE 33.5 Bringing business to Washington

② **a** Which attractions do all areas mention?

b Which attractions are specific to the individual places?

c Imagine you are a foreign industrialist thinking of setting up a company in one of these areas. Which advertisement would you find most attractive? Why?

d Would the financial advantages of the Assisted Areas affect your choice?

Government help in the Assisted Areas takes different forms. It may help by building factories or even industrial estates. In other cases it may help with the costs of moving, buying machinery, borrowing money, or paying the rent. Job creation, Manpower Services Schemes and Youth Opportunities Schemes all help to provide jobs in Assisted Areas. In some cases the government may improve communications to an Assisted Area or provide special help for companies in particularly difficult times. In addition, EEC funds are available in places following industrial closures. An example of this was seen in Scotland after the closure of the aluminium smelter at Invergordon.

Not everyone agrees about creating areas for special help. Usually people living in the Assisted Areas are in favour of the idea, but people in other places are not so sure. Figure 33.6 summarises some of the arguments for and against a policy to help specific areas.

3 **a** List the main arguments in Figure 33.6 for and against government help to the Assisted Areas, under two headings *For* and *Against*.

b Explain why *you* are for or against aid to Assisted Areas.

c Put the following list of people into groups for or against government help to Assisted Areas. In each case, explain the reasons for your choice.
- A politician from the West Midlands
- A politician from East Anglia
- An unemployed person in Wales
- An unemployed person in Inner London
- The Industrial Development Officer of Peterborough

FIGURE 33.6 Government aid to Assisted Areas: what people think

We are not an Assisted Area but unemployment here is just as high, and we have just as much derelict land. It is unfair to give them advantages that we do not have.

We in Scotland and Wales feel that the people in London do not really care about our problems. We are too far away from them and they are not really interested.

We need better roads and motorways to stop the quality of life from getting worse.

Why should the South East get all the best paid jobs, new airports and even the Channel Tunnel? What about the rest of the country?

It seems silly to spend so much money helping Assisted Areas when we could have created many more jobs by spending the money in the South East.

Many parts of Europe are richer than South-eastern England, so why not encourage the South East to keep on growing?

The government is only trying to win votes and prevent social unrest by spending money in the Assisted Areas.

We need more jobs in the Assisted Areas to reduce unemployment.

The government should help firms in Assisted Areas to prevent even more closures and higher unemployment.

There will always be differences between areas – you cannot ever make them all equal.

34 Enterprise Zones: the debate

The government is particularly keen to encourage industrial growth in areas of high unemployment. Such areas often have other problems, such as old, derelict factories, acres of waste land, unattractive Victorian housing and an ageing, disadvantaged population. ENTERPRISE ZONES were set up to attract firms and to create jobs in areas with particularly severe problems. The most important questions to ask about Enterprise Zones are shown opposite (Figure 34.1).

Case study: the Telford Enterprise Zone

Telford (population 110 000) is a New Town, 48 kilometres north-west of Birmingham (see Figure 34.2). In some ways it is unlike other towns with Enterprise Zones as there are no areas of nineteenth-century housing, derelict factories or polluted land. However, there are other problems. Telford grew in the 1970s by taking people who moved out of Birmingham and the West Midlands.

Unfortunately many of the firms established there in the 1970s were forced to close in the economic recession of the early 1980s. As a result, unemployment rose to 25 per cent by 1983, because there were not enough jobs either in Telford or the West Midlands. In January 1984, part of Telford became an Enterprise Zone.

ENTERPRISE ZONES: KEY QUESTIONS

- Are they *creating* new jobs or simply moving existing jobs from one place to another?
- Are they unfair to areas just outside the Enterprise Zone boundary, where it is hard to attract new companies?
- Are the financial attractions large enough to bring in big firms?
- Is 10 years tax relief long enough to attract most companies?
- Are some of the environments with decaying housing, empty factories and derelict land the best places to create new industry? Might not greenfield sites be better?
- Will the companies stay when the financial incentives end?
- Will the new companies create many jobs, and will they develop new skills in their workforce?

FIGURE 34.1

FIGURE 34.2 Telford, in the West Midlands

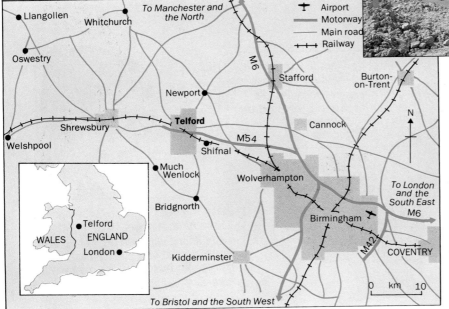

FIGURE 34.3 New units in Telford's Enterprise Zone

Telford has been able to create its Enterprise Zone on a greenfield site. Other Enterprise Zones such as Dudley nearby do not have greenfield sites but have had to clear derelict factories and warehouses in order to create space. The M54 motorway has helped Telford develop its contacts with Birmingham and the rest of the UK motorway system.

By 1987 the Enterprise Zone had attracted some large foreign companies, such as Ricoh (a Japanese firm producing photocopiers), which built its European headquarters in Telford, together with Tatung (a Taiwanese firm producing electrical equipment), Bendix (washing machines) and Unimation Europe (a robot manufacturer). Queen's Moat, a leading UK hotel group, have built a 100-bedroom hotel within the zone.

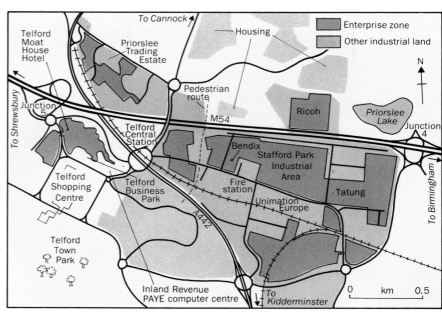

FIGURE 34.4   Telford Enterprise Zone

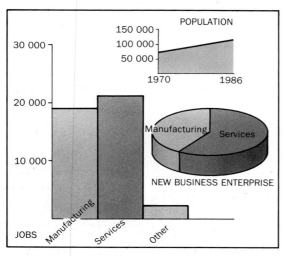

FIGURE 34.5   Population and employment in Telford

By 1987 unemployment had fallen to 18 per cent, partly as a result of jobs created in the Enterprise Zone, and partly as a result of jobs created elsewhere in Telford and the West Midlands. Telford Development Corporation maintain that most of the firms moving into the Enterprise Zone are creating *new* jobs, not simply moving jobs from another part of the West Midlands. However, while it is true that some firms such as Tatung and Ricoh have created new jobs, others, such as Brintons Carpets and Pelloby Engineering, have simply moved their jobs out of the West Midlands and into Telford.

Companies in Wolverhampton, Stafford, Cannock and even other parts of Telford do complain because they do not receive the freedom from rates and other Enterprise Zone advantages. They claim that the competition they face from firms in the Enterprise Zone is unfair.

The companies already attracted to Telford's Enterprise Zone clearly feel that the financial incentives are good, and that 10 years' freedom from rates is a distinct advantage. However, some firms such as Cinzano (making wine), Clifford Williams (making clothing) and Hitachi-Maxell (making video tapes) have located in Telford but not within the Enterprise Zone. In their cases, the general attractions of the area were more important than a site within the Enterprise Zone.

1   Imagine that you have to write a dialogue for a short TV documentary about Enterprise Zones. There are two main characters, one in favour of Enterprise Zones and the other against them. Work in pairs, and use the key questions from Figure 34.1 and the data on Telford to write two sets of dialogue in answer to each question, for example:

35 Urban industry: renew or replace?

The role of Development Corporations

Urban DEVELOPMENT CORPORATIONS were set up by the government to redevelop urban areas, particularly those in the North and in the Midlands where there has been a rapid run-down of traditional industries. These areas desperately need new jobs and an improved environment. Figure 35.1 describes the main ways they aim to encourage people to live and work in their regions.

The Merseyside Development Corporation

In 1981 when the Corporation was established, it took over the area of dockland shown in Figure 35.2. Of the 410 hectares covered by the Corporation, 25 per cent were former docks which had closed in the 1970s. This was an area of empty docks, demolished factories, empty goods yards and railway sidings with many other buildings in a poor state of repair. The whole impression was of a run-down area which was a danger to the public, and prone to

- helping local industries
- attracting new industries and services
- improving the environment by schemes to revive derelict land
- attracting new housing development

The Corporations receive some funds from the government, but also have to attract considerable private investment to achieve their aims.

vandalism. Of the 2 million square metres of buildings only 60 000 square metres were relatively new, and most of the rest was too poor to renovate. Only a few warehouses were worth retaining and improving because of their historic importance. The docks were in a poor state of repair, with broken gates, and deposits of silt 10 metres deep, left by the tides. The water in the docks was polluted by sewage and industrial waste.

FIGURE 35.1 The role of the Development Corporation

FIGURE 35.3 Liverpool docks before redevelopment. What evidence is there of disuse?

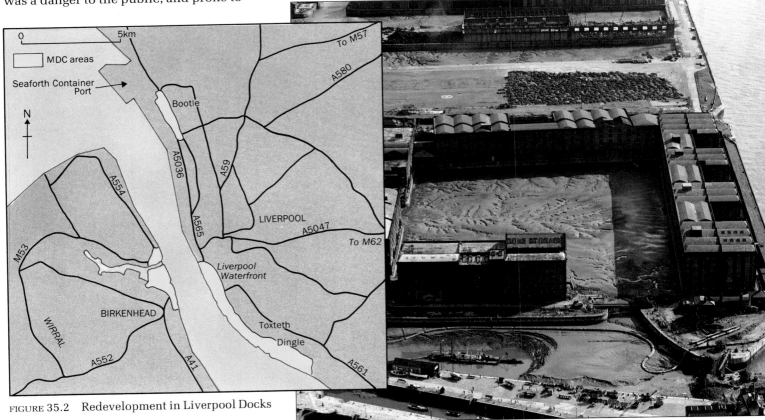

FIGURE 35.2 Redevelopment in Liverpool Docks

FIGURE 35.4   Albert Dock after redevelopment.
The warehouse on the left now houses the
Merseyside Maritime Museum. The building with
the green domed roof is the former Dock Office

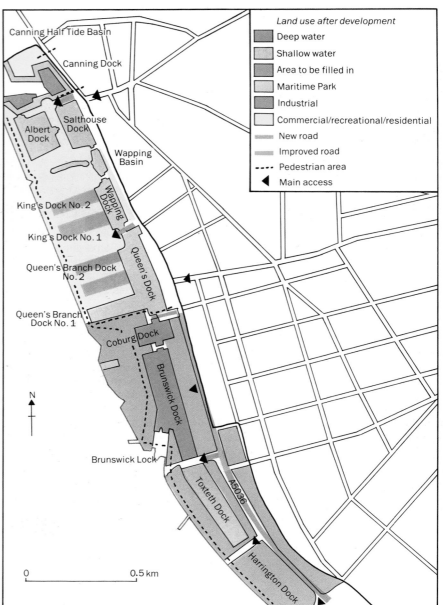

FIGURE 35.5   Liverpool Waterfront Area, showing
the redevelopment land use plan. Parts of
Wapping and Queen's Docks were found to be in
particularly poor condition. What is the proposed
land use for them?

By 1988 there were considerable signs of
progress, particularly in the Liverpool
Waterfront area. Here, the Albert Dock had
been transformed at a cost of £110 million
into a waterfront village with shops, wine
bars, offices and restaurants (these last four
uses were particularly attractive to private
investors). In 1986, 1.8 million tourists
visited the Albert Dock, one of the key
attractions being the Merseyside
International Maritime Museum. In 1988 the
Tate Gallery North opened its exhibits of
modern art to the public, and private
companies are now developing hotels, flats
and houses around the Dock. Granada TV
now occupies the modernised Dock Traffic
office next to the Albert Dock.

Twenty-five hectares of water space has
been created for leisure use, by
improvements to the lock gates, and anti-
pollution measures to clean up the water.
Albert and Canning Docks are to be used for
prestige and historic vessels, Salthouse,
Wapping and Kings/Queens Docks are being
redesigned for dinghy sailing, rowing,
canoeing and windsurfing, and the Coburg/
Brunswick Docks are to be for large yachts
with a 500 berth marina.

Other planned developments include an
ice rink, a national aquarium, a water theme
park, a cinema complex, a roller skating
centre and an hotel around the Queens Dock.
The Merseyside Development Corporation
calculate that tourism brought in £250
million during 1986, and 14 000 jobs are
supported by tourism. However, the
redevelopment has aroused mixed feelings
amongst local people (see Figure 35.7).

1 a Compare the photograph of the Liverpool Waterfront Area (Figure
    35.6) with the above map (Figure 35.5). On a tracing of the picture
    in Figure 35.6 mark and name the following:

    Albert Dock   Queens Dock
    Salthouse Dock   Coburg Dock
    Canning Dock   Brunswick Dock
    Canning Half Tide Basin   The A5037 main road
    Wapping Basin   The edge of the Development
    Wapping Dock (Kings Dock)   Corporation area

  b What if people want more space in Liverpool Waterfront for
    commercial, recreational and residential land uses? From your
    map and Figure 35.6 which area would you recommend for a
    change of proposed use? Give the reasons for your choice.

FIGURE 35.6 Liverpool Waterfront, viewed from the northern end. Here you can see the Dock Office at the bottom of the picture

All this development is not creating many new jobs, but it's making a lot of money for large companies.

I was unemployed for two years when the local sugar refinery closed, but now I have a job in the Maritime Museum. Liverpool needs new jobs, whoever is creating them.

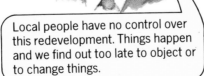

Local people have no control over this redevelopment. Things happen and we find out too late to object or to change things.

It's nice to see the area coming to life again.

FIGURE 35.7 Liverpool's dockland redevelopment: what the people think

2 Imagine you are the Development Adviser to a British city of 200 000 people which has problems similar to those of Merseyside. In particular, your city has high unemployment, empty factories and warehouses, areas of derelict land, and a polluted estuary (narrower than the Mersey) with two abandoned docks.

Write a report for the Council's Planning Department urging them to persuade the government to set up a Development Corporation in your city. Include the following points:
- What has been achieved on Merseyside between 1981 and 1988.
- What might have happened there without a Development Corporation.
- The role of private investments and the types of project they support.
- How local people might be more involved in the projects.

Finish with a summary of what might be possible in your own city (such as development of tourism, for example).

36   *Co-operating to create jobs*

One method of providing jobs starts with people, rather than with the government. This is the establishment of co-operatives. A CO-OPERATIVE is simply an organisation in which people join together to help both themselves and others. More and more groups of people, often in areas of high unemployment, are starting their own factories or running their own shops or nurseries.

In a co-operative, the company belongs equally to all members of the group. They share the work and the profits (Figure 36.1). Some of the main advantages of co-operatives are:

- All people can have a say in the running of the firm.

- Profits are shared equally.

- The wealth usually stays in the local community.

- The members can decide to put profits into projects which may not earn much money but which benefit the community. (Helpline telephone services, for example.)

- The people involved know the problems of the area at first hand and the types of firms and services that are really needed.

- The company belongs to the people who work in it.

- Members are kept informed of the state of the business so unexpected redundancies are less likely.

① Using the list of advantages above, compare the structure of a co-operative with a commercial company, owned by shareholders and run by managers.

FIGURE 36.1   Community co-operatives, as suggested here, can be set up and run by local people to benefit their own communities

Through co-operation breathe new life into your community

Your community may need a good shop, a nursery, or bus service, for example. You might want to repair household goods, or provide help for older people . . .

Whatever your community needs, you could provide it yourselves through a co-op.
You, your friends and neighbours can all become members of the community co-op and have an equal say in how it works.

You keep control by voting at regular meetings for the things you want to see happen. You might want to create full- or part-time jobs in your community, to provide goods or services.

And if the co-op makes money, it stays in your area. You choose how to spend it. It can always be used to fund other activities which benefit the community.

FIGURE 36.2 The Three Is, a vegetarian restaurant co-operative in North London is based in a small business unit rented from the local council. The founder members, shown here, obtained free financial advice from the government

2 Read the article in Figure 36.3 which describes how one co-operative started in Durham. Use the information to draw a flow diagram of the stages necessary in establishing a co-operative. Here is a suggestion for starting your diagram.

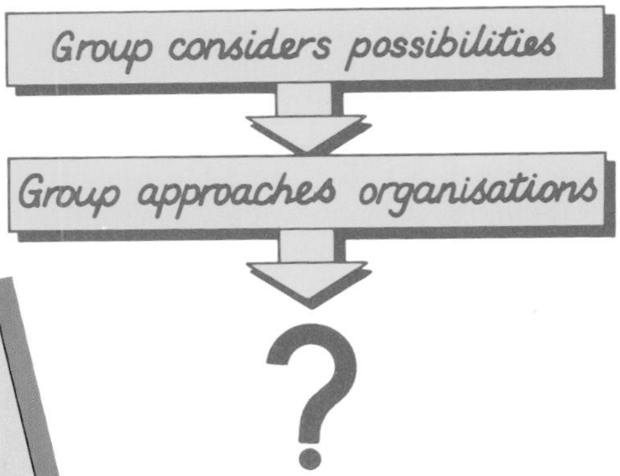

Group considers possibilities

Group approaches organisations

?

FIGURE 36.3 A co-operative business venture gets going in County Durham

Lois Engineering established itself in County Durham in 1986. Its three founder members are Linda Clayton, Dave Mason and Ron Laidow. Linda explains how they managed to get started.

In March 1986, we considered the possibility of forming a common ownership company. We approached various organisations including Cleveland Co-operative Agency. A meeting with Peter Smith of Cleveland Co-operative Agency gave us guidelines as to the correct procedure to follow.

We contacted a number of potential customers outlining the wide range of engineering services we had to offer and received an excellent response.

We arranged a meeting with Mr. Stewart Watkins of the Industrial Bureau, County Hall. The response we received from customers led to Durham County Council appointing Mr Gordon Scott Management Consultant to work with us on a feasibility study. Further research into our market led to cash flow figures being produced. This gave us a basis to apply for premises and finance.

We had meetings with most of the main banks, and a meeting with The Manager of the Co-operative Bank, Durham resulted in us obtaining an overdraft arrangement. This, together with our own investment, left us looking for finance to purchase our machinery. BREL purchased the machinery on our behalf, to be repaid over three years. Within six months we commenced trading as Lois Engineering Limited occupying Unit 2 on the Chilton Industrial Estate, Chilton, Co. Durham.

People involved in co-operatives have to LEARN

How to think positively about fellow workers and customers
How to control finances
How to work together efficiently
How to advertise their goods or services
How to make decisions and choices
How to take responsibility for their actions.

They have to UNLEARN

Ripping off the boss or company
The attitude that 'the world owes me a living'
Maximum reward for minimum work
Muddling through
Walking away from problems
Using time badly
Wondering why customers do not turn up
Passing the buck
Taking minimal responsibility

FIGURE 36.4 Guidelines in co-operative thinking

Co-operatives clearly represent a very different approach to providing jobs to that of Development Corporations, Assisted Areas or Enterprise Zones. There were about 1500 co-operatives in England and Wales in 1987, employing 6800 people. Partly because of their small size, they have not had a huge impact on the unemployment figures. Raising money to start any new business remains the main problem. Co-operatives have flourished in areas where the local authority has been prepared to take risks, and make loans to small groups who have often been turned down by commercial banks. The driving force, though, must come from the co-operative members themselves (see Figure 36.4).

37 *Revival with micro-electronics?*

The micro-electronics industry did not exist 25 years ago, yet now it is one of the few rapidly expanding sections of manufacturing industry. Britain's future as a manufacturing nation depends on its ability to specialise in HIGH TECHNOLOGY (high-tech) industries such as aerospace, biotechnology, computers, electronics and telecommunications. In 1987, 6 per cent of all UK jobs were in high-tech industries, and they accounted for 28 per cent of all manufacturing exports.

However, as in other cases, jobs in high-tech industries are not distributed evenly across the country. The largest concentration of firms is in a belt between London and Bristol (see Figure 37.3). Other concentrations are in East Anglia and Central Scotland. In contrast some areas of Britain actually lost jobs in high-tech industries. These areas were mainly in Yorkshire and Humberside, the North West and the Midlands (East and West).

FIGURE 37.1   This industrial area in Reading, Berkshire, houses a number of high-tech industries. It offers a clean, well-placed working environment, just off the M4. What could happen to the field in the centre of the picture, and why?

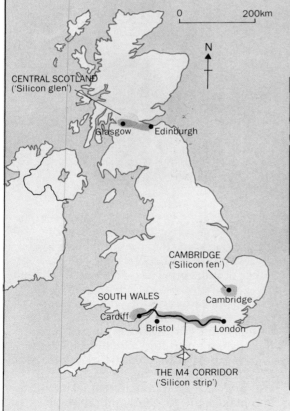

FIGURE 37.3   High-tech areas of England and Wales

FIGURE 37.2   The girl in the picture is carrying out a circuit board check in a telecommunications factory. What do you notice about the work surfaces, the operating equipment and the worker's clothing?

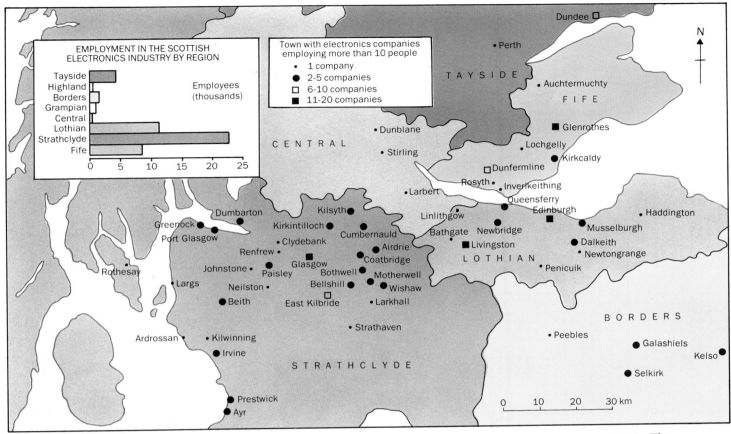

FIGURE 37.4   The electronics industry in central Scotland

The new manufacturing industries are called high-tech because they use a great deal of expensive and sophisticated research and development techniques. The new, expanding companies are also called 'sunrise' industries, in contrast to the older, declining 'sunset' industries such as textiles, coal and steel.

The micro-electronics firms seek modern, attractive premises near to international airports. They also require access to universities with their research and development facilities, and a local environment which will be attractive to technical, scientific and professional staff.

A 1987 analysis of the largest 150 British cities showed that those urban areas with older, declining industries did badly in attracting high-tech firms. New Towns throughout the country, together with pleasant residential areas like Cambridge and the Thames Valley towns do well in attracting high-tech firms.

If too many high-tech firms locate in southern England problems might arise. Overcrowding, for example, could lead to an increase in production costs, caused by higher business rents and warehousing costs. Companies may decide to relocate to another part of the EEC rather than an alternative site elsewhere in the UK. There is a need to attract high-tech industry away from the South if problems such as overcrowding are to be avoided.

Electronics in central Scotland

The map shows the distribution of electronics companies in central Scotland, one of the few areas away from southern England to succeed in attracting firms. Study Figure 37.4 then answer the questions which follow.

 a Which towns and cities have between 11 and 20 electronics companies?
b Which towns have between 6 and 10 electronics companies?
c Which three Scottish regions have most electronics workers?

 On an outline tracing of Figure 37.4, use an atlas to add:

- Motorways (M8, M80, M74, M90)
- International airports (Glasgow)
- Main railway lines
- Main roads (A1, A74, A9)

Locate the major electronics centres on your map.

③ Use the map you have drawn for question 2 plus the data on Glenrothes New Town in the fact file to list the attractions of the area for high-tech companies.

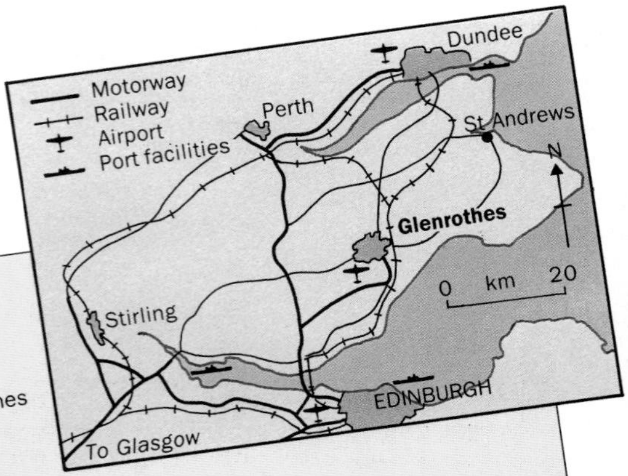

Map legend:
— Motorway
+ Railway
✈ Airport
⚓ Port facilities

Dundee, Perth, St Andrews, Glenrothes, Stirling, To Glasgow, EDINBURGH
0 km 20   N

Glenrothes Fact File

EDUCATION
Glenrothes has 14 primary schools, three secondary schools and one College of Technology, noted for its close links with industry. Of the eight Scottish universities, five are within easy travelling distance of Glenrothes.

HOUSING
The town has been built in precincts or 'villages' to retain an element of local character. There are many house types suitable for most needs. The owner-occupation rate is now almost 40 per cent.

SHOPPING
The Kingdom Centre is one of the largest enclosed shopping complexes in Scotland, with an extensive range of shops. Each precinct has its own neighbourhood shopping centre with community facilities.

LEISURE AND RECREATION
Extensive facilities are available to suit almost every sporting taste: badminton, squash, snooker, ice-skating, bowling, curling, football, rugby, flying, parachuting, swimming, golf, riding.

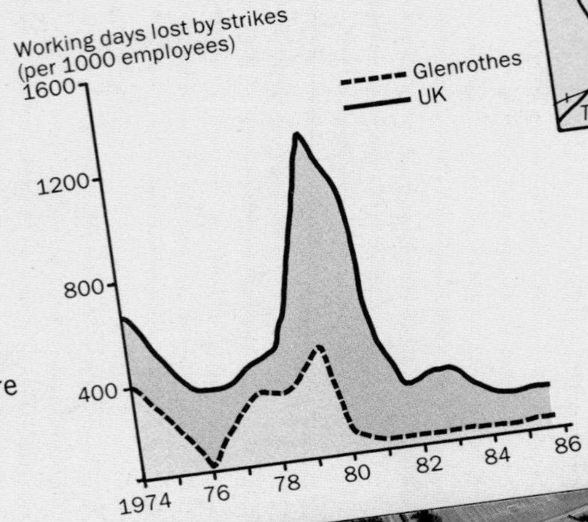

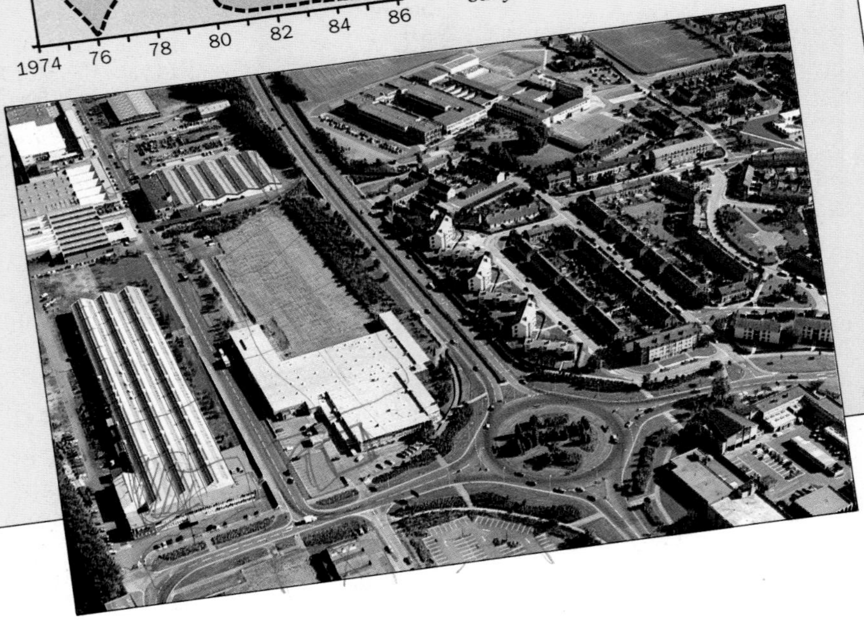

Working days lost by strikes (per 1000 employees)
- - - - Glenrothes
——— UK
1600, 1200, 800, 400
1974 76 78 80 82 84 86

FIGURE 37.5   Queensway industrial estate, Glenrothes. Work, home and community facilities are all planned to be within easy reach

Glenrothes is typical of the towns which are attracting high-tech industries. It became a New Town in 1948 based on its high unemployment. By 1963 its future was switched away from local coal-mining towards new industries. GEC located here to produce telecommunications equipment, followed by ACT, computer manufacturers. The town had a population of 40 000 in 1987, which is projected at 45 000 by 1996 and eventually to 55 000 by 2000.

Some people argue that towns like Glenrothes have been *too* successful in attracting high-tech firms. Over 25 per cent of the workforce is employed by such companies. They feel this represents an over-dependence on one type of industry, which could be dangerous if that industry declines.

A further worry is that 90 per cent of the high-tech firms are American- or Japanese-owned. The rest are Dutch or West German, with Britain coming a very poor fifth. The factories in Britain mostly assemble imported parts, and so rely heavily on the parent company for know-how and key decisions about investment and product development.

④ Write two short paragraphs headed *The Rocks Ahead* explaining the possible future problems for the high-tech industry in
a Britain as a whole,
b Central Scotland.
Outline ways in which these problems could be avoided by careful planning.

KEY POINTS

- Areas with high unemployment receive government help to try and attract new industries. These ASSISTED AREAS are competing against each other to attract a limited number of companies.

- ENTERPRISE ZONES are another government attempt to stimulate industrial growth. They have attracted firms and created jobs, but some people argue that the companies will leave once the financial incentives end.

- Large-scale DEVELOPMENT CORPORATIONS have begun to improve derelict land, attract new housing and industry whilst supporting existing local concerns. The rapid pace of such development has made some local communities feel excluded from important decisions that affect their lives.

- Not all schemes designed to create jobs depend on government initiatives. CO-OPERATIVES are one important way in which people come together to provide goods and services and so create jobs.

- Expanding manufacturing industries such as micro-electronics tend to be highly automated and create relatively few jobs. They are rarely located in areas of high unemployment.

IDEAS FOR COURSEWORK

 Examine the impact of a factory (new or old) on an area near you. Carry out a traffic census at different times over a period of a few weeks.
- At what times of the day does the factory most influence local traffic patterns? Why is this?
- What types of traffic does the factory generate?

Carry out a survey of housing around the factory.
- What percentage of people surveyed work in the factory?
- How do local people feel about the factory? For example, do they find it a nuisance and a source of pollution, or a useful source of jobs?

 You could compare two factories in different parts of a city. Use maps to identify earlier land uses. Use questionnaires to compare factories under headings:
- Age, size, height of buildings
- Extent of on-site car parking
- Main products
- Surrounding land use, road widths
- Possible problems created by the factories

 If you live near an Enterprise Zone or visit one on fieldwork, you could carry out a survey of the reasons why firms had located there. You could also survey surrounding firms and shops to establish their views about the Enterprise Zone:
- Do they feel it represents unfair competition?
- Has it created traffic problems?
- Does it provide much-needed jobs?
- What types of companies have located in the Enterprise Zone?
- What percentage are manufacturing firms, or service firms?
- Why was the Enterprise Zone created?
- What was the previous land use?

 You might study an industrial estate in your area. Map the type and location of companies.
- What are the commonest types of firm? Why is this?
- What was the previous land use? Use a questionnaire on a sample of companies to establish where they have come from and why they chose this estate.
- Have most moved over 5 kilometres?
- Are most branches of bigger firms in local cities?
- What are the three most important factors which have attracted firms to this estate?

38 Service industries

If you refer back to Figure 28.2 (page 96) showing expanding and declining industries between 1978 and 1986 you will be reminded that most of the SERVICE INDUSTRIES grew rapidly during this period.

Many people see service industries as a natural progression from manufacturing industries. However, you need to be clear about the exact nature of service industries. Three broad sections make up the services:

- Transport and public utilities (gas, water, electricity, telephone)
- Insurance, finance, trade, property
- Education, government, health, recreation and research

In this sense, the service industries affect us all when, for example, we visit a shop, use a telephone, have a car repaired, turn on gas, water or electricity, go to school, visit the dentist, go to a bank or to a social security office. They all provide a *service* which people need.

FIGURE 38.1 These pictures all show people working in service industries. Name each industry you recognise. Which broad section of the services (see main text) does it come under?

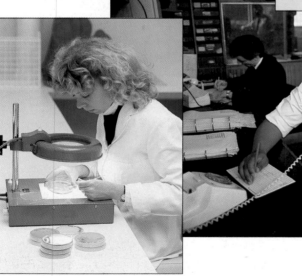

As Figure 38.3 shows, jobs in the service industries are not spread evenly across the areas of Britain. Between 1979 and 1987, service industries as a whole expanded by 7 per cent or 867 000 jobs. Ninety-one per cent of these new jobs were in the South East, South West, East Anglia and the East and West Midlands.

② Study Figures 38.2 and 38.3 which show the distribution of service industries in Britain and the likely changes in employment between 1985 and 1990.
  a Rank the regions of Britain in order of their total employment in services. (If in doubt, measure the circles.)
  b Which two regions have the largest percentage of their employees in public administration? Can you suggest why this is the case?
  c Which region has the largest percentage of its employees in the banking, finance and insurance group? Try to explain this.
  d Which region has the largest percentage of its employees in transport and communication jobs?
  e Which three groups of service industries show the largest increase for 1990?
  f How many more employees in the business services group are forecast for 1990?
  g How many more employees in (i) the banking and (ii) the insurance groups are expected by 1990?
  h How many new jobs in total are expected in service industries by 1990?

① Refer back to Figure 28.2 (page 96).
  a Which group of services grew most between 1978 and 1986?
  b How many thousand more employees were there in 1986 in the following groups?
    Retail distribution
    Hotel and catering
  c Which service industries experienced a decline in employment between 1978 and 1986?

FIGURE 38.2   Workforce increase in the growth industries (1985–90)

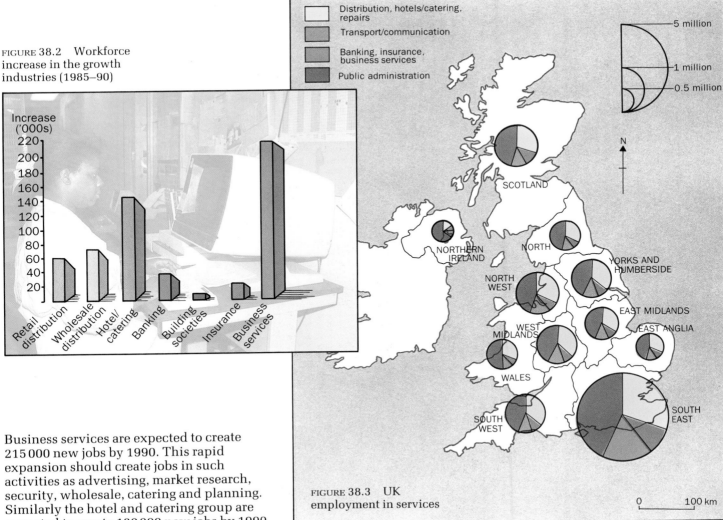

FIGURE 38.3   UK employment in services

Business services are expected to create 215 000 new jobs by 1990. This rapid expansion should create jobs in such activities as advertising, market research, security, wholesale, catering and planning. Similarly the hotel and catering group are expected to create 120 000 new jobs by 1990.

Three main groups of people are likely to benefit by this expansion of service industries:

- women
- part-time workers
- young people

Unfortunately these groups do not necessarily include people who have been unemployed for a long time. Although service industries are growing rapidly and creating new jobs, areas of high unemployment are not likely to benefit as much as the South and East.

 Outline a series of measures that the government could take to
  a direct new service jobs to areas of high unemployment.
  b fill more of the new service jobs by people who have been out of work for over 18 months.

 The growth in services has sometimes been called 'the Second Industrial Revolution'. Why do you think this is so? Do you agree?

FIGURE 38.4   The former Greater London Council headquarters on the south bank of the Thames is considered by some to be ideal for conversion into a top-class hotel, business centre and luxury flats. Do you agree? What other uses could you suggest?

39 Beauty or the Beast?

Case study: Ashford, Kent

One of the main problems connected with industrial growth is its effect on the environment. Areas of scenic beauty and scientific interest may be sacrificed in the rush to develop new companies and the jobs they bring.

One area where there is great pressure for extra land for industrial expansion is Ashford in Kent. The completion of the M25 London Ring Road and the proposed Channel Tunnel with an important station at Ashford have made this a very attractive area to companies.

The newspaper extracts (Figure 39.2) outline the type of development proposed and some of the objections raised by the Council for the Protection of Rural England (CPRE). Study these and then answer the questions which follow.

FIGURE 39.1   Under threat? Ripening wheat fields and lush hedgerow just outside Ashford

1) Make a list of the proposed developments in Ashford.

2) Now make a list of the groups of people likely to benefit from the developments, and a second list of groups who are likely to oppose the Ashford developments.

FIGURE 39.2   Plans for change in Kent (1987)

Chunnel boom comes to Ashford

A Disneyland-style theme park, a replica of the Cambridge Science Park, and a possible new village built by Consortium Developments, are planned at Ashford, in Kent.

The two developments will create 1,000 construction jobs and 1,300 permanent jobs in the town and have sparked a 50 per cent rise in industrial rents and 20 per cent rise in house prices in the past year.

Industrial units which have been lying empty for up to five years have been snapped up, mainly by firms wanting to capitalise on the potential of a town where 1.8 million passengers are expected to board or leave tunnel trains each year.

Trinity College Cambridge, which owns land in the north of Ashford, has already drawn up proposals for a science park which would be modelled on the Cambridge Science Park, which has successfully brought together high-technology industrial units and university research establishments on a single attractive site.

Kent ready to trim green belt for growth

Pulling back the boundaries and allowing "prestige" businesses within the green belt, and giving generous land allocations for housing and industry are proposed by Kent County Council in a bullish response to the growth potential of the M25 and the Channel Tunnel.

Its structure plan review, which also canvasses the idea of free-standing new settlements near Ashford and Canterbury, was described by the Council for the Protection of Rural England (CPRE) yesterday as containing "some of the most alarming proposals to come out of a county council."

The CPRE says that area of Kent does not need the jobs, and development will create extra demand for housing land.

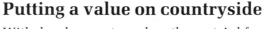

COUNTRYSIDE SCORE SCALE

ADD

10 for mountains

8 for hills

6 for plateaux

2 for lowland

10 for wild, uncultivated landscape

6 for water

6 for natural or landscaped forests

4 for farmland with hedges

2 for farmland with no trees or hedges

SUBTRACT

10 for industrial area

10 for urban area

5 for continuous forests

FIGURE 39.3   Mountain river, Derwentwater

3 Make a copy of the diagram shown below (Figure 39.4). Fill in each box with the correct entry from the list below, to show the sequence of events. Label your diagram *Ashford: a Spiral of Growth*.
  ● More companies move into area
  ● More houses are built
  ● Channel Tunnel built
  ● More factories built
  ● Ashford becomes more accessible to new people and companies.
Write two or three sentences to describe your diagram.

4 Explain why you think the developments at Ashford should be encouraged or should be opposed.

Putting a value on countryside

With developments such as those at Ashford it is important to identify which areas of countryside are particularly valuable and need conserving. There may be other, less valuable areas of countryside where development would do far less harm. Therefore planners need to be able to measure countryside and put a value on it.

Measuring the attractiveness of countryside can be very difficult. Areas which appeal to some people are disliked by others. The score scale above shows one method of measuring a section of countryside.

5 Look at Figures 39.1 and 39.3. Use the method outlined in the countryside score scale to measure the attractiveness of the two landscapes. What does each landscape score?

FIGURE 39.4

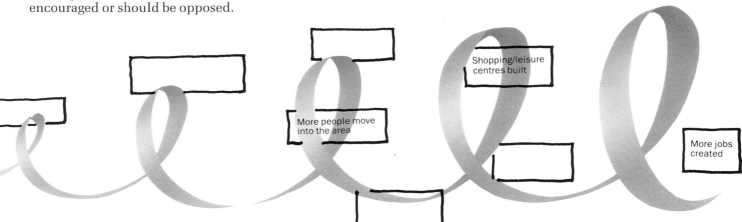

Shopping/leisure centres built

More people move into the area

More jobs created

KEY POINTS

- The growth of SERVICE INDUSTRIES has created many new jobs especially in office blocks. Jobs in service industries tend to be concentrated in the South East.

- The pressure to build new factories, offices and houses may lead to environmental damage, by sacrificing green belts or other areas of scenic beauty and scientific interest.

IDEAS FOR COURSEWORK

 You might make a study of a local office block. Use a questionnaire and a map to establish where most companies came from and why they chose this particular office block.
- Is it near the railway station, with easy parking for clients, or close to main roads?
- Is the rent low?
- Is the block near to competitors?
- Is it close to many customers?
- Have most companies come from the surrounding area, or from over 20 kilometres away?

 If you live near an area of new factories or if you visit one on fieldwork, you could map the type and location of firms.

You could also question the local people on the impact they feel the factories have had on them (such as new job opportunities, loss of farmland).

Question some of the factory managers about their attitude towards the local environment and their attempts to reduce disturbances created by the factory.

Managing urban environments

Urban living

Housing and redevelopment

Urban services

City limits

This view of Leeds shows many of the changes that have affected British cities since the end of the nineteenth century. What evidence of change do you notice?

40 *Flight from the city*

Three out of four people in Britain live in towns or cities but, as Figure 40.1 illustrates, the pattern is changing. During the nineteenth and early twentieth centuries, towns and cities became the destination for thousands of migrants from the countryside during a period of URBANISATION. Now these same towns and cities no longer have the same attraction. London in the 1980s has 2 million fewer people than at its peak in the 1950s.

Figure 40.3 on the page opposite shows just how people began leaving large urban areas between 1971 and 1981. All the CONURBATIONS (groups of towns which have grown together) lost population in the 1970s and 1980s, and in general, the larger the conurbation, the greater the loss of people.

FIGURE 40.1 Changing numbers in town and country

1 Study Figure 40.1
  a In which year was Britain's urban population more than 50 per cent?
  b What percentage of Britain's population lived in towns and cities in 1800? And in 1950?
  c What percentage of Britain's population is likely to live in towns and cities in AD 2000?

Greater London	−10.5 million
Merseyside	−9.5 million
Tyne and Wear	−5.2 million
West Midlands	−5.0 million
Greater Manchester	−4.8 million
South Yorkshire	−2.1 million
West Yorkshire	−2.0 million
Central Clydeside	−2.1 million

2 a Use an atlas and a copy of Figure 40.2 to mark and name the following conurbations:
  Clydeside   Tyne and Wear
  West Yorkshire   South Yorkshire
  Merseyside   Greater Manchester
  West Midlands   Greater London
  b Draw a bar graph next to each conurbation to show the *percentage decline* between 1971 and 1981 based on Figure 40.2. You will need to choose a suitable scale.

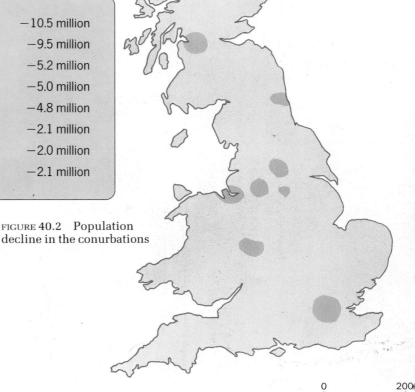

FIGURE 40.2 Population decline in the conurbations

0   200

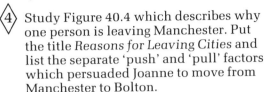

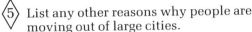

3 Study Figure 40.3.
a Which types of towns grew most in population between 1971 and 1981?
b Which other types of towns grew between 1971 and 1981?
c Can you suggest reasons for your answers to **a** and **b**?
d Which other types of area grew in population between 1971 and 1981?

Why are people leaving?

4 Study Figure 40.4 which describes why one person is leaving Manchester. Put the title *Reasons for Leaving Cities* and list the separate 'push' and 'pull' factors which persuaded Joanne to move from Manchester to Bolton.

5 List any other reasons why people are moving out of large cities.

The same everywhere?

Although cities such as London show a rapid population decline between 1971 and 1981, not all areas of the city were equally affected. Figure 40.5 shows Greater London, together with the population change for each borough (1971–1981).

6 a On a copy of Figure 40.5 shade in each borough according to its population change, using the following key:
Yellow Increase
Green Decrease 0–9 per cent
Red Decrease 10–19 per cent
Blue Decrease 20 per cent and over
b Which areas of London lost most people between 1971 and 1981?
c Why do you think the areas shaded in blue lost so many people?
d Why do you think the area shaded in yellow actually grew?

FIGURE 40.3 Flight from the cities, England and Wales (1971-81)

FIGURE 40.4

FIGURE 40.5 Population change in Greater London (1971-81)

		Gain/Loss %			Gain/Loss %
1	City	+32	17	Ealing	−7
2	Islington	−20	18	Brent	−10
3	Hackney	−18	19	Harrow	−3
4	Tower Hamlets	−15	20	Barnet	−5
5	Southwark	−20	21	Enfield	−4
6	Lambeth	−20	22	Redbridge	−6
7	Westminster	−23	23	Barking	−8
8	Camden	−18	24	Havering	−4
9	Haringay	−15	25	Bexley	−1
10	Waltham Forest	−9	26	Bromley	−4
11	Newham	−11	27	Croydon	−6
12	Greenwich	−2	28	Merton	−8
13	Lewisham	−14	29	Sutton	−1
14	Wandsworth	−16	30	Kingston	−5
15	Kensington and Chelsea	−29	31	Richmond	−10
16	Hammersmith	−21	32	Hounslow	−4
			33	Hillingdon	−3

Joanne – leaving it all behind her

Computer programmer Joanne Boyd (26) has just given up her job in Manchester after four years of sharing a flat there. She has decided to seek refuge from the high rents and high commuting costs of the big city. 'I have had enough,' she said. 'It was so noisy where I lived either from the traffic, the neighbours or the 'planes overhead. I am glad that at last I can buy my own house and live in a place where I can really get to know people. I will also be able to go out without fear of being mugged or attacked.' Joanne is moving to Bolton where house prices are lower than Manchester and traffic problems are far fewer.

0 10 km

41   *Inequalities within cities*

Many studies and reports have been made of the social conditions in Britain's cities. They are often very long and detailed, so that they can give a full and accurate picture. This unit uses a model – the city of 'Manford' – to illustrate the type of data that is collected in such studies, which planners need to analyse and interpret before making suggestions for change and improvement. 'Manford' is typical of a number of British cities.

People in different parts of the same city often live in very different conditions. For example, houses are generally classified as overcrowded if there are more than 1.5 people per room. Figure 41.1 shows the pattern of variation in overcrowding in the city of Manford. Study this, then answer the questions which follow.

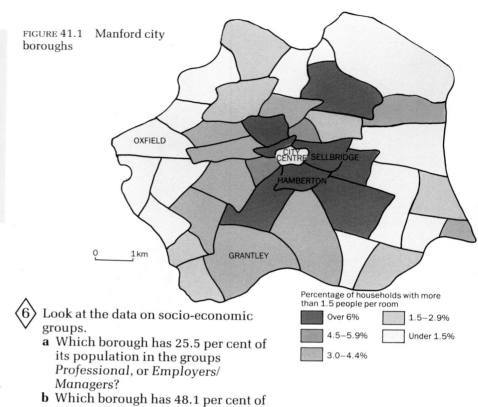

FIGURE 41.1   Manford city boroughs

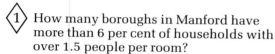

Percentage of households with more than 1.5 people per room

- Over 6%
- 4.5–5.9%
- 3.0–4.4%
- 1.5–2.9%
- Under 1.5%

1 How many boroughs in Manford have more than 6 per cent of households with over 1.5 people per room?

2 Where are these boroughs within the city?

3 In which parts of the city are boroughs with less than 3 per cent of their households overcrowded?

4 How many boroughs have less than 1.5 per cent of their households overcrowded? Where are these boroughs in the city?

Now study Figure 41.2 which gives more detail about the four boroughs shown on the map, and answer the questions. Use your answers to prepare a fact sheet for each of the four boroughs.

5 Look at the data on age structure in Figure 41.2.
   a Which borough has the highest percentage of people under 14?
   b Which borough has the highest percentage of people over 65?
   c Which borough has the largest percentage of people of working age?

6 Look at the data on socio-economic groups.
   a Which borough has 25.5 per cent of its population in the groups *Professional*, or *Employers/ Managers*?
   b Which borough has 48.1 per cent of its population in the *Unskilled* and *Semi-skilled* groups?
   c Which borough has most of its population in the *Skilled workers* group?

BOROUGHS	AGE STRUCTURE			SOCIO-ECONOMIC GROUPS	
	0-14	*15-65*	*Over 65*	*Professional*	*Employers/ Managers*
Hamberton	22.7	55.3	22.0	1.3	5.5
Sellbridge	20.9	65.1	14.0	2.0	3.7
Grantley	29.2	58.3	12.5	1.7	6.5
Oxfield	21.9	66.1	12.0	6.9	18.6

	HOUSING			
	Owner- occupied	*Private rented*	*Council rented*	*With no bath or shower*
Hamberton	6	19	75	3.4
Sellbridge	22	60	18	9.3
Grantley	15	2	83	0.4
Oxfield	60	2	38	0

	INFANT MORTALITY
	Death under 1 year per 1 000 population
Hamberton	15
Sellbridge	21
Grantley	12
Oxfield	10

FIGURE 41.2   Manford: selected statistics

7 Look at the data on housing in Figure 41.2.
   a In which two boroughs are most houses owned by the council?
   b In which borough do most people own the houses in which they live?
   c In which borough do most people rent their homes from private landlords?
   d Which borough has the highest percentage of houses lacking basic amenities?

8 In which two boroughs do over half the households own a car?

9 Describe the location within the city of the two boroughs with the highest rates of infant mortality.

10 Describe the location within the city of areas with less than 50 per cent of their population unemployed.

11 Use the information in Fig. 41.2 to draw pie graphs showing house ownership in each of the four boroughs. What are the main differences shown in your diagrams?

12 Use the information from your fact sheet to help you complete the following sentences:
   a Two similarities between Hamberton and Sellbridge are . . .
   b Two similarities between Grantley and Oxfield are . . .
   c Two differences between Hamberton and Sellbridge are . . .
   d Two differences between Grantley and Oxfield are . . .

FIGURE 41.3   Housing in Manford

FIGURE 41.4   Living in Manford. What people think

JOHN

It's a great part of Manford to live in – we have lots of good neighbours, the houses are small but easy to maintain and the shops are close by.

I hate living in the tower blocks – it is very noisy and usually the lifts do not work. We have a long walk to the shops.

JULIE

It's boring where I live, lots of big houses and gardens but people do not mix, and they go everywhere in their cars.

MARTIN

PAULINE

I like our part of Manford. We have some nice old trees and big gardens, and there are lots of other kids to play with.

13 Study Figure 41.3, which shows photographs of Sellbridge, Hamberton, Grantley and Oxfield. Match the photographs A, B, C, D to the correct borough, and justify your choice.

14 Figure 41.4 shows some comments made by people who live in the four selected boroughs of Manford. In which part of Manford do you think each person lives? Explain carefully the reasons for your choice.

15 Make a list of all the complaints people might have who live in
   a Hamberton.   b Sellbridge.

Skilled workers	Non-Manual	Semi-skilled workers	Unskilled
32.2	13.3	27.8	20.3
31.6	24.0	23.1	15.5
44.9	16.0	20.9	10.0
31.4	26.0	13.0	4.5

CARS Households with no car	UNEMPLOYMENT Unemployed
96	53
76	62
45.7	45
26	8.2

42 *Communities in the city*

City populations are made up of a large number of local communities. In British cities, these communities often include people who have migrated to the city from another part of Britain, or from other countries. All the people in these communities share the same basic needs: jobs, decent housing, and a secure environment in which to live.

There are many reasons why people MIGRATE from one place to another. Some of these have been discussed earlier in this book (see Units 2, 4 and 31, for example). Similar 'push' and 'pull' factors influence people to move from one country to another.

Over the years from 1972 to 1983 there were 430 000 fewer immigrants than there were emigrants who left the country, mainly to live in Canada, Australia and New Zealand.

 List four 'push' and four 'pull' factors that a person might consider before migrating from one country to another.

Britain's ethnic minorities

Immigration

Until the 1950s, Afro-Caribbean and Asian communities were not widely known in Britain. During the 1950s and the early 1960s Britain encouraged people from the West Indies, India, Pakistan and Bangladesh to live and work here. Britain was suffering from a labour shortage, and welcomed a supply of labour, both from New Commonwealth and European countries. These immigrants helped to rebuild the economy after the Second World War.

London and Birmingham were two of the main destinations for New Commonwealth immigrants because there were many job vacancies in these cities, both in manufacturing (engineering works) and in the service industries (especially health and transport). Most of the jobs were unskilled and poorly paid.

Housing was in short supply and no extra provision was made. As a result, many of the newcomers and their families were forced to live in overcrowded conditions in run-down parts of the towns and cities where they worked. At times they also faced prejudice at work and in the community. Most British people knew little about the immigrants, or their countries of origin.

FIGURE 42.1 (*Above*) Local shopping in a Manchester street market. (*Top right*) Indian wedding, North London. (*Right*) Surburban primary school in the South East.

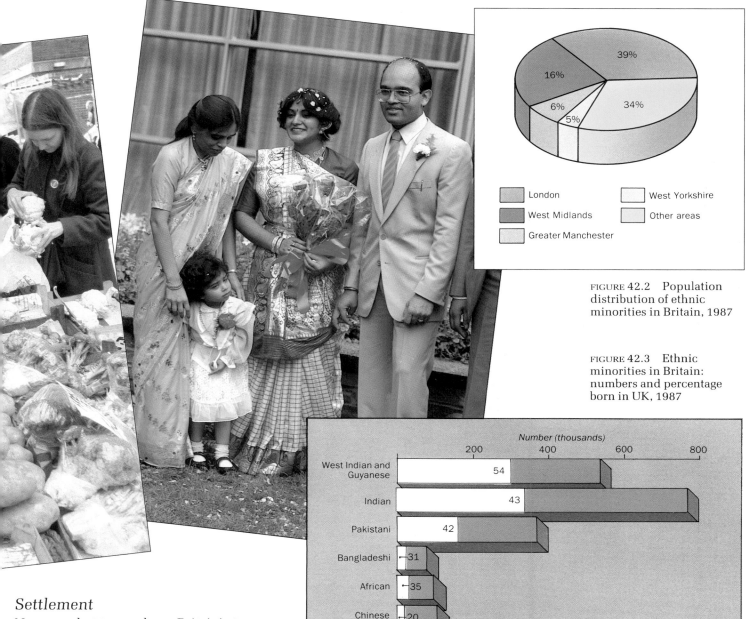

FIGURE 42.2   Population distribution of ethnic minorities in Britain, 1987

FIGURE 42.3   Ethnic minorities in Britain: numbers and percentage born in UK, 1987

Settlement

Now, nearly 30 years later, Britain's 2.4 million Afro-Caribbean and Asian population forms 4 per cent of the national total. Forty per cent of the 2.4 million were born in Britain and have never lived anywhere else. Due to government restrictions, immigration from the New Commonwealth countries is now very low indeed.

Although many of Britain's ethnic minority groups still live in inner-city areas, the pattern is changing. A number of suburbs now have a multi-racial population, as the picture of the school playground on the left shows. There have also been changes in employment, with an increasing number of people from ethnic minorities working in skilled jobs in offices, and factories, and in the professions as lawyers, doctors, engineers or accountants, for example.

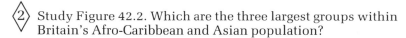

⟨2⟩ Study Figure 42.2. Which are the three largest groups within Britain's Afro-Caribbean and Asian population?

⟨3⟩ Study Figure 42.3. Name the main conurbations in which most of Britain's ethnic minorities live.

⟨4⟩ What percentage of Britain's ethnic minority population live in areas *other than* the four major conurbations?

Working for equality

Although there have been a number of outward changes since the 1950s, many people born in 'multi-racial' Britain still do not get equal treatment. Figure 42.4 describes some of the ways racism still operates in Britain.

'British newspapers distort the truth about race in this country. They make headlines out of 'racial' unrest and crime. They want sensation more than reality. How about some more stories on the positive things that are happening with the community?'

FIGURE 42.4 Racial inequality: what people think

'Although we have laws for equal opportunities, there should be more checks made. A recent government report admitted that at least one in three British employers discriminates against black applicants. We need more help to start local businesses that can guarantee equal opportunities.'

'Too often I'm seen as a black rather than as a teacher. I was turned down for one job because they told me there weren't many black children in the school! People need to be more aware of how racism affects the professions.'

'We have a neighbour whose family got racially bullied when they first moved to our estate. We residents knew who the troublemakers were, so a group of us got together and told them we wouldn't stand for it. Once they knew that most of the tenants here were prepared to stand by our neighbour, the trouble stopped.'

'We get labelled as "a problem" by people who know nothing about us. The real problems on our estate are long-term unemployment and overcrowding. If more people knew that, maybe the government would do something.'

5 Name the views in Figure 42.4 which are concerned with:

a housing
b jobs
c violence
d the media

The statements in Figure 42.4 also suggest some ways of tackling the different aspects of racism. Make a list of these. For each item on your list, suggest which group of people you think should get involved.

6 **a** Why do you think it is important for planners, working on the future development of towns, to collect information about ethnic minorities?

b What sort of information would planners require about the *whole* population of an area in order to produce a realistic plan for future development? (Think about retired numbers of people, birth rate, numbers of single-parent families, for example.)

Planning: the human factor

The photographs shown in Figure 42.5
illustrate several different aspects of
everyday life within Britain's inner cities.
They can be interpreted in different ways,
but each of them underlines the importance
of the community's needs in developing, or
redeveloping, for the future.

 Study the photographs in Figure 42.5.

a What does each photograph show?

b What does each photograph *imply*
about the needs of the community?

c What significance is there for planners
in the information you have collected
so far? Give reasons for your answer.

FIGURE 42.5   Living in
Britain's cities

IDEAS FOR COURSEWORK

 Make a study of four or five
administrative units of a
town. Choose the units from
different parts of the urban
area. (For example, in a
transect from the centre
outwards.) Use population
data from the census or local
planning department to
compare the changes in total
population since 1961. Can
you explain the variations
you observe?

 Urban planning
departments usually have
detailed socio-economic
data for different wards or
administrative areas.
Compare four or five wards
with regard to

- overcrowding
- age of buildings
- car ownership
- infant mortality
- housing
- employment

Try to explain the patterns
you have described.

 Over a period of two weeks,
make a collection of
newspaper articles. They
could be about any of the
following:

- housing, administration
or jobs in the inner city

- an event within an urban
community (a ceremony,
festival, parade or
demonstration, for
example)

- an individual person or
group within the city

Prepare a short analysis of
each article, using the
following questions as a
guideline:

- What is the main subject
of the article?

- Is the article critical? In
what way?

- Do you think the article is
biased in any way? If so,
why?

- Are there any
implications for planners?
If so, what are they?

- To investigate the subject
further, what questions
would you ask?

If you prefer, you could
make a collection of
different articles about the
same subject.

- What difference in
approach or treatment do
you notice? Can you
suggest any reasons for
this?

- Why is it important for a
planner to be aware of
these differences?

43 More offices?

Theory . . .

The CENTRAL BUSINESS DISTRICT (CBD) of most cities usually consists of a mixture of shops and offices housed in tall buildings (see Figure 43.1). This is because the CBD is at the centre of road and rail networks, and so is the most accessible part of the city (see Figure 43.2). It is the area which most people can reach most easily. Land in the CBD is expensive because it is so accessible. Shops and offices can afford to pay the high rents for land in the CBD but industry and housing cannot. In order to get the maximum use from such expensive land, buildings have become taller and taller.

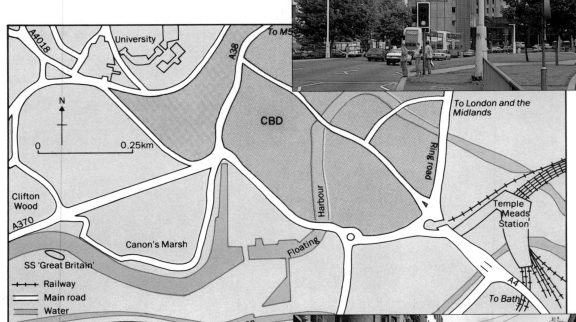

FIGURE 43.1 (*Above*) Central Business District, Bristol

FIGURE 43.2 (*Left*) Access to Bristol CBD. What are the main communication links?

FIGURE 43.3 (*Below*) An older street in Bristol's CBD. More human in scale, but what are the problems?

However, many people argue that there are too many offices in city centres. They point to the fact that the CBD often becomes dead at night because people do not live there. They argue that offices in the CBD also add to traffic congestion, push up land prices and drive out local people. They claim that there is a need to build more houses on land in or near the CBD rather than more offices.

Their opponents argue that offices are vital; they create new jobs and bring in a high income to local government from the rates. They argue that firms wanting offices are not monsters who fail to value human beings. Rather, they are trying to improve conditions for many more people from all walks of life.

FIGURE 43.4 Town centre, and (below) redevelopment proposals

Study Figure 43.4 which shows land close to the CBD of a town. There are already lots of shops and offices in the town, and now a site next to the river has been cleared for development. The town has high rates of unemployment amongst semi-skilled and unskilled workers, and there is also a shortage of council houses close to the CBD. As you can see, there are five different proposals for redeveloping the site.

1 Build a marina for pleasure boats. This would provide some employment for unskilled people and could be fairly profitable for developers.

2 Build a shopping complex with riverside cafes and restaurants, together with underground parking. This would create work for skilled and semi-skilled people and be profitable for developers.

3 Build an office block. There is a demand for more office space and it would create jobs for skilled managers plus professional and clerical workers. It would be very profitable for developers.

4 Build council houses to reduce homelessness and council waiting lists. This would create no long-term jobs, and would not be attractive to developers.

5 Build a motorway to relieve traffic congestion in the CBD. This would not create long-term jobs but might help existing shops by attracting more people.

1 Different groups support the different projects. Complete a copy of the table below suggesting which of the land uses each group might prefer and why.

Interest groups	Do want	Do not want
Families with young children	Houses (Why?)	Offices (Why?)
Unemployed people		
Shopkeepers	The motorway (Why?)	
Homeless people		
Developers		
Office workers		

2 Is there any agreement amongst the groups?

3 Generally the most powerful groups in society win conflicts, so people who lack power usually have to accept the poorest land and locations. Status, money and power generally influence decisions rather than *need*. State what is the main *need* of each of the groups in the table, and then explain which of the five proposals you think would eventually be successful.

...and practice

Coin Street is the name given to a 5 hectare site in central London, close to Waterloo station on the Thames South Bank. It used to be an area of warehouses, factories and a few flats, but by the 1980s it had fallen into disrepair. Being in central London it would be an ideal site for a large office and hotel complex. Figure 43.5 shows a plan of the area and some of the main commercial proposals for redeveloping Coin Street.

In contrast, the local council and community groups wanted to build 360 houses on the site.

  Outline the arguments that each of the following groups would put forward in support of their redevelopment plan:
   a The Heron Corporation
   b Greycoat London Estates
   c Local community groups

5 Decide which group you think would be most likely to succeed, then compare your answer with Figure 43.6 below. Why do you think this decision was reached?

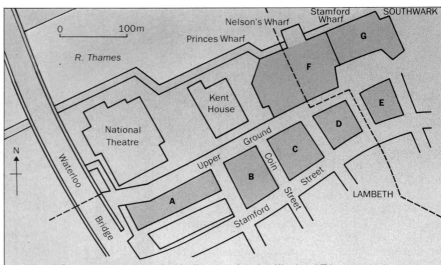

Heron Corporation: wants to build offices on Sites B and C with showrooms, 228 homes. Also wants to build Europe's tallest hotel plus offices and flats on site A and has existing planning permission for hotel and flats on same site.
Commercial Properties: wants to build showrooms, leisure facilities including a cinema and 54 flats on sites E and D. On F and G they want more offices, plus pub, theatre, and 108 homes.

London Weekend TV: wants studio complex with offices on part of site E.
Greycoat London Estates: want to build offices and warehouses plus 170 homes and six shops on sites A, B and C and perhaps a 100 room hotel.
GLC: owns sites A, B, C, part of D and E.
Guardian Royal Exchange Insurance: owns site F.

FIGURE 43.5 Proposals for redeveloping Coin Street

Real community values

Coin Street Community builders recently revealed an impressive array of housing, communal gardens, playgrounds and river walks on London's prime South Bank site. They have achieved all this in the three years since the GLC sold them 5.2 hectares of land between Blackfriars Bridge and Waterloo Bridge on the Thames.

The land lay idle for years, while a succession of would-be builders of office blocks tried and failed to come up with schemes that would appeal to Lambeth, Southwark and Greater London council offices.

At the same time, a local action group who believed the area should be a human community 24 hours a day, rather than an office desert alive only between the hours of nine and five, kept raising patient objections, arousing public interest and, more usefully, producing practical plans.

Coin Street's Mulberry Housing Co-op (illustrated) will provide 56 homes around a square – 10 one-bedroom ground floor flats for singles or couples, two two-bedroom bungalows for people in wheelchairs, and 44 houses for families of up to eight – with a garden and play area in the centre.

Rents are likely to be about £50 a week. The co-op is earning some further rent from car parking for the nearby office workers. Later there will be industrial units, at least 70 more domestic units in the same block as the (preserved) Oxo tower, and exhibition spaces, open market facilities and shopping.

FIGURE 43.6 Coin Street Co-op: a community victory

44 *Redevelopment: phase one*

Most British cities have an inner ring of nineteenth-century houses and factories around the CBD. Past rapid industrial growth demanded large areas of cheap houses which were quick to build, and within walking distance of the factories. Long, straight terraces of houses (or tenement blocks in Scotland) were the result of the process, often built back-to-back, with up to 20 houses sharing one cold water tap and only four toilets between them.

After the Second World War, when many of these areas had been bomb-damaged, cities had to decide how to redevelop these inner areas. The process of redevelopment still continues today, as this unit and Unit 45 illustrate.

1 Study Figure 44.1 which shows an inner city area before redevelopment. Write a short report of the area under the following headings:
Housing (type, materials, age of houses)
Land use (for roads, buildings, open space/waste land)
Amenities (car parking, shops etc)

FIGURE 44.1   Typical inner city area (Leeds), prior to redevelopment

FIGURE 44.2   Highgate, Birmingham, before and after redevelopment. What major differences can you see?

Birmingham takes action

A report on Birmingham in 1947 identified 30 000 houses in need of repair, mostly built between 1830 and 1875 in a zone 3 kilometres from the city centre. Of these, 18 185 were back-to-back, 3879 had no internal water supply and 19 821 shared a toilet. Hundreds of homes had no electricity and some had no gas supply. Factories, engineering works and foundries were scattered amongst the houses spreading noise, dust and pollution.

Only months earlier Birmingham had compulsorily purchased 507 hectares of land which it sub-divided into five COMPREHENSIVE DEVELOPMENT AREAS (CDAs). The five CDAs in 1946 housed 103 000 people in 30 000 houses, with 4000 shops and 2300 industrial or commercial buildings.

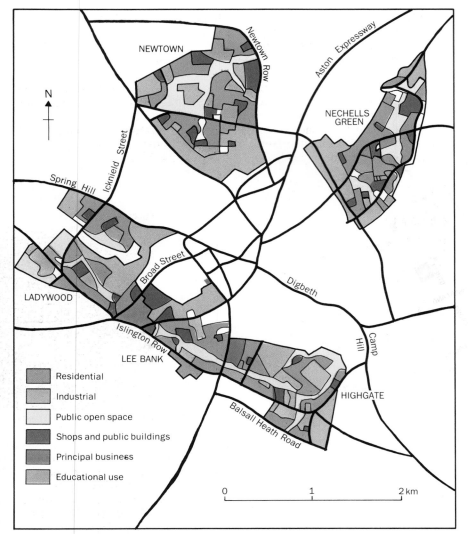

FIGURE 44.3
Redevelopment in inner
Birmingham

Residential
Industrial
Public open space
Shops and public buildings
Principal business
Educational use

0   1   2 km

The old houses, shops and most of the factories were demolished. The number of through routes was reduced and traffic concentrated on improved ring roads. More open space was introduced and the tall blocks of new flats were designed to give most people a view of some green space. The flats all had hot and cold water and a toilet; many had central heating. The tower blocks were relatively cheap and quick to build, and saved space.

The CDAs (see Figure 44.3) were designed as a series of neighbourhoods each grouped around a primary school and a shop, sometimes with a pub, a church and a community centre. Open space was created between the blocks of flats, which was free from industrial traffic such as lorries. Figure 44.4 shows how population and land use in the CDAs changed between 1947 and the present.

② Study the map in Figure 44.3.
  a What type of land use is often used to separate residential from industrial land?
  b What roads would be most used by industrial traffic? Are the residential areas protected from this? How?

③ Use Figure 44.3 to draw a sketch map showing the main roads and the outline of each CDA. Use the population change figures in Figure 44.4 to add two bar graphs for each CDA showing its population before and after redevelopment. How has their rank order of population changed?

④ Use the data from Figure 44.4 to answer the following:
  a Which CDA had the largest percentage decrease in its residential area after redevelopment?
  b In which CDAs has the industrial area remained the same?
  c In which part of the city (north/south/east/west) are the CDAs with a reduced industrial area?
  d Which CDA has the largest increase in open space?
  e In which CDA has the area of public buildings and roads increased?

POPULATION OF CDAs		
	Before	*After*
Newtown	28 125	15 400
Nechells	19 072	12 537
Ladywood	24 418	12 448
Lee Bank	14 797	6 531
Highgate	16 484	10 080

LAND USE IN CDAs
(% of total)

	Newtown Before/After		Nechells Before/After		Ladywood Before/After		Lee Bank Before/After		Highgate Before/After	
Residential	41	26	44	30	48	30	45	24	43	29
Industrial	30	30	24	24	21	21	24	21	22	21
Open space	2	16	1	16	1	17	0	13	4	17
Schools	3	10	3	10	2	9	2	7	3	14
Others (public building, roads)	24	18	28	20	28	23	29	35	28	19

FIGURE 44.4   Population
and land use in
Birmingham's CDAs before
and after redevelopment

Glasgow: clearing the tenements

In the early 1950s, the inner city areas of Glasgow had possibly more problems than those of Birmingham. Throughout the nineteenth century Glasgow had housed its workers in tenement blocks like those shown in Figure 44.5. There was no alternative to demolition in order to redevelop these areas. Figure 44.6 shows part of the Gorbals area before and after redevelopment.

⑤ Study Figure 44.6. Write out only the *true* statements below:
  a There were fewer railway lines in 1984 than 1965.
  b The bus depot was closed by 1984.
  c Large areas of housing around Cumberland Street had been demolished by 1984.
  d Factories were built along Ballanter Street between 1965 and 1984.
  e Land which in 1965 was open space along Cathcart Road was used for factories by 1984.
  f The pattern of roads remained unchanged between 1965 and 1984.
  g There were more cemeteries, gardens and parks in 1984.
  h There were more public buildings in 1984 than in 1965.

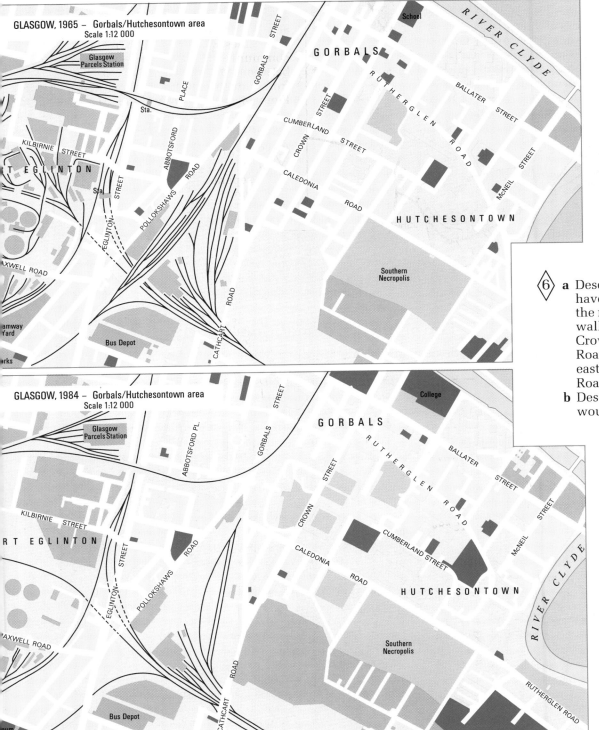

FIGURE 44.5   The Gorbals

⑥ a Describe what you would have seen on both sides of the road in 1965 if you walked from the junction of Crown Street and Caledonia Road, along Caledonia Road eastwards to Rutherglen Road.
  b Describe how the views would be different in 1984.

URBAN LAND USE

Industrial

Residential and commercial

Cemeteries, gardens and parks

Open space

Public building (schools, places of worship, etc.)

Other specified use

COMMUNICATIONS

Road

Tunnel   Railway

FIGURE 44.6
Redevelopment in Central Glasgow

45 Redevelopment: phase two

Unfortunately the estates of tower blocks built in cities like Liverpool, Manchester, Glasgow, Birmingham and London did not provide a long-term answer to living in the inner cities. Although the flats often have superb views across the city, the lifts are frequently out of order and there is a lack of play areas for children. Blocks of flats do not encourage the sense of community the old terraced houses had. Elderly and infirm people feel trapped on the upper stories and are afraid to venture out for fear of muggings. There are also problems of noise and vandalism.

The poor quality of some tower blocks was shown by the collapse of part of a block at Ronan Point in London in 1964 after a gas explosion. Figure 45.2 below highlights some of the other problems facing people in the redevelopment blocks.

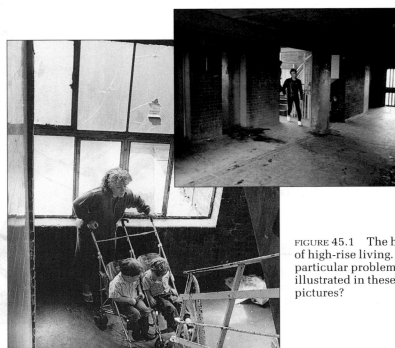

FIGURE 45.1 The hazards of high-rise living. What particular problems are illustrated in these pictures?

Estate tenants in Glasgow cannot heat their homes because architects installed expensive underfloor electric heating systems. Now the council cannot afford to carry out repairs. Leaking roofs add to the disaster. On estates where half the tenants are out of work, they heat one room for a few hours at a time with a one bar electric fire. So, with the growth of unemployment, has come the spread of dampness and the growth of mushrooms on the bathroom floor. A night in an icy bedroom on a Glasgow housing estate – big rooms, built for a hopeful future – is one to remember, giving point to the rising figure of hypothermia, and heart attacks or strokes. Glaswegians, according to a Glasgow Health Board survey, face a higher risk of death before 65, 50 per cent higher than in England, and higher than Scotland as a whole. It has the highest early death rate in the western world.

FIGURE 45.2 Problems in Glasgow flats

FIGURE 45.3 Low-rise housing, 1970s. What improvements are there?

Tower blocks: demolition . . .

Some high-rise tower blocks in inner city areas have already become impossible to live in and have been demolished. In their place, low-rise houses, with gardens and garage or parking space have been built (see Figure 45.3). Some streets have been PEDESTRIANISED, shops have been built and play areas created for children. This approach is the second attempt at improving the quality of life for people in the inner city.

. . . or luxury for some?

However, not all tower blocks have been demolished. Some have been sold by local councils to property developers who have converted them into luxury flats for the rich. Moravian Tower (shown in Figure 45.4) is one example of this trend.

1. Why do you think Kensington and Chelsea Council sold Moravian Tower rather than improving the flats itself?

2. Do you think that the people who used to live in Moravian Tower will now be able to afford a flat there?

3. Write a letter to Kensington and Chelsea Council *either* supporting the sale of tower blocks such as Moravian Tower *or* opposing it. In either case give reasons for you views.

Improving on the past

In some inner city areas the nineteenth-century houses still stand and are of good quality. In these areas, houses are being improved, not demolished. In HOUSING ACTION AREAS (HAAs) grants are available to help people install new bathrooms or to improve the kitchen and the bathroom. GENERAL IMPROVEMENT AREAS (GIAs) involve the improvement of the whole area as well as individual houses. This may take the form of tree planting, pedestrianisation and the provision of garages or parking spaces. Figure 45.6 shows what has been done to such an area in Eastleigh in Hampshire.

4. What are the main advantages of improving an inner city area rather than demolishing it?

FIGURE 45.4   Moravian Tower, council block near the Thames, in fashionable Chelsea. How much has its position influenced its future?

Come to the so-called 'gardens in the sky' to be planted in Chelsea by Ideal Homes of Woking.

It is an outlandish name designed to give a very necessary new look to Moravian Tower, a 1969 red-brick high-rise block of council flats abandoned at the bend of the Kings Road.

The block suffered the fate of many such towers in London and other big cities. Its inhabitants were afraid because there was no ground-floor supervision.

Tower blocks also notoriously create a bleak mini-climate of gusting winds that gather scraps of paper and grit into small whirlwinds and fling them in the faces of residents.

The developers are investing £6 million in the building to create one-, two- and three-bedroom flats selling for between £100,000 and £400,000.

What will make this building unique, though, will be those hanging gardens, planted on every third floor of the tower. They will be set behind glass and clearly visible to passers-by in King's Road. It promises to be a spectacular sight.

FIGURE 45.6   Improving inner cities (*below*). Which improvement do you think has the greatest effect on the environment here?

New roofs

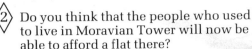

Pavement widened and renewed with contrasting paving materials

Residential pedestrian area, with seating

Road closed to through traffic

New street lighting

Trees planted along road

Central tree planter

Modern poster display boards

46   *Profit before people?*

The case of London's Docklands

Between 1700 and 1900 London grew to be the busiest port in the world, employing thousands of labourers to load and unload the ships. People lived in small terraced houses, packed together around the docks. This was London's Docklands. Until 1967, the dockers had no job security, but each day had to queue to get work if a ship had arrived. If there was no ship or if there were too many people, then there was no work and no pay. Life was hard, and even when work was available it was dangerous and often unpleasant.

Other people living in Docklands worked in port-related industries such as flour-milling, sugar-refining and ship-repairing. For every job in the docks there were three more in related industries. However, things changed from 1968 onwards when London's docks began to close, starting with those furthest upstream. By 1981, all the docks shown in Figure 46.1 had closed. As a result the number of dockers declined from 25 000 in 1960 to 22 800 in 1967 and a mere 4100 in 1981. The only dockers still employed today work downstream at the modern, automated Tilbury docks.

When the docks closed, so did many local industries and people began to leave the area. Figures 46.2 and 46.3 show the changing population and employment structure of London's Docklands.

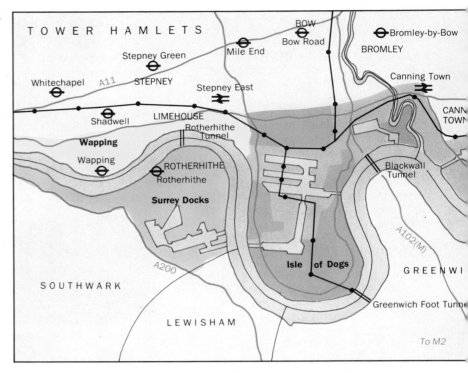

FIGURE 46.2   Changing employment in Docklands

FIGURE 46.3   Population change in Docklands

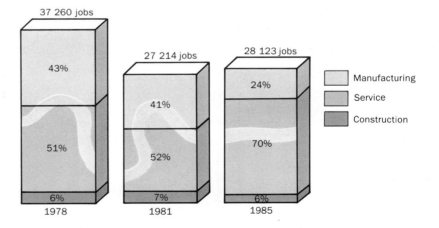

1 Use Figures 46.2 and 46.3 to answer the following:

  a What was the population of Docklands in 1961? In 1981? In 1986?

  b What is the expected population of Docklands for 1991?

  c What percentage of jobs in 1978 were in manufacturing?

  d How many jobs were there in 1978 in manufacturing?

  e What percentage of jobs in 1985 were in manufacturing? How many jobs was this?

  f By how many per cent had the service jobs increased between 1978 and 1985?

  g How many more service jobs were there in 1985 than in 1978?

FIGURE 46.1 London Docklands

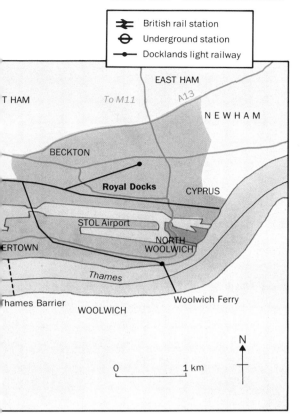

Deciding to redevelop

By 1971, the problems of industrial and population decline forced parliament to consider how best to redevelop the 2000 hectares of Docklands. There were two alternative strategies:

A *needs-based* approach, recommended by the local councils. They stressed the importance of stopping job losses and bringing in new jobs to match the skills of the local people. In 1981 there were 71 000 unemployed people in Docklands. The idea was to meet the needs of the local people and was set out in the *London Docklands Strategic Plan* of 1976. The emphasis was on building more houses (which were in very short supply), and making the area more attractive.

A *market forces* approach which aimed to attract as many new jobs as possible to the area. New houses and flats would be built and sold to those working in the new offices, shops and high-tech factories. This view was adopted by the government, which in 1981 set up the London Docklands Development Corporation (LDDC). This single agency, financed by £60–80 million of government money was charged with co-ordinating the rebuilding of Docklands and attracting extra money from private investment.

FIGURE 46.4 Docklands Light Railway operates along the network shown in Figure 46.1. It provides a quick connection to central London and the City

FIGURE 46.5 The new Docklands City Airport show here has 300 airline staff and 70 airport workers. Less than a third of the jobs are unskilled. Passenger throughput is 3–4000 per week (1988)

Achievements of the LDDC

In order to revive the area (economically, socially and physically) the Corporation has spent money on buying land and building a better INFRASTRUCTURE such as new roads and sewers. Docklands has not been well connected with the rest of London, so the Docklands Light Railway (see Figure 46.4) opened in 1987 to improve links. A water bus service is also planned to run from Greenwich to Chelsea. The STOL (Short Take Off and Landing) airport (see Figure 46.5) in the old Royal Docks carries over a million passengers each year. In 1982, part of Docklands became an Enterprise Zone with freedom from planning restrictions and rates, together with tax benefits for the developers and occupiers.

The LDDC has attracted industries to Docklands, especially printing, media communications and leisure companies, together with some large retail firms such as ASDA. Between 1981 and 1986, 8000 new jobs were created and another 25 000 are planned by 1991. Similarly between 1981 and 1986, 6000 new homes were built by private developers, mostly in Wapping, the Surrey Docks and the Isle of Dogs. Another 9000 more homes should be built by 1991.

Who benefits?

At first sight the LDDC seems to have made great progress in redeveloping the area and in attracting investment. However, there are important questions concerning those who have profited from the redevelopment.

Most of the new flats and houses are occupied by people in their twenties or thirties, usually with no children. These newcomers mostly have well-paid office jobs locally or in the City of London to which they commute each day. Local people complain that the newcomers have forced up house prices beyond their reach. Figure 5.30 shows how the pattern of house ownership in Docklands changed between 1981 and 1985, and the expected pattern for 1991.

2 Use the data from Figure 46.8 to answer the following:
   a Which type of housing decreased between 1981 and 1985?
   b Which type of housing increased most rapidly between 1981 and 1985?
   c Roughly what percentage of homes in Docklands in 1991 will be owner-occupied, and what percentage will be council rented?

Local people are pleased to see new life coming to the derelict land and they support developments such as the Docklands Light Railway. Their main concerns are rising house prices, the lack of consultation over new developments and the mismatch between the available jobs and the skills of local people.

Some writers point out that the growth of Docklands has actually led to job losses. For example, when the News International printing group (who publish *The Sun* and *The Times*) moved out of Fleet Street into Wapping, 3500 jobs were lost. These writers argue that many so-called job *gains* in Docklands are simply job *transfers* from other parts of London.

3 Imagine you are employed in the public relations section of the LDDC. What arguments would you use to defend the work of LDDC?

FIGURE 46.6   Riverside flats such as these sold for over £200 000 in 1988

FIGURE 46.7   The STOL airport runway lies in the centre of the Royal Dock area, still to be developed. Who will benefit?

Future Docklands

The pattern of future development in Docklands remains uncertain. Will it follow the existing pattern of attracting offices, shops, hotels, water sports and exhibition centres? Or will it try to meet the needs of the local community by building cheaper houses and flats for rent, and making waterside space open to everyone, not simply those who can afford to pay?

The Royal Docks (Figure 46.7) have yet to be redeveloped. Current plans include a shopping centre, hotels, an exhibition centre, a sports stadium, high-tech factories, warehouses and 4000 new homes. LDDC favour these plans, together with a new East London River Crossing (bridge) to link the M11 with the A2. In contrast, the *People's Plan* (for the Royal Docks) produced by local groups, stresses the opportunity provided by the docks to solve some of the area's economic and social problems. They argue redevelopment should be for people, not simply for profit.

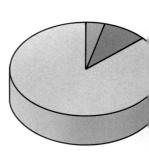

Docklands 1981

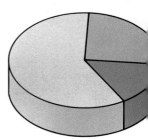

Docklands 1985

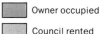

Owner occupied

Council rented

Other

KEY POINTS

- Land close to city centres is very valuable. As a result, when this land is redeveloped there are often conflicting plans for its use.

- Often, but not always, more profitable land uses such as offices and shopping centres replace housing close to city centres.

- Inner city redevelopment in the 1950s concentrated on wholesale demolition of slums to be replaced by tower blocks of flats.

- Tower blocks of flats have many advantages and some council blocks have been privatised. However, the problems associated with tower blocks and their rising building costs made them unpopular with many people.

- The redevelopment of London's Docklands is creating new jobs in SECONDARY, TERTIARY and QUATERNARY industries. Most of the new flats are occupied by people from outside Docklands. The original community feels excluded from both jobs and housing by the newcomers.

IDEAS FOR COURSEWORK

 It may be possible to consider the alternative uses for a stretch of land in your area. In many towns redevelopment has created a gap-site which could be used in different ways, to provide playing fields, or as the site for a supermarket, or as the site for a mosque, temple or church, for example. Measure the site and consider the surrounding land use.
- Interview local residents on how they would like to see the site developed.
- Consult the planners for their views on the future of the site.
Summarise the possibilities, outlining the advantages and disadvantages of each, perhaps ending with reasons for your own recommendation.

 If there are tower blocks of flats in your area, carry out a survey of some of the residents.
- What do they like/dislike about the flats?
- Do they want to stay in the flats?
- How would they like to see the flats improved? You might produce a list of possible improvements.
You might also compare a sample of residents in two blocks of flats – do they agree or disagree? Try to explain your findings.

 Make a study of part of an urban area in the past. Local reference libraries usually have maps going back many years. Use the maps to show how the area developed from, say, 1900 to the present.
- Which areas have been built up? Can you explain this?
- Where was industry located in the past? How has this changed?

 Compare two types of urban redevelopment, one which created tower blocks of flats, and one which created rows of terraced houses with small gardens. You could interview a sample of people (different ages and genders) from each area.
- What do they like about their area?
- What do they dislike?
- What changes would they like to see?

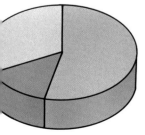

Greater London 1981

Docklands 1991
(estimate)

FIGURE 46.8   Changing patterns of house ownership in Docklands

47   *On the move, but at a price*

Traffic is constantly on the move in towns and cities, as people travel to and from work, visit friends, go shopping or make business calls. There are distinct patterns to this movement, as Figure 47.1 illustrates.

 1 Study Figure 47.1 which shows weekday traffic flow in a town of 500 000 people.
   a Use the graph to describe the flow of traffic during the day.
   b Explain the steep rise on the graph at A, the short peak at B, the rise at C and the peak at D.

 2 What problems of traffic flow does the graph suggest occur each day?

In fact, the way people travel to work has been changing in the last 20 years as Figure 47.3 shows.

 3 Study Figure 47.3, then answer the following:
   a Which was the most popular means of transport used to and from work for men and women in 1970? What was it in 1988?
   b Which means of transport to and from work increased for women but not for men between 1970 and 1988?
   c Which means of transport to and from work increased for both men and women between 1970 and 1988?
   d Which two means of transport to and from work showed the greatest decrease between 1970 and 1988?
   e What are the implications of the changes shown for car traffic in towns, bus transport, and rail transport?

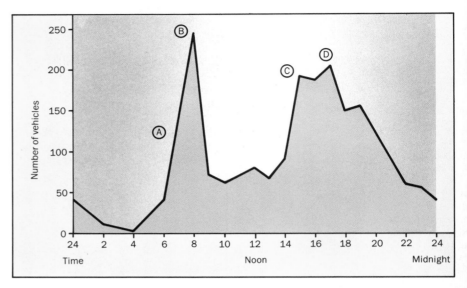

FIGURE 47.1   Daily traffic flow in a typical British city (population 500 000)

FIGURE 47.2   Morning traffic builds up in a London street. What measures have been taken to improve traffic flow? What problems might be experienced by those who live in this street?

FIGURE 47.3   Methods of transport to and from work (% of total)

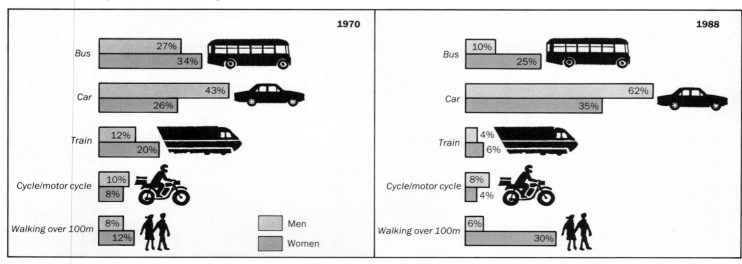

FIGURE 47.4 Traffic flow into the city (8 to 9 a.m.)

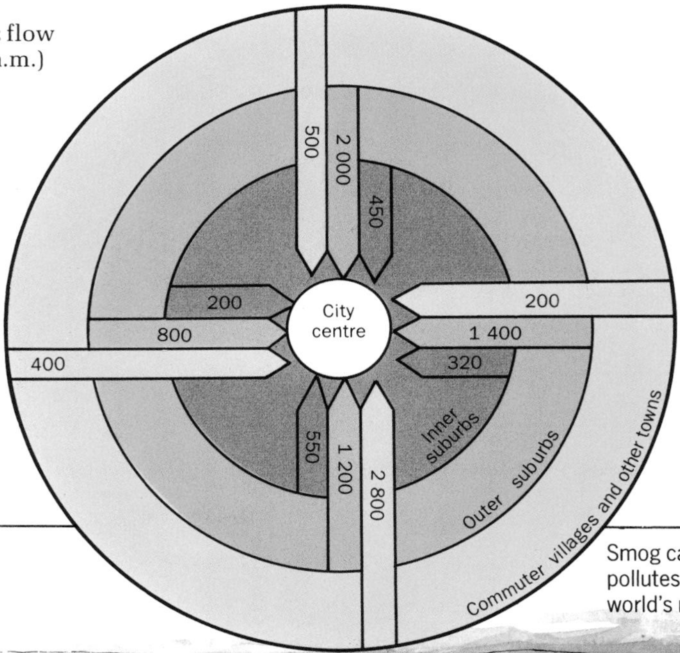

N

500
2 000
450
200   200
800   City centre   1 400
400   320
550
1 200
2 800

Inner suburbs

Outer suburbs

Commuter villages and other towns

The volume of cars travelling into and out of cities is not the same in all parts of the urban area. Figure 47.4 shows the flow of cars into a large city between 8 and 9 a.m. Use the data to answer the questions which follow.

④ **a** What proportion of all cars travelled to the city centre
  ● From the commuter villages and other towns?
  ● From the outer suburbs?
  ● From the inner suburbs?
b From which direction were most cars travelling into the city?
c From which part of the city and from which direction was the largest single group of cars?

FIGURE 47.5 The price of motoring

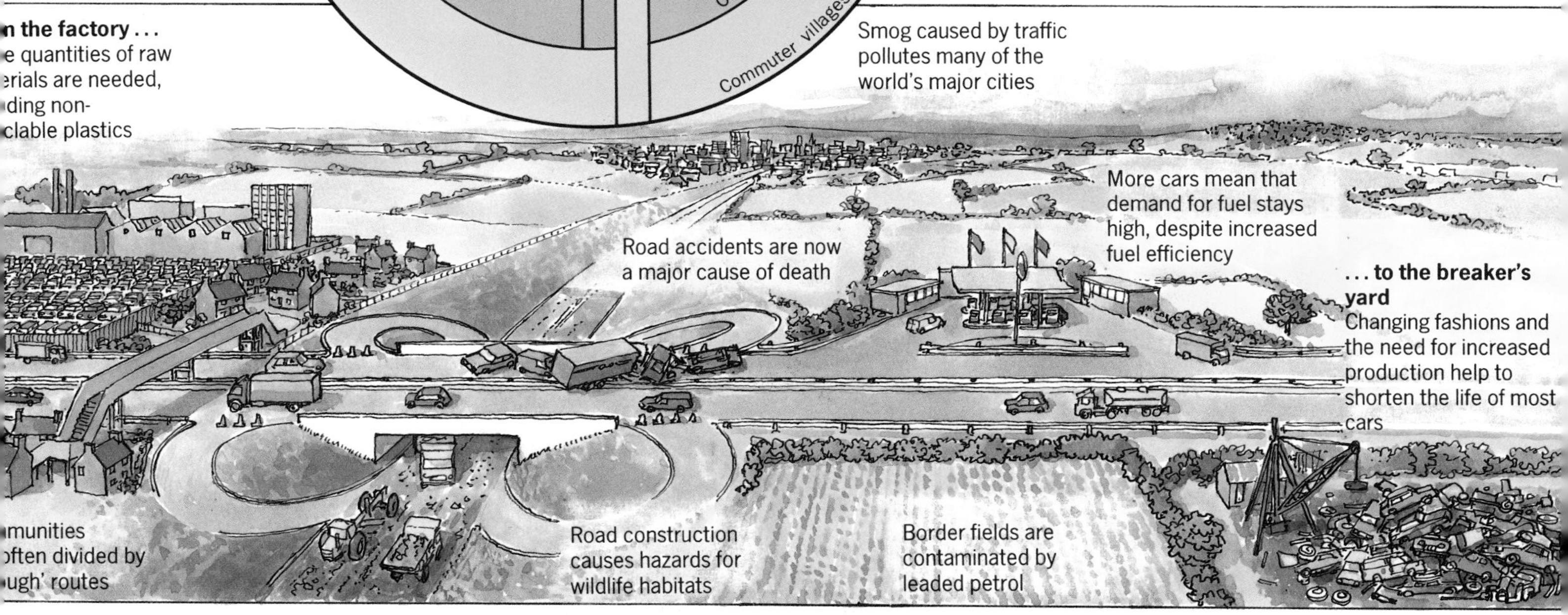

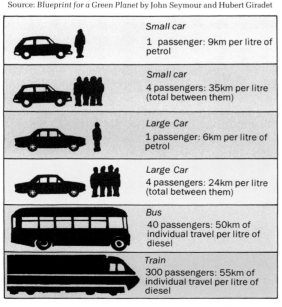

n the factory …
e quantities of raw
erials are needed,
ding non-
clable plastics

Smog caused by traffic pollutes many of the world's major cities

More cars mean that demand for fuel stays high, despite increased fuel efficiency

Road accidents are now a major cause of death

… to the breaker's yard
Changing fashions and the need for increased production help to shorten the life of most cars

munities
ften divided by
ugh' routes

Road construction causes hazards for wildlife habitats

Border fields are contaminated by leaded petrol

Source: *Blueprint for a Green Planet* by John Seymour and Hubert Giradet

The effects of increased traffic

As more and more people use their cars for travelling to work, so problems of noise, traffic jams, accidents, air pollution and parking become more serious. Figure 47.5 summarises some of the main problems people face as a result of the increased numbers of cars.

⑤ Study Figure 47.5, 'the price of motoring'.
  a Write a short account for a daily newspaper pointing out the dangers of so many cars.
  b Draw a flow diagram which shows what would happen at each stage from factory to breaker's yard if we reduced the numbers of cars.

⑥ Study Figure 47.6 which shows how far a person can travel on a litre of petrol using different methods of transport. Use the information to draw a bar graph comparing the efficiency of the different methods of transport.

⑦ Why is it difficult to persuade people to make more use of buses and trains?

FIGURE 47.6 How far for a litre of fuel? Transport and fuel efficiency
Source: *Blueprint for a Green Planet* by John Seymour and Hubert Giradet

	Small car 1 passenger: 9km per litre of petrol
	Small car 4 passengers: 35km per litre (total between them)
	Large Car 1 passenger: 6km per litre of petrol
	Large Car 4 passengers: 24km per litre (total between them)
	Bus 40 passengers: 50km of individual travel per litre of diesel
	Train 300 passengers: 55km of individual travel per litre of diesel

Urban traffic schemes: do they solve the problem?

Parking systems

In many city centres traffic is excluded altogether, or controlled by disc parking schemes or parking meters. Traffic-free, pedestrianised city centres can create a much safer, pleasanter environment for large numbers of people. However, there may be long walks to car parks or bus stops, whilst the parking restrictions may make some visitors go instead to other, less congested towns. The bridges and underpasses necessary to cross roads in pedestrianised city centres often have many steps and are unpopular with elderly people and families with pushchairs.

Multi-storey car parks above or below ground are another solution to city centre parking problems. Where old factories, warehouses or derelict houses near the CBD are demolished, temporary car parks spring up. However, both multi-storey and temporary car parks are often expensive and are not necessarily close to the main shops and offices.

Park-and-ride schemes, where people leave their cars in a large car park in the suburbs and catch a frequent shuttle bus service to and from the centre have been tried in many towns. Unfortunately these schemes do not seem to have attracted many customers. People find the transfer from car to bus time-consuming and inconvenient.

FIGURE 47.7   The multi-storey car park is a central feature in this Sunderland shopping centre. What factors do you think are important in planning an urban car park like this one?

FIGURE 47.8   Newcastle's metro system

The railway alternative

Underground railways, such as the extensive tube network of London, allow many people to make journeys in and out of the city without adding to the congestion on surface roads. In Newcastle-upon-Tyne, the metro scheme uses specially built supertrams on the former British Rail network to connect commuter villages and suburbs with the city centre. New stations have been built and old ones renovated, and the supertrams travel both above and below ground. It is a fast, clean, relatively cheap service to help reduce road traffic.

Flow systems

One-way streets are used to speed the movement of traffic in and around the CBD of many towns. Urban motorways and inner ring roads are designed to allow traffic to move quickly around the CBD without having to go through it. Building such urban motorways often arouses great opposition because it is very expensive and involves the demolition of homes, factories and offices. These roads also create additional noise and air pollution and are difficult for pedestrians to cross.

Bus lanes which operate either all day or at rush-hour peaks, allow the buses faster journeys to and from the centres. However, these lanes reserved solely for buses do cause longer tailbacks of cars and vehicles in the other lanes.

In some cities such as Birmingham and Manchester a *tidal flow* system operates, freeing three out of five lanes for traffic travelling into the centre in the morning and out again in the evening. The schemes do speed the traffic flow, and careful use of controlled lights has helped to prevent accidents in the alternating third lane.

Case study: the A660 corridor in Leeds

Leeds is typical of large cities with traffic problems. Recently the City Council has been considering how to improve conditions in the north/west part of the city, along what is called the A660 corridor. This belt of land has severe problems of traffic congestion. Three schemes have been proposed to improve the area (see Figure 47.9).

	SCHEME 1	SCHEME 2	SCHEME 3
A Changes in roads involved (e.g. widening)			
B Environmental effect (noise and pollution)			
C Road safety effect			
D Effect on traffic flow, especially buses			
E Land and property affected			
F Cost			

⑧ **a** Study the three schemes, then complete a copy of the table to identify the likely effects of each scheme.

b Now rank the six factors A to F in what you consider to be their order of importance.

c On the basis of your answers, state clearly which scheme you favour and why.

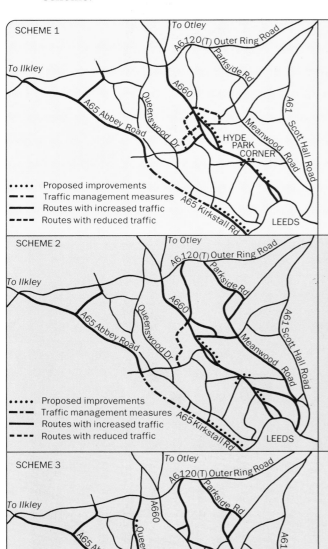

SCHEME 1

To Otley · A6120(T) Outer Ring Road · To Ilkley · Parkside Rd · A660 · Queenswood Dr · A65 Abbey Road · A61 Scott Hall Road · HYDE PARK CORNER · Meanwood Road · A65 Kirkstall Rd · LEEDS

····· Proposed improvements
--·-- Traffic management measures
—— Routes with increased traffic
---- Routes with reduced traffic

Most of the traffic would be carried by the main roads (A65 and A660). In order to cope with the extra traffic, both roads would need widening. This would involve the compulsory purchase and demolition of some houses and warehouses. Trees along the roads would be cut down, gardens reduced, and a new by-pass built at Headingley. The other roads in the area would be largely unchanged. The scheme would give much quicker journey times for buses using the A65 and A660. Noise, pollution and safety would be improved at Headingley, though there would be an increase in noise levels along the A65 and A660. Shoppers at Headingley, Hyde Park and Clarendon Road would be able to cross the roads in safety. Thirteen houses and 44 commercial properties would be demolished. Cost: between £5.6 million and £10.7 million.

SCHEME 2

To Otley · A6120(T) Outer Ring Road · To Ilkley · Parkside Rd · A660 · Queenswood Dr · A65 Abbey Road · A61 Scott Hall Road · Meanwood Road · A65 Kirkstall Rd · LEEDS

····· Proposed improvements
--·-- Traffic management measures
—— Routes with increased traffic
---- Routes with reduced traffic

The increased traffic flow would be spread over a greater number of major and minor roads. The A65 would be improved by widening. This would involve some compulsory purchase and demolition of houses. Many minor roads such as Queenswood Drive, Cardigan Road would be improved by widening, but this would not involve demolition of property. More traffic would use the Meanwood area. Spreading the traffic would give some improvement in bus journey times along the A660 and A65. Only four houses and approximately four warehouses would be demolished. Road safety would be improved at Headingley and Hyde Park but the increased use of minor roads could lead to more accidents. There would be little improvement in levels of noise and pollution along the A65 and A660, and in fact noise and pollution would be spread over a wider area under the scheme. Cost: between £4 million and £5.4 million.

SCHEME 3

To Otley · A6120(T) Outer Ring Road · To Ilkley · Parkside Rd · A660 · Queenswood Dr · A65 Abbey Road · A61 Scott Hall Road · Meanwood Road · A65 Kirkstall Rd · LEEDS

····· Proposed improvements
--·-- Traffic management measures
—— Routes with increased traffic
---- Routes with reduced traffic

This is a variant on Scheme 2. Most of the increased traffic would use the improved A65, with its widening and compulsory purchase and demolition of two houses. Conditions on the A660 would be improved by reducing traffic flow and diverting it on to minor roads (especially Meanwood Road). The scheme would allow buses faster journeys on the A65, but not on the A660 nor on the minor roads. Noise and pollution would be spread to minor roads where accidents might also increase. The main benefits would be to people living along the A660. Cost: £2.5 million.

FIGURE 47.9 Three plans for relieving congestion on the A660

48 Urban shopping centres

Patterns . . .

Items such as bread, meat and vegetables which people buy regularly (see Figure 48.1) are called 'low order' or CONVENIENCE GOODS. In contrast, things like furniture or carpets which people buy much less frequently are called 'high order' or COMPARISON GOODS (because people like to *compare* prices and qualities).

The movement of people purchasing these goods and services creates a pattern within the urban area. A recent survey of the shopping habits of a representative cross-section of people in a city of 500 000 gave the results shown in Figure 48.2 below.

 Draw a line 20cm long, where 1cm = 1 km. Label one end of the line *Home*, and then mark on your line the location of each of the shops listed above.

 Now add the following shops to your line on the basis of how far *you* would be prepared to travel: butchers, sportswear, jewellery store, fish and chip shop, shoe shop, newsagent, men's/women's clothing shop.

 In what ways do you think the results of the survey would have been different
a if the shoppers lived in a rural area?
b if only people over 60 were interviewed?

The pattern of shopping centres in large towns is usually like that shown in the map opposite (see Figure 48.3). Notice that some areas of the town are well served by shopping centres, but others are not. Study the map and then answer the questions which follow.

 From the evidence on the map, why do you think the largest centre has developed at A?

 How many shopping centres have
a 1–10 shops?
b 11–20 shops?
c 21–50 shops?
d over 50 shops?

FIGURE 48.1   Shopping locally for everyday needs

Shops	Distance prepared to travel (km)
Dry cleaners	8
Baker	3
Electrical	15
Shoe shop	18
Post Office	3
Greengrocer	2

FIGURE 48.2   Acceptable travel distances for shopping (survey)

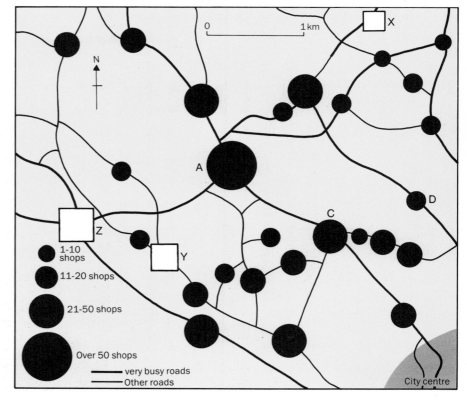

FIGURE 48.3   Urban shopping centres: size and position

6 Write down only the *true* versions of these statements:
  a Centres with 1–10 shops are close together/spread out.
  b Centres with 21–50 shops are close together/spread out.
  c There are fewer/more centres with 1–20 shops than with 21–50 shops.

 7 Find centres X, Y and Z on the map (Figure 48.3). Use the data from Figure 48.4 to estimate the number of shops in each centre (1–10, 11–20, 21–50).

 8 What things would shoppers from centre X need to buy elsewhere? Measure the distance on the map that they would have to travel. Is this within an acceptable limit (see Figure 48.2)?

9 Figure 48.5 shows survey results for how often people visited different shopping centres.
  a What percentage of people used centre X every day?
  b What percentage of people used centre X less than once per month?
  c Centre Y has more shops, so why do you think 47 per cent of people only visit it once a week?
  d Compare the pattern of visits to centre Z with that of centre Y. Try to explain the differences you have identified.

10 In centres C and D on Figure 48.3 there is an empty shop. For each centre, choose one of the following types of shop which you think would be best suited to the area:
  DIY shop
  Post Office
  camera shop
  women's clothes shop
Explain the reasons for your choice.

The pattern of shopping centres in Figure 48.3 is not the result of chance. It is the result of people's shopping behaviour, and there is a clear relationship between the number, size and composition of the centres. If you look at Figure 48.6 you can see the structure of this relationship is like a pyramid.

At the base of the pyramid is a large number of small shopping centres. At the top of the pyramid is the town centre, with over 50 shops, selling mostly comparison goods. People only visit the town centre once every two or three weeks because of the distance and effort involved.

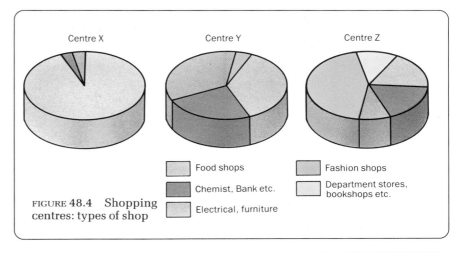

FIGURE **48.4**   Shopping centres: types of shop

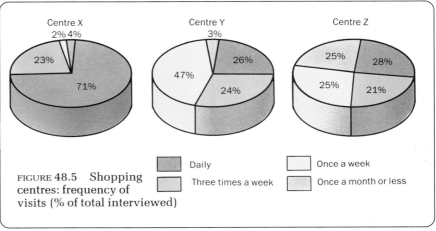

FIGURE **48.5**   Shopping centres: frequency of visits (% of total interviewed)

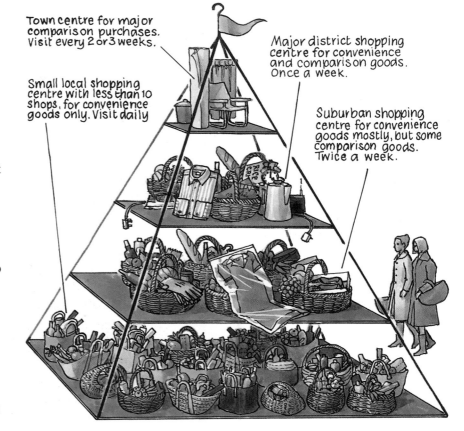

FIGURE **48.6**   The shopping pyramid

...and problems

Many urban shopping centres have grown up along main roads that lead out of the city. The largest centres are usually found at the points where the main roads cross a ring road, because then they are more accessible.

Figure 48.7 illustrates some of the problems facing people in many urban shopping centres.

 11 Study the picture in Figure 48.7 then make a list of all the problems you can identify.

FIGURE 48.7　Problems in an urban shopping centre

FIGURE 48.9　Inside the Kingfisher Centre (*below*). Shopping is all under cover, parking is provided in the multi-storey park (*below left*), and there is a free wheelchair/scooter scheme (*left*) for disabled shoppers

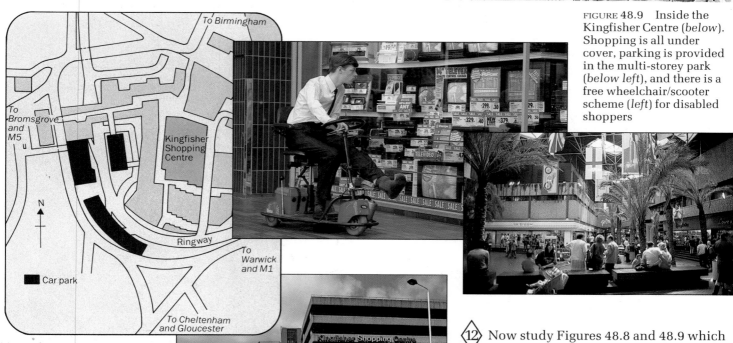

FIGURE 48.8　Kingfisher Centre, Redditch. Shopping centre plan

12 Now study Figures 48.8 and 48.9 which show one attempt to solve the problems of shopping centres. Use your list of problems from question 11 to show how these have been overcome in Redditch. Are there any remaining problems? What new problems might be created by centres like Redditch?

49 Superstore now open

One of the most important shopping changes in recent years has been the growth of superstores and hypermarkets. Sections of traditional shopping streets have been demolished to make way for giant new stores, but most recently, even larger out-of-town sites have been used. A SUPERSTORE is a single level, self-service store, selling a wide range of food and non-food (e.g. household) items with 2500 square metres of net floor space, plus car parking. Stores with over 5000 square metres of net floor space are called HYPERMARKETS. (Net floor space refers to the selling area and excludes warehousing and storage areas or space for staff facilities.)

Figure 49.1 shows the interior of a typical hypermarket. Their main characteristics are:
- Large volume of sales 'pile it high, sell it cheap'.
- Price cuts on selected items. These are called 'loss leaders', designed to attract a lot of people.
- A wide range of goods (25000–30000 items).
- Both food and non-food goods.
- Bulk buying, to keep prices low.
- Restaurants, play areas, rest rooms.
- Free car parking.

FIGURE 49.1　Shopping in a superstore

FIGURE 49.2

SUPERSTORES/HYPERMARKETS

ADVANTAGES	DISADVANTAGES
• One-stop shopping. People can usually do all their shopping in one store.	• They occupy a lot of valuable land. Sometimes this is former farmland where the countryside borders on the town.
• Ease of car parking.	
• Traffic jams in traditional shopping centres may be reduced as customers are attracted to the superstore/hypermarket.	• They create a demand for services such as new bus routes, which may be expensive to meet.
	• They may create traffic jams on their access roads.
• As more and more people are living in out-of-town locations, they are closer to the new superstores/hypermarkets.	• They favour car owners, not the elderly, the poor and non-car owners.
	• They are a threat to existing supermarkets and other stores.
• The competition of new stores may bring about improvements in existing shops.	• They create more cross-town car journeys and so may add to the overall traffic problems.

Assessing the impact

To examine the impact of such hypermarkets it is helpful to compare the cases of the Carrefour store, which opened in 1986 at Brierley Hill near Dudley in the West Midlands (see Figure 49.3), and the Presto store, opened in 1984 at Halesowen (see Figure 49.4) 9 kilometres south-east of Brierley Hill.

The Carrefour store, built in an Enterprise Zone on the site of a former steelworks, is part of a large out-of-town development with many other large stores on the same site. The Presto store by contrast was built within the existing shopping area of Halesowen.

Environmental impact

 1 Study the photographs of each store then carry out an environmental impact assessment using a copy of the table opposite.
Which store seems to blend into its environment better?

 2 What suggestions would you make for improving the appearance of either store?

Social impact

A survey in 1987 of over 200 customers at each store produced the results shown in Figure 49.5. The survey was taken over a three-week period at different times of day to ensure accurate results.

 3 a Using data from Figure 49.5, draw pie graphs for each store to show how people travel there.
b At which store do over three quarters of customers arrive by car? Suggest reasons for your answer.
c Which store has the highest percentage of people walking to do their shopping? Why might this be so?
d What methods of travel would come under the heading *other*?

 4 Which store attracts
a the most people over 65?
b The most aged 16–29?
Give reasons for your answer.

5 Which store attracted more female shoppers. Why might this be so?

FIGURE 49.3   Carrefour store, Brierley Hill

ENVIRONMENTAL IMPACT ASSESSMENT		
Feature	Carrefour	Presto
A Style of architecture. (Assess each store on a scale of 0–5 where 0 = blends in well, and 5 = very intrusive.)		
B Car park. (Assess as for **A**.)		
C Impact on skyline. (Assess each store on a scale of 0–5 where 0 = no impact and 5 = great impact.)		
D Advertisements. (Assess as for **A**.)		
E Other features. (Assess on a scale of 1–5 where 1 = good and 5 = poor.)		

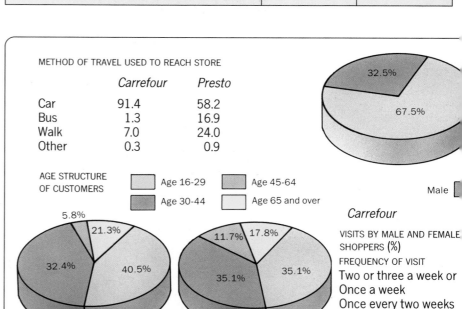

METHOD OF TRAVEL USED TO REACH STORE

	Carrefour	Presto
Car	91.4	58.2
Bus	1.3	16.9
Walk	7.0	24.0
Other	0.3	0.9

AGE STRUCTURE OF CUSTOMERS — Age 16-29 — Age 45-64 — Age 30-44 — Age 65 and over

Carrefour: 5.8%, 21.3%, 40.5%, 32.4%
Presto: 11.7%, 17.8%, 35.1%, 35.1%

32.5% 67.5%

Male

Carrefour

VISITS BY MALE AND FEMALE SHOPPERS (%)
FREQUENCY OF VISIT
Two or three a week or
Once a week
Once every two weeks
Once a month
Less than once a month
Don't know

FIGURE 49.5   Shoppers to Carrefour and Presto: social data

FIGURE 49.6   Economic impact of Carrefour and Presto

TRADE DIVERSIONS	Carrefour	Presto
(percentage of customers previously using other stores)		
Asda Superstore, Brierley Hill	25.2	1.4
Sainsbury Supermarket, Brierley Hill	17.4	1.3
Waitrose Supermarket, Stourbridge	9.3	8.2
Presto Supermarket, Stourbridge	8.5	2.0
Sainsbury Supermarket, Halesowen	9.6	26.3
Other shops in Brierley Hill	10.2	Other shops in Halesowen 28.4
Shops in other areas	19.8	32.4

0-10 minutes drive   Over 20 minutes drive

10-20 minutes drive

6.3%
30.1%
63.6%
Carrefour

13.8%
31.8%
44.4%
Presto

FIGURE 49.4   Presto store, Halesowen. Front entrance, and rear view showing car park

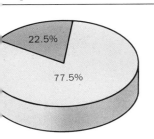

22.5%
77.5%

Female

Presto

Carrefour	Presto
14.7	45.2
44.0	35.5
11.4	6.4
11.2	5.1
8.5	3.1
10.2	4.7

6 a Draw pie diagrams to show how the frequency of shoppers' visits varies between the two stores.

b Which store do the largest percentage of people visit most frequently? Why might this be so?

c Which store has the greatest proportion of its customers visiting on a monthly basis? Suggest reasons for your answer.

7 Summarise your findings on the social impact of the two superstores, by completing a diagram for each, like the one below:

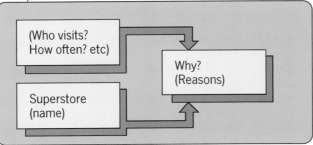

(Who visits? How often? etc)

Superstore (name)

Why? (Reasons)

Economic impact

The growth of superstores usually means that other local shops lose trade. These trade diversions (the amount of trade diverted to the Carrefour and Presto stores) are shown in Figure 49.6 which also records which stores and areas lost most.

8 a Which area of the West Midlands was most affected by the Carrefour store? And by Presto?

b What types of shops (superstores, supermarkets, other shops) were most affected by Carrefour? And by Presto?

9 a Has Presto affected shops within 0–10 minutes driving time more than shops 10–20 minutes driving distance?

b Has Carrefour had the same effect?

10 Write a short paragraph based on the exercises and data in this section, explaining why you think more superstores and hypermarkets should or should not be built.

KEY POINTS

- Traffic flow in cities creates problems of pollution, parking and congestion. Different approaches have been taken to solving these problems such as developing flow systems or metro schemes.

- The pattern of shopping centres in a city is usually a pyramid. There are many small centres at the base of the pyramid, selling mostly CONVENIENCE GOODS. The city centre at the top of the pyramid sells mostly COMPARISON GOODS.

- Shopping centres experience such problems as congestion (traffic and pedestrians,), pollution, parking and exposure to the elements. New, purpose-built, under-cover centres are designed to solve these problems.

- In recent years SUPERSTORES and HYPERMARKETS have grown up, often at the expense of smaller, traditional shops which have not been able to compete.

- Superstores and hypermarkets have an important environmental social and economic impact and thus such new developments require careful planning.

IDEAS FOR COURSEWORK

 Carry out a series of traffic surveys on the roads in part of a town. You may need help to cover a number of roads, and you should vary the time and the day of the survey to make your results more accurate.
- Which are the busiest routes? Why is this?
- Are the same routes always the busiest (day and night/at different times in the day)?
- Why do some routes always have little traffic?
- Which routes carry most heavy lorries? Why is this?
- Which routes are most used by buses? Are these the busiest routes?

 Carry out a comparison of several different streets using a 'streetometer' as shown below. You have to give each street a score out of ten, for each of the factors such as parked cars, litter etc. Give low scores for 'poor' aspects (such as a great deal of litter/decaying buildings), and high scores for 'positive' aspects.

 Make a comparison of two or more shopping centres in a town. Points of comparison could be:
- How many shops in each centre?
- How many shops of different types at each centre?
- How many bus services?
- Number of parking spaces?
- Is one centre pedestrianised?
- Is one centre under cover?
You could interview a sample of shoppers at each centre to compare the following:
- How far people had travelled.
- What methods of transport people used.
- What type of goods most people bought.
- How often most people visited each centre.
Try to explain any contrasts you may find.

 If a hypermarket or superstore has been built in your area, you could analyse its impact on surrounding shops. Use a questionnaire on a sample of shops to establish the effect (if any) of the hypermarket.
- What has been the effect on trade/on types of goods sold/on types of customers (age/gender)?
- Has the effect changed over time? (Have lost shoppers returned?)

 Carry out a comparison of two superstores or hypermarkets similar to that in Unit 49. Consider their environmental, social and economic impact. Try to explain any differences you discover.

STREETOMETER

Factors	Poor (0,1,2)	Average (3,4,5)	Good (6,7,8)	Excellent (9,10)
1 Litter.				
2 Cars parked along the road.				
3 Buildings in a poor condition (e.g. holes in roof).				
4 Amount of traffic.				
5 Evidence of vandalism (e.g. broken bus shelter).				
6 Any trees or grass.				
7 Other factors selected by you.				

50 New towns, old problems

Britain began to build NEW TOWNS after 1946, when the aim was to create new, planned centres which would relieve the overcrowding and poor housing conditions in large cities like Liverpool, Glasgow and London. Slum clearance schemes moved out many people who were attracted by the idea of new houses with all amenities in a semi-rural environment. These 'first generation' New Towns (see Figure 50.1) were intended to have a population of 80 000 and to be self-contained, balanced communities.

The second generation of New Towns was built between 1966 and 1970. These spread over a wider area of Britain and were mostly designed as OVERSPILL SETTLEMENTS for large conurbations. Skelmersdale (see below) was one of this generation. Others such as Craigavon (Northern Ireland) were built in areas of high unemployment.

Since 1970, the third generation of New Towns has really produced New Cities, designed to take 250 000 people. Like Telford, for example (see Unit 34), they bring together existing small centres. They are designed to become growth points for their areas and are located close to motorways.

By contrast EXPANDED TOWNS like Ashford are mostly in the South East. They already existed before 1970, but were chosen to grow because this was less costly than to create totally new centres.

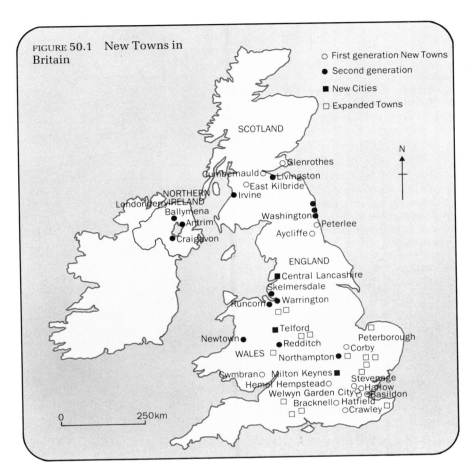

FIGURE 50.1 New Towns in Britain

○ First generation New Towns
● Second generation
■ New Cities
□ Expanded Towns

FIGURE 50.3 Office building and surroundings, Peterborough town centre. What factors (design, use of materials) contribute to the more relaxed atmosphere here?

FIGURE 50.2 Bus station, Harlow, Essex. Notice the use of concrete in all the buildings, typical of the time they were built

Skelmersdale: what went wrong?

Skelmersdale is a New Town 24 kilometres north-east of Liverpool (see Figure 50.4). Many of the 42 000 people who live there wish they could move elsewhere, but they are trapped in an environment of poverty and deprivation. Yet this is not how things started . . .

In the 1960s many people left over-crowded, sub-standard houses in Liverpool for Skelmersdale. They usually found semi-skilled work in the new factories which had been attracted by government grants. Large estates, complete with shopping parades, parks, pubs, community centres and other facilities were rapidly constructed.

From the 1970s, though, things changed:
- Skelmersdale, like other New Towns, did not become SELF-SUFFICIENT in employment. People still had to commute to Liverpool, Wigan or St Helens.
- When factories in other parts of Britain began to close in the 1970s and 80s those in Skelmersdale employing semi-skilled labour were particularly hard hit. There was no work to be found on Merseyside in Wigan or St Helens either. Factories attracted by government grants closed when the grants ran out.
- The planned hospital was never built and key stores such as Marks and Spencer did not arrive.
- Many people began to feel isolated and trapped in Skelmersdale. Most could not afford a car to visit surrounding towns; prices in Skelmersdale shops often increased because of the 'captive' population.

Unemployment, lack of local job opportunities and poor local services are just a few of Skelmersdale's problems. Read the newspaper articles in Figure 50.6 which describe the situation in 1987.

① Write a report to the government as if you lived in Skelmersdale. Your report is designed to persuade the government to provide more financial help for Skelmersdale. Use the information given in this unit to illustrate your report. It should include the following sections

  a The nature of the problems:
     Employment
     Housing conditions
     Estate design
     Poverty
     Social and health factors
     Other factors
  b Point out how many of these are problems people tried to escape from by moving to Skelmersdale.

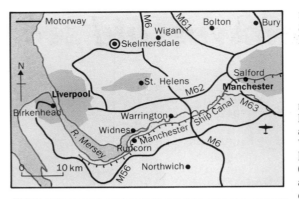

FIGURE 50.4 Location of Skelmersdale New Town, Lancashire

FIGURE 50.5 (*Below left*) Empty houses such as these are quickly vandalised. What do you think of the housing layout? (*Below*) One of the local shopping arcades. What differences do you notice between this and the picture on page 156?

FIGURE 50.6 Reports on Skelmersdale

SKELMERSDALE – like much of Mrs Thatcher's other Britain – is blighted first and foremost by the lack of jobs. 'There's no-good dose of employment thing,' people like to say, 'that a wouldn't cure.' The big factories will never come back.

The disaster of Skem is that it was designed as a series of villages each separated from the others and from Skem's 'centre' by the elaborate road network.

The footpaths are not entirely ornamental, but they take the decorative, planners' route, with the result that residents walk on the roads.

The planners recreated some-thing of the street structure of the industrial North, with the result that the view from one house is frequently the back of another; that people walk directly past each other's windows; and that the houses open on to complex warrens rather than on to streets. Such a layout is bliss for vandals and almost impossible to police. Most of the houses are poorly built; some genius even thought that flat roofs were appropriate in a region of gales, rain and snow.

Doreen's husband had walked out five years before, owing she said, 'a gas bill,' as a result of which her gas had been discon-nected. Three years later the council had installed gas central heating: radiators that had never been used were now rusting while carpets rotted with damp and walls went green. One child was so severely asthmatic that she was in a residential school, coming home at weekends. Doreen heated the child's bed with an electric blanket, and kept two fires burning round the clock. When I visited, her meter had just been emptied – £253 since Christmas, all in 50p pieces.

  c Possible solutions: outline the priorities you would establish for using government funds. For example, you might decide to tackle the problem of unfit housing first, so give this first priority and then list the others in order of importance. Explain the reasons behind your order of priorities.

51   Green belt conflict

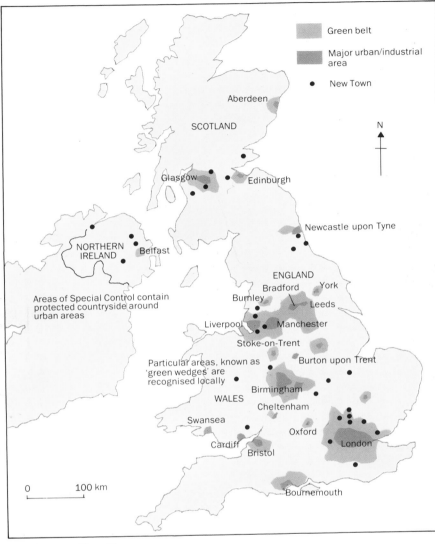

FIGURE 51.1   New Towns and green belts in Britain.

The idea of a GREEN BELT, that is an area made up mainly of agricultural land encircling a town, is centuries old. This idea was renewed in Britain by Ebenezer Howard at the end of the nineteenth century, and it was applied to London in the Greater London Plan of 1944. At the same time that London's green belt was established, a ring of New Towns was created beyond the belt partly to take people from the bomb-devastated areas of the inner city. These early green belts had three main functions:

- To check the spread of urban development.
- To prevent towns merging.
- To preserve the special character of towns.
- In 1984 a fourth function was added, namely to assist urban renewal.

1 Study Figure 51.1 which shows that most large cities are surrounded by green belts.
  a Name those New Towns situated within green belts.
  b List the three largest New Towns based on their current population.
  c Why do you think there are no green belts in south-western England?

Green belts cover 11 per cent of England's land area, and within them housebuilding has been strictly controlled. The boundaries of the green belts are not fixed, for example London's green belt expanded from 307 000 hectares in 1976 to 572 000 hectares in 1986. Figure 51.2 lists several problems resulting from green belts:

Green belt problems

FIGURE 51.2

1 There is great pressure to release land for house-building and other commercial and industrial development on the inner edge of green belts, closest to cities.

2 The restrictions on development may force house prices to rise, due to a shortage of homes.

3 Some farmland on the inner edge of green belts is not very productive and is used as pasture for stables and riding schools. This type of land use is sometimes called 'horsiculture'. If the farmer obtains planning permission to sell the land for development, its value is likely to rise from £8–9000 per hectare (near London) to £500 000 per hectare.

4 Some motorways such as the M25 already run through green belts.

London's green belt

London's green belt is under particular pressure because there is such a huge demand for more housing. Builders and developers argue that even if they were allowed to build all the houses they wanted, it would still only take up a further 1 per cent of Britain's land by the year 2000. A survey in 1986 concluded that London alone would need 884 000 new homes by 1991.

FIGURE 51.3 Proposed new settlements in the South East

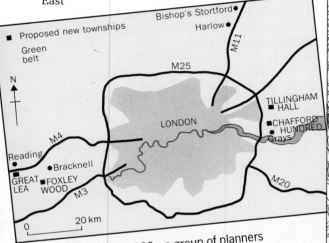

- ■ Proposed new townships
- Green belt

During the 1980s, a group of planners proposed a series of *New County Towns* around London. Each County Town would have a population of 12–15 000 with 5000 homes covering 344–405 hectares. The housing would range from cheap 'starter homes' to more expensive properties, together with sites for factories, warehouses, schools, health centres and recreation facilities. There would also be a small number of council housing and Housing Association developments.

FIGURE 51.4 Undeveloped land status in the South East

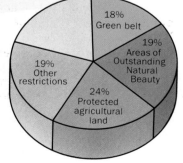

18% Green belt
19% Areas of Outstanding Natural Beauty
24% Protected agricultural land
19% Other restrictions

② Study Figure 51.3. How many homes would the proposed New County Towns provide overall? What proportion of London's housing needs does this represent?

③ Study Figure 51.4. What restrictions do the developers face?

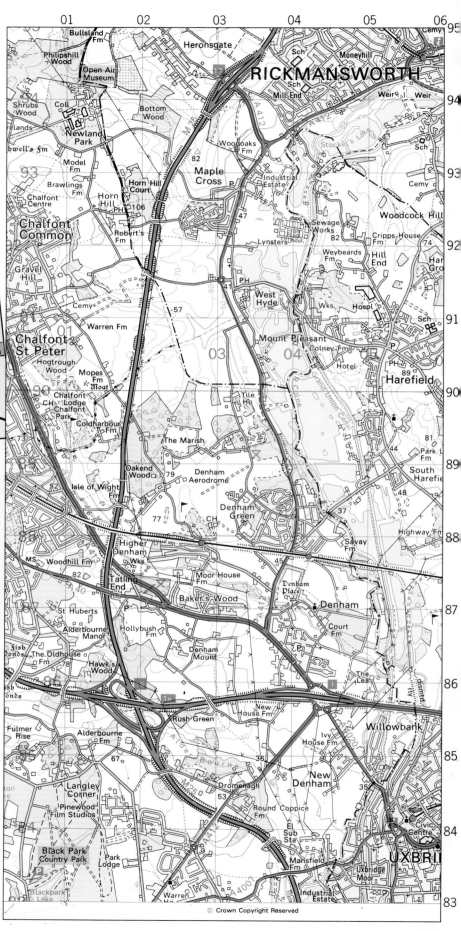

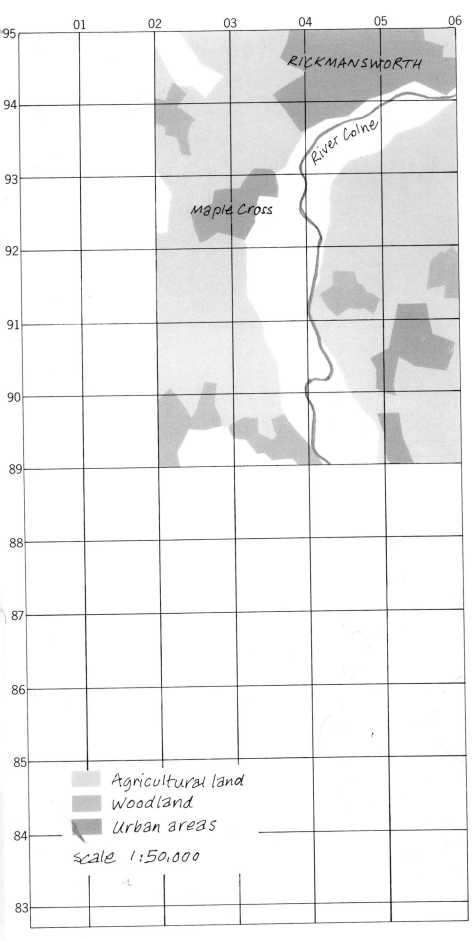

RICKMANSWORTH

River Colne

Maple Cross

Agricultural land
Woodland
Urban areas

scale 1:50,000

Case study: the green belt near Rickmansworth

Figure 51.5 shows part of London's north-western green belt, at a scale of 1:50 000. Study the map, together with Figure 51.6 which indicates some of the area's land uses.

④ Use the 1:50 000 map to complete a copy of Figure 51.6

⑤ List all the different land uses found in this area of green belt.

⑥ Which of the land uses could create noise and pollution?

⑦ There is a proposal to expand Denham Green (035 883) by building houses in the remaining open space of map square 0388. An Advisory Group has been invited to consider the proposals and suggest whether planning permission should be given. The Group members are:

- The manager of a local supermarket in Uxbridge
- A local builder
- The president of the Denham Golf Club
- A nurse working at Harefield Hospital, looking for a house
- A civil servant, living in Rickmansworth and commuting to London.
- A widow, who has retired to Denham Green from London

a Write a role profile for each member of the Advisory Group. It should include (i) whether the member is for or against the development, (ii) the reasons given to support this view, (iii) what group of opinion, if any, the member represents.

b If there is time, hold a class planning enquiry into the proposed development. Each member of the Advisory Group should put their case, then take a class vote on whether the development should be allowed.

FIGURES 51.5 AND 51.6 Part of the green belt near Rickmansworth, Hertfordshire

The future of London's green belt

The attraction of people and firms to London and the South East will continue to grow with the proposed airport at Southend and the Channel Tunnel. Many high-tech companies in the South East already say they have problems in recruiting staff due to the high house prices.

A recent survey of people in the South East (including London) showed that 83 per cent wanted to retain green belts. However it is significant that 55 per cent of those interviewed in the same poll were also in favour of allowing more house-building in their area.

Some pressures on the green belt are easing. Less land will probably be needed for farming and some quarries (for sand, gravel, chalk) are nearing the end of their useful life. One solution to the search for more development land would be to use sites of former mineral workings for new housing and to use low-grade farmland for recreation development.

FIGURE 51.7   What point is the cartoonist making? In what ways would you agree or disagree with this view?

IDEAS FOR COURSEWORK

 You may live in a New Town (or an Expanding Town), or you may visit one on fieldwork. Here are some possible topics for study:
- A comparison of streets using the streetometer (see page 160).
- A comparison of shopping centres (see Unit 48).
- A comparison of different sections of the town with regard to unemployment, housing quality, housing type, etc. (see Unit 41).
- Research why the town was built and what was here earlier (see Unit 50).
- Compare the views of residents in different types of housing (see Unit 41).
- Compare traffic flows on different routes (see Unit 47).
Alternatively, write a report similar to that in question 1, Unit 50 (page 162), pointing out the nature of any problems, and outlining possible solutions.

 You may live in an area of green belt, or you may visit one on fieldwork. Map the land use of a small section of the green belt close to the city.
- What are the main uses (farming/forestry/water supply/ sewage farms/riding schools/golf courses)?
- What percentage of your sample area is covered by each use? Try to explain the pattern (think of geology, soils, climate, local agriculture, local pressures for more houses/ supermarkets/golf courses, etc).
- Are there conflicting views amongst local people about how the area should be developed?
- What do the planners think?
- What do you think?

PART E

Managing hazards

**Environmental
precautions**

**Dealing with
hazards**

This picture of the Thames
flood barrier illustrates an
attempt to manage the
flooding hazard for
London. How effective do
you think it would be
against some of the results
of the greenhouse effect
(see page 92)?

52   *Slope hazards*

We are surrounded by slopes. Some are entirely natural whilst others have been influenced by human activities such as building, farming or mining. Slopes usually look fixed and stable, but they are constantly changing.

When slopes change *slowly* there is not usually a problem. These slow changes involve material creeping down the slope, and may only be visible as soil piled high on the upslope side of a tree. If topsoil is lost by this SOIL CREEP over a long period of time, then soil fertility will decline. Eventually walls have to be built across the slope to prevent soil creep, or in other cases, trees and shrubs have to be planted to hold the soil together.

However, when slopes change *rapidly* the effects can be dramatic and disastrous. On 21st October 1966, 147 people, 116 of them children, died in the Welsh town of Aberfan when a former colliery spoil heap collapsed. This was a human disaster, created by people failing to see or take action over the problem of piling up colliery waste so close to local homes. In the event, heavy rain set off the disastrous flow of material down into Aberfan.

Despite this tragedy, spoil heaps can still be found very close to towns and villages as Figure 52.1 shows. The newspaper article (see Figure 52.2) indicates that the dangers of rapid change on steep slopes still remain. Study Figure 52.3 and locate the places mentioned.

FIGURE 52.1   A china clay tip towers over these cottages in Penwithick, Cornwall. Can you estimate its height? What are the risks to the householders?

 1   What factors contributed to the movement of the Little John spoil heap?

 2   What created the waste tips originally?

 3   What attempts had the mining company made to prevent such mass movement in their spoil heaps?

 4   Make a set of 1 kilometre grid squares for the area of Figure 52.3. Calculate how many kilometre squares are covered by
   a spoil heaps
   b pools associated with the china clay workings.

 5   Why do you think villagers in the St. Austell area are so concerned about the incident?

 6   Could the collapse of the tip have been predicted?

Village in fear after clay tip collapses

A china clay tip which collapsed and swept through a Cornish farm, depositing hundreds of tons of mud and boulders has renewed local arguments for greater safety measures.

There are hundreds of tips of the sandy material left over from china clay mining in the St Austell area, some at the very heart of villages. The tips tower over the villages, and every week get higher and higher. Some villagers even have tips in their gardens.

The collapse of the 15 metre Little John tip, near the village of Roche, was caused by heavy rain. The built-in drainage system could not cope and a cascade of water, sand and rocks poured 100 metres down a country lane. 'It happened incredibly quickly,' said Mr Peter Rawlings, whose year's supply of silage at Coldwreath Mill Farm was destroyed by the landslide. 'If I'd been in the way of it, I'd have been killed.'

FIGURE 52.2

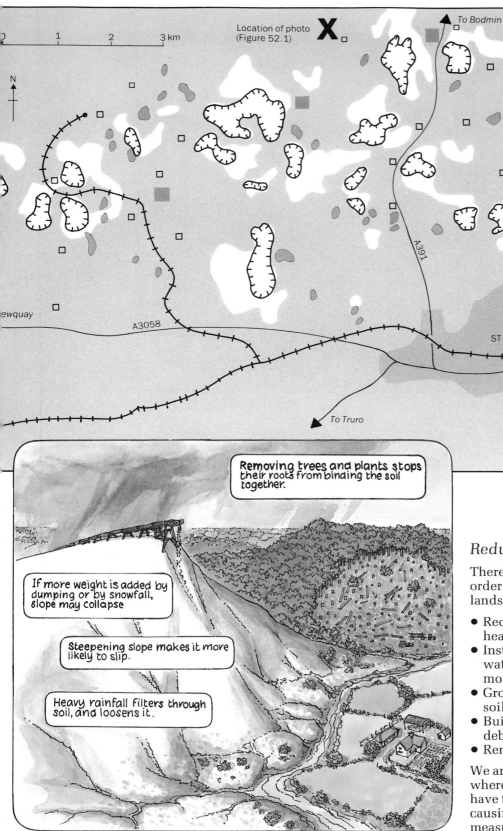

FIGURE 52.3   China clay workings in the St. Austell area

Movement of material on slopes may be triggered by the events shown in Figure 52.4. When the slope 'fails', the material in it slips downwards and settles at a new, gentler angle.

FIGURE 52.4   Causes of landslips. Which of these are natural causes, and which are caused by people?

Reducing slope hazards

There are several ways to manage slopes in order to reduce the danger of landslips or landslides like those at Aberfan or Roche:

- Reduce sleep slopes – in the case of spoil heaps by levelling the tips.
- Install drainage to prevent the build-up of water which could lubricate the movement.
- Grow plants or trees to hold the surface soil together.
- Build walls or fences to hold back the debris.
- Remove loose rock and soil.

We are now able to identify those areas where slope movements could occur, and we have the technology to prevent most of them causing damage. The problem is that these measures are expensive, and people are often unwilling to undertake such precautions when there is nothing positive to show for them. It is difficult to assess the value of avoiding a *possible* (but not definite) disaster.

53 *The silent crisis*

> By the end of the century there will be one third less topsoil per person in Britain than there is now.

Soil erosion

In the past, farmers kept the soil fertile by using farmyard manure and crop rotation. Now they more often apply large quantities of artificial fertilisers. This may not be enough to prevent soil loss, or EROSION. If not properly maintained, soil will deteriorate and eventually be removed by water or wind.

People in Britain think soil erosion usually occurs in other countries, such as the USA or China. Unfortunately, soil erosion occurs increasingly in our own country, in areas like East Anglia. It is often increased by activities such as removing hedges which provide shelter and help break the force of the wind. Look at the landscape in Figure 53.1. How well protected is it against erosion?

There are three main types of soil erosion:

- *Sheet erosion.* Large areas of topsoil are removed from the whole field by the effects of prolonged rainfall.
- *Gullying* is more localised in effects. It occurs when heavy rainfall moves downslope and in so doing erodes channels. These gullies or rills become deepened with successive storms.
- *Wind erosion.* When the topsoil is dry it becomes crumbly and is easily blown away. (See Figure 53.2.)

Soil erosion is an increasing problem in many parts of Britain. In Cambridgeshire and Bedfordshire, 1.1 tonnes per hectare are being lost each year. On sandy soils in Shropshire 3–4 tonnes per hectare are lost each winter. This means that, on average, the surface is lowered by 1.9 millimetres per year! This figure is much higher than the amount of soil being formed by the continuing weathering of rock.

Soil erosion has been referred to as the 'quiet crisis'; we are not usually aware that it is taking place, but its effects can be devastating. This is a hazard which requires very careful management.

FIGURE 53.1 (*Top*) Wind erosion in Oxfordshire

FIGURE 53.2 (*Above*) Cambridgeshire: danger zone for soil erosion

The disappearing planet

The Soil Survey of England and Wales recently studied an area of sandy and silty soils mainly in arable use. Some 40 fields were chosen randomly and monitored for soil erosion monthly.

Most erosion occurred under winter cereal crops, and least from bare ploughed land. The mean soil loss from fields under cereals was 4.2 tonnes per hectare, compared with 2.3 tonnes per hectare under maize, 1.7 tonnes per hectare under potatoes, but only 0.2 tonnes per hectare from bare ploughed land.

Most erosion occurred with the coarser textured, sandy soils which generally had lower organic carbon contents and, in consequence, a poorer soil structure. Losses were highest in the fields subjected to the greatest use of wheeled agricultural equipment.

Increasing erosion was also connected with increasing field slope; less than 3 degrees of slope resulting in an average loss of 3.4 tonnes per hectare compared with 4.9 tonnes of soil per hectare in fields with a slope greater than 3 degrees.

By January small rills started to develop in areas of field slope, many of which were eventually etched by heavy rainfall into channels of more than 100cm^2 cross section. Water flow in these rills then continued to move soil downslope until late March when rapidly growing crops and a drying soil again reduced water runoff.

FIGURE 53.3

KEY POINTS

- HAZARDS are events posing possible threats to people's lives. Hazards may be natural or the result of human interference. DISASTERS occur when people fail to take enough precautions against the danger of a hazard.

- Material in slopes is frequently moving under the influence of gravity and other factors such as water. Slow slope movements can usually be corrected quite readily, but rapid movements can create disasters. Slopes require careful management to reduce dangers.

- Because SOIL EROSION takes place relatively slowly, the scale of the problem is not always appreciated. Action to reduce and prevent soil erosion is urgently needed in many parts of Britain.

Study Figure 53.3 which describes an investigation of sandy soils in Somerset. Forty fields were chosen at random, and soil erosion was measured each month for a year.

 1 Was there more soil erosion from bare ploughed fields or from those with winter cereal crops?

 2 How much soil was lost from the following types of land use?
a maize   **b** potatoes   **c** bare ploughed land

 3 Which soils experienced most erosion?

 4 What other factors increased soil erosion?

 5 When did rills (small gullies) start to develop?

 6 How large did the channels become?

 7 Why was erosion reduced from March onwards?

 8 The survey listed the following practices as being responsible for increasing soil erosion:
a Ploughing up and down the slope of the land.
b Using heavy, wheeled machines.
c Removing last year's stubble (remains of cereal crops).
d Failing to replace organic matter in the soil.
e Cultivating steep slopes.

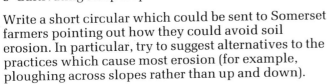 **9** Write a short circular which could be sent to Somerset farmers pointing out how they could avoid soil erosion. In particular, try to suggest alternatives to the practices which cause most erosion (for example, ploughing across slopes rather than up and down).

IDEAS FOR COURSEWORK

 1 Carry out a survey of some slopes of varying steepness in your area. You may select a valley or simply a long slope. Use measuring tapes, poles and a clinometer to produce a map of varying slope angles. Use your own observations of soil, water, geology, human impact and other factors, together with any maps (such as geology maps) to explain the slope variations you have mapped.

 2 Study a steep slope where soil movement is taking place.
a Map the evidence for slope movement (soil piled up against walls or tree trunks, soil overflowing on to a road or into a stream).
b Measure the steepness of the slope and draw a diagram to show how its shape varies from top to bottom.
c Collect samples of soil and rock along the slope:
- How do these vary?
- What action have people taken to reduce soil movement, such as building retaining walls/ planting trees or grass to bind the soil together?
- Have such measures been effective? If not, why not?

Try to explain fully why the slope is unstable and what has been done to manage the possible hazard.

54 The fog hazard

'Dense fog in the Midlands last night led to an early morning pile-up which closed two northbound lanes of the M6 near Coventry. Birmingham airport was closed and flights had to be diverted to Glasgow.'

Headlines such as this tend to be a regular feature of news and travel bulletins especially in autumn and spring. Fog consists of tiny droplets of water, suspended in the air close to the ground. These water droplets limit visibility and create numerous hazards. The Meteorological Office, which provides weather forecasts, has very precise definitions of 'fog' and 'mist':
Mist: visibility between 1000 and 2000 metres
Fog: visibility less than 1000 metres
Thick fog: visibility between 40 and 190 metres
Dense fog: visibility between 0 and 39 metres.

The hazard forms

Fog often forms after sunset on fine days with clear skies and no wind. The surface of the ground loses heat rapidly because the skies are clear (see Figure 54.1). As the ground cools it also cools the air in contact with it. Eventually the water vapour in the air condenses into droplets and forms fog. These droplets form around nuclei such as dust particles or the salt from sea spray.

If the air is still and the fog is very thick, the sun may not have enough power to evaporate the water droplets. In this case, the fog may persist for several days until the wind blows it away. In very cold conditions during the winter, freezing fog sometimes forms with temperatures below 0°C.

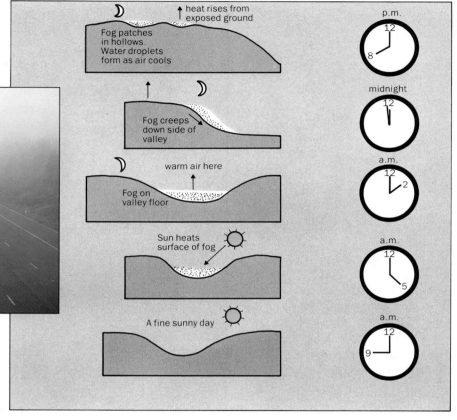

FIGURE 54.1 Fog formation and dispersal

The hazard strikes

The effects of fog are often spectacular and frequently dangerous:
- Fog contributes 1 per cent of all injuries in road accidents. It is especially dangerous on motorways where it occurs in patches, so vehicles may enter it at high speed with no warning. Motorway 'pile-ups' are the result.
- Airports may be closed by fog and flights delayed.
- More people postpone their journey for fog than for any other weather reason.
- In freezing fog, ice forms on aeroplane wings so creating dangerous extra weight and making manoeuvring difficult.

Managing the fog hazard

People have tried various methods of dispersing fog such as:
- Burning petrol or running jet engines near airport runways to evaporate the water droplets.
- Spraying silver iodide or dry ice pellets, or calcium chloride into fog. This provides nuclei around which the water drops can accumulate, become larger and fall as rain or snow.

Most of the schemes have been tried at airports. The methods are all expensive and not very successful, but the costs of delays or, even worse, the accidents resulting from fog are even greater, so experiments continue.

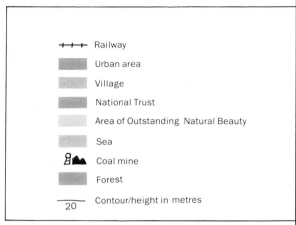

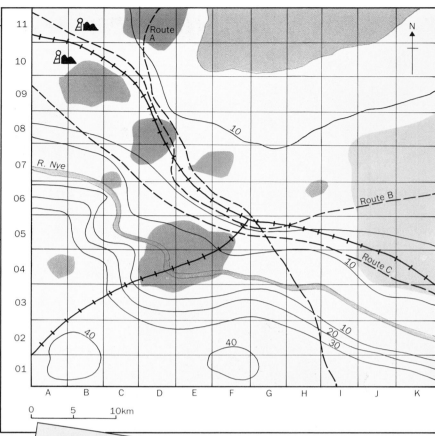

FIGURE 54.2 Fact file for estimating motorway costs

Other solutions to the fog hazard include:
- The use of Instrument Landing Systems (ILS) now installed at all major UK airports. These allow aeroplanes to land in fog using just instruments.
- Better planning of road and motorway routes to avoid areas subject to fog.

Costing the fog hazard

Study Figure 54.2 which shows three possible routes for a motorway through the region. The motorway has to pass close to the two main towns, and must also run NNW→SE.

1. Calculate the construction costs for each of the three routes on the basis of £6 million for each grid square crossed. Which route works out cheaper?

2. Now add the environmental costs for each route, using the costs in Schedule A for each grid square. On the basis of your calculations which is now the cheaper route?

3. Before the route is finalised, the government wish to include estimated additional costs of fog hazards. Schedule B is based on local weather records which show areas close to the river or to the estuary have more fog days each year. Add the costs of fog hazards to your grid square calculations using the figures in Schedule B. Which is *now* the cheapest route? Explain the effect of including fog hazard statistics.

4. On a copy of Figure 54.2 draw your own route for the motorway which would *minimise* the total cost (construction, environmental, fog hazard). Describe the route you have drawn.

SCHEDULE A
Environmental costs
If the proposed motorway route crosses a square containing the following features add on the costs shown

	per square
Coalmines	£1 million
Industrial area	£1 million
Flat or gently sloping land	£5 million
Steeply sloping land	£10 million
National Trust land	£15 million
Nature Reserve	£10 million
A.O.N.B.	£20 million
Forestry	£4 million

SCHEDULE B
Fog hazard costs
1 If part of the proposed motorway route passes within 5 kilometres of the river or the estuary, add £4 million per square.
2 If part of the proposed motorway route passes between 6 and 10 kilometres from the river or estuary, add £1 million per square.
3 There is no fog hazard cost for sections of route over 11 kilometres from the river or the estuary.

55 Adjusting to floods

 1 Study the newspaper extract here (Figure 55.1).
   a What was the cause of the flooding?
   b Give two examples of things that happened to people.
   c Why were there still problems on the roads after the flooding?
   d What did people do to try to prevent further flooding?

2 Write a short, lively account for a newspaper as if you were staying in Appley Bridge when the floods hit.

What causes floods?

Floods are the result of rapid and excessive run-off. If ground in the drainage area of a river is dry it can, like a sponge, absorb many millimetres of new moisture. However, if the ground in the drainage area is already saturated as a result of earlier rainfall then further heavy rain or rapid snow-melt will not sink into the ground but will run off into rivers and streams. The area alongside rivers and streams is termed the FLOOD PLAIN because this is the first zone to suffer flooding from the rising waters.

Figures 55.2 and 55.3 show the relationship between rainfall and stream flow for the River Stour, in Dudley in the West Midlands.

 3 Complete a copy of the graph (Figure 55.3) using the data in Figure 55.2.

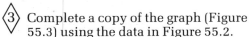 4 Describe the pattern of rainfall over the 28 hour period as shown in your graph.

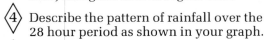 5 In what ways is the pattern of stream flow different from that of rainfall over the 28 hours?

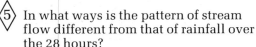 6 What must the rainfall level have been like before 4 a.m. on 15th November?

FIGURE 55.2   Rainfall and run-off, River Stour, West Midlands (1986)

A rescue launch passes a submerged car as residents are ferried to safety at Appley Bridge.

BRITAIN's worst thunderstorms this year left a trail of damage over the weekend with one man killed and hundreds of homes flooded.

Essex was badly hit by the storms with flooding in several villages and in Chelmsford town centre, which was under 2 metres of water.

Police and firemen handed out cups of tea and coffee to stranded motorists, advising them to abandon their vehicles. Shops and homes were flooded and householders were up all night baling out water.

Essex firemen, who answered more than 600 calls, used sandbags to hold back the banks of the River Roding, and an amber alert was declared when water flooded down the village streets into homes.

Some minor roads in the county were still affected yesterday by mud, surface water, and debris as the drying up operation continued.

Hundreds of villages in Appley Bridge, near Wigan, Lancashire, had to be rescued through their bedroom windows by police and firemen after a freak deluge swamped the tiny village forcing people to race upstairs for safety.

FIGURE 55.1   Storm damage, August, 1987

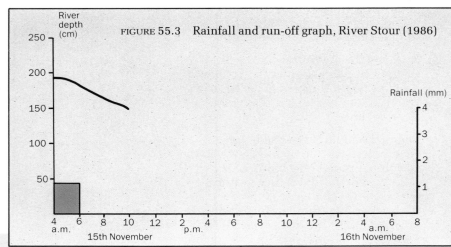

FIGURE 55.3   Rainfall and run-off graph, River Stour (1986)

River depth (cm)

Rainfall (mm)

15th November

p.m.

16th November

	15th November										16th November			
	a.m. 4-6	6-8	8-10	10-12	p.m. 12-2	2-4	4-6	6-8	8-10	10-12	a.m. 12-2	2-4	4-6	6-8
Rainfall in mm	1	3	2	1	2	0	0.2	1	3	3	2	1.5	0.5	0.7
Depth of river in cm	190	160	150	160	155	160	140	143	144	140	150	180	210	190

The price of using flood plains

Most flood damage takes place on the flood plain. If this is occupied by towns or villages the damage can be costly in human and economic terms. The financial loss from floods also includes the extra costs of disrupting transport systems, industrial production and everyday life.

Despite these hazards, people continue to farm on flood plains. Fields on flood plains are often high-yielding and floods occur infrequently, so many farmers are prepared to take the risk. People are also willing to build housing and factories on the flood plain, because the risk element from flooding is balanced by advantages such as cheaper, flat building land, or space for expansion.

Floods: should they be controlled?

Some of the issues arising from the use of flood plains are shown in Figure 55.4 above. It is proposed to 'improve' this section of the River Rushmore by straightening it, dredging a channel for barges and building higher banks to prevent flooding.

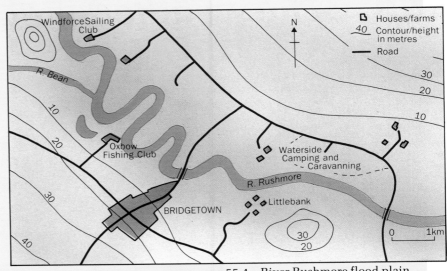

FIGURE 55.4   River Rushmore flood plain

⑦ Make a copy of the map in Figure 55.4. Show
* where the river could be straightened,
* where the banks could be raised to prevent flooding,
* the areas that are normally free from flooding.

When the river floods, we have hardly enough helpers to rescue trapped people and animals. We welcome the idea.

I have a quarry near Bridgetown. The Rushmore Channel would mean I could use barges to transport the sandstone more cheaply.

I'm in favour of controlling the river. My cellar floods every year, and it's no joke.

I make a living from repairing flood damage to homes and roads. What will happen to me?

The floods keep my soil fertile. Who will pay for the extra fertiliser if the flooding is stopped?

FIGURE 55.5   Controlling the Rushmore. What the people think

⑧ Figure 55.5 shows what some local people think of the Rushmore proposal. What do you think the following people would think?
a Members of the Windforce Sailing Club
b Oxbow Fishing Club members
c Bridgetown Construction and Engineering Company Ltd.
d The River Rushmore Conservation Society
e Villagers from Littlebank
f The owner of Waterside Camping and Caravanning

56   'The weather outlook . . .'

People talk about Britain's weather so much because it changes so rapidly. In the course of one day the morning may be foggy, by lunchtime it may be raining and by evening it may be sunny. The different elements of weather, such as wind, hail, snow and frost all produce hazards which have to be managed. The main effects of these hazards are summarised in Figure 56.1. Read this carefully before answering the questions which follow.

FIGURE 56.1   Weather hazards and their effects

Frost

Long periods of frost increase heating bills in most homes. The extra expense can be a serious problem to low income groups.

Frost is a hazard to people and vehicles on untreated roads and pavements. It can lead to falls, accidents and travel delays.

High winds create problems for shipping.

High-sided vehicles may be blown over on exposed bridges or stretches of motorways. Other vehicles have to travel more slowly.

May cause damage to property especially roofs, chimneys and fences.

Overhead power lines may be blown down; people have to manage with no electricity until repairs can be carried out.

Crops may be flattened at harvest time.

High winds

Sheep and other animals may be buried in snowdrifts, or die from exposure. Sheep, cattle and deer cannot find grazing and may go hungry unless supplies are airlifted to them.

Snow and ice

Domestic heating bills are higher as people struggle to keep warm and dry.

 1 Redraw the diagram for each hazard and add labels describing how the harmful effects may be overcome. (For example, sand and salt are sprayed on roads and motorways to prevent accidents and delays.)

 2 Add to your diagrams some of the *positive* effects of frost, high winds and snow and ice. (For example, sharp frosts kill many pests which affect crops; high winds may be used to generate electricity; snow and ice provide the necessary conditions for skiing.)

 3 Draw a diagram to illustrate the effects of *drought*. Add to your diagram ways in which the negative effects have been overcome.

 4 Choose one of the hazards and write a short paragraph summarising how successful (or otherwise) people have been in managing and containing its effects.

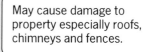

Frost may cause burst pipes in many homes.

Crops may be destroyed; frost may kill the blossom on fruit trees, so the crop may be poor.

Traffic is forced to move slowly on roads causing delays and accidents. Some roads may be blocked completely, and villages cut off for several days.

Large snowfalls may bring down overhead power lines and cause electricity cuts.

Winter vegetables may be buried in frozen ground, so supplies in the shops are expensive and poor quality.

When large falls of snow melt, rivers flood, and farmland, animals and people may be lost.

KEY POINTS

■ Fog is an important HAZARD which, despite much research, regularly continues to create problems for people in all walks of life.

■ Managing hazards to reduce their effects can be very expensive and people have to weigh such costs against the likely impacts of the hazard.

■ Hazards occur with varying frequency and varying severity, so attempts to calculate their probable effects are very difficult.

■ The positive effects of some hazardous weather conditions are frequently forgotten in favour of their negative aspects.

IDEAS FOR COURSEWORK

 Maintain weather records for your home or school over three or four weeks. You may be able to record temperature (maximum and minimum), rainfall, wind (speed and direction), cloud cover and visibility. Draw graphs to show the weather changes over the three or four weeks. Collect daily weather forecasts from the local paper at the same time.
● How often were they correct?
● How often were they wrong?
● Why is weather forecasting so difficult?
Use the weather maps from the local or national paper to explain your recordings in terms of the movement of depressions or areas of high pressure affecting the British Isles as a whole.

 Measure temperature and wind speed at a selection of points (about 20) around your school. At each point take three measurements, one close to the ground, one about a metre above the ground and one about 2 metres above the ground. Plot your observations on graphs located on a school plan or map. Try to explain the variations in temperature, and wind speed and direction you have observed.

 You may live close to a stream or visit one on fieldwork. You may take a variety of measurements at the stream such as depth (at a series of points across it and along it) and speed of flow (on the edges and near the centre). You may also record the material forming the stream bed, and how this varies both across and along the stream. You may do the same with plants growing in the stream.

In processing all the collected data it may be best to set up a series of key questions to ask such as
● How does the speed of the stream vary with its depth?
● How does the material on the stream bed vary with stream depth/stream speed?
● How do the plants growing in the stream vary with stream depth/stream speed/material forming the bed?

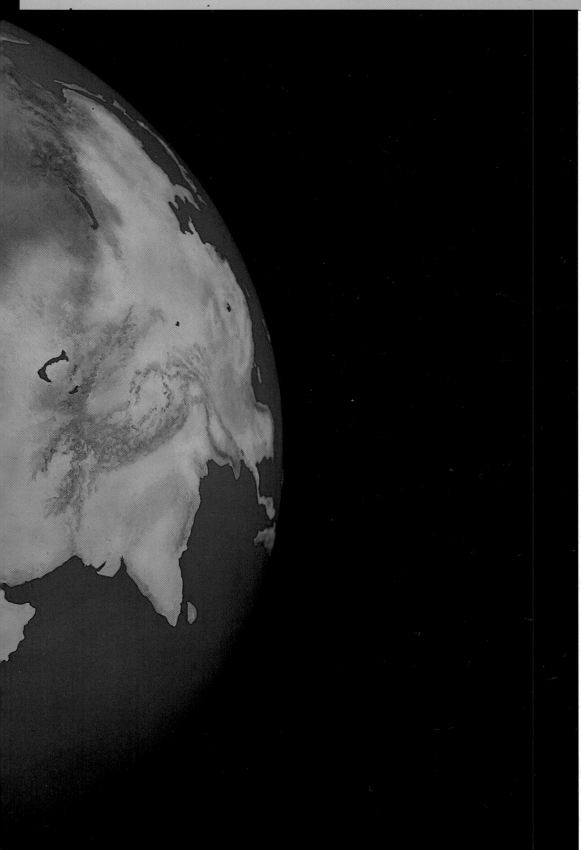

Conclusion

Fragile planet. Without
this, there is no future.
Planning decisions made in
Britain today need to take
into account the future of
the Earth and its population

Present trends, future outlook

This book has concentrated on examining current geographical trends which have controversial results. However, it is also important to look ahead and consider what the future holds for Britain and for the world. This is not as simple as it sounds because people have different ideas about what 'the future' actually means.

The future unfolds like a dice game. This view suggests that the future is entirely a matter of chance, just like a turn of the dice. We have to learn to accept whatever comes our way, whether it be good or bad.

What is the future?

We need to be aware of what we mean by the future, especially in planning situations. A decision that has short-term benefits, for example, may turn out to bring disadvantages in the longer-term future.

How are we connected to the future? What responsibilities do we have? Four common views are shown here.

① Which of the four views about the future is closest to your own? Explain why you hold this view and why you reject the others.

The future is like a roller-coaster. This view suggests that our future is a fixed track which we have to follow. The future is determined but we do not know where the track leads because it is night. Occasionally we get glimpses of the future in flashes of lighting, but we are locked into our seats so cannot do anything.

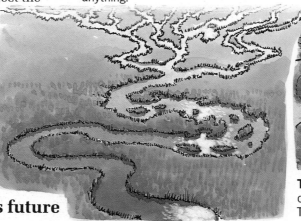

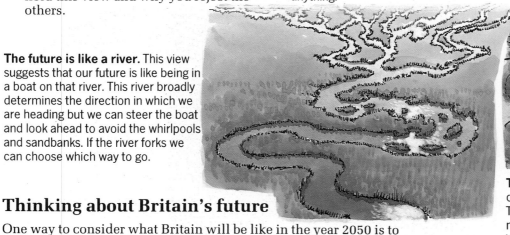

The future is like a river. This view suggests that our future is like being in a boat on that river. This river broadly determines the direction in which we are heading but we can steer the boat and look ahead to avoid the whirlpools and sandbanks. If the river forks we can choose which way to go.

The future is like an ocean. In this view our future is like a ship on that ocean. There are many possible destinations and many different routes to each destination. We can choose whatever future we want, if we work for it.

Thinking about Britain's future

One way to consider what Britain will be like in the year 2050 is to examine current trends, and then decide if they are likely to continue.

② Think carefully about what you read in Parts A to E of this book. Turn to page 182, which shows a summary of some of the key trends you have examined.
  a On your copy of the table shown here put a tick in the appropriate column if you feel the trend is *either* possible *or* probable. Then decide whether the *probable* events you have identified are desirable or not. Finally, briefly outline the likely effects for planners who will have to consider Britain in 2050.
  b Add more trends to your table based on your own re-reading, and outline their effects.

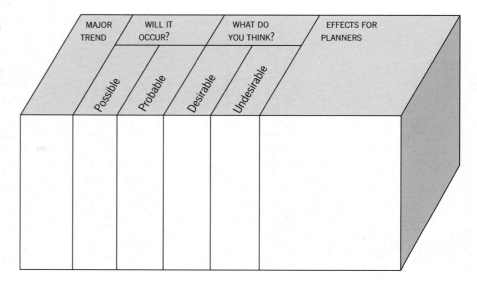

MAJOR TREND	WILL IT OCCUR?		WHAT DO YOU THINK?		EFFECTS FOR PLANNERS
	Possible	Probable	Desirable	Undesirable	

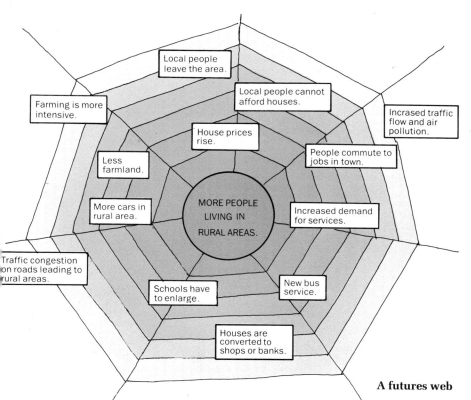

A futures web

The way ahead

In order to consider the future results of today's trends in more detail, it is helpful to use a Futures Web like the one shown here which illustrates the effects of rural population growth. The boxes closest to the centre indicate the *immediate* results, or consequences, and they are arranged in a roughly circular pattern. Each of these consequences in turn generates further results so there may be second, third and even fourth order consequences resulting from an event.

③ Select one of the most important trends you identified in question 2. Produce a Futures Web similar to the one shown on this page. It should illustrate the first, second and third order consequences of this trend.

Future news and comment?

ROW OVER NEW MOONBUS LAUNCH SITE

Angry protesters voiced their disapproval last night at a public meeting concerning the new Moonbus site in Dithwyn. They say that the development will introduce a level of noise pollution unrivalled even by Heathrow airport. They were not reassured by the Transport Authority's assurance on traffic levels either. As one resident told me, 'Dithwyn will just become another space transit town for rich tourists.'

The Great Escape

The town of Waddington on the East Coast was evacuated by air yesterday after a freak storm. No loss of human life was reported, thanks to the emergency bunker system installed five years ago at the recommendation of the North West Europe Planning Board. Scientists have always maintained that freak storms such as the one experienced in Waddington are the direct result of the overheating of the earth's atmosphere due to the use of fossil fuels.

Inventing the future

It is important to consider how things will change in the future, often as a result of decisions made now. We too shall need to adapt to cope with these changes. The 'press cuttings' shown here are fictional, but they describe events which may form news items in the future. What do they tell you about the planning issues of their time?

④ Imagine that you are living in Britain in 2050. You are 18 years old and are part of a team collecting information on geographical issues. Write a series of headlines and short reports on the main issues of the day. In each case outline the background to the issue and the different views about its effects.

⑤ Design three new, wordless signs that you think might be necessary or relevant in the year 2050.

Architects Stone and Wall unveiled plans today for a revolutionary floating housing complex to be built adjoining the Isle of Wight. They are confident that their scheme will not only attract local developers but would be suited to areas elsewhere along British and European coasts where infill is acceptable and where there is a pressure for retirement housing.

MAJOR TRENDS IN BRITISH GEOGRAPHY

Rural environments

1 Declining population in some areas

2 Increasing population in areas of commuter settlement and retirement homes

3 Difficulty in providing services

4 Increasing numbers of people seeking recreation in the countryside

Natural resources

1 More intensive farming methods

2 Less land under cultivation

3 Fewer farmers, large farms

4 Disappearing countryside

5 Organic farming

6 Pressure to plant more forests

7 Problems of water supply

8 Water pollution

9 Demand for more estuary barrages

10 Attempts to drill for oil and gas on land and sea

11 Fewer coal mines

12 Pressure to build more nuclear power stations

13 Development of alternative energy – wind, water, tides, geothermal

Industrial environments

1 Deindustrialisation continues

2 Government aid to the regions

3 Growth of even larger transnational companies

4 Growing unemployment

5 More part-time, low paid workers

6 Growing division between rich and poor people

7 Development of Enterprise Zones

8 More Development Corporations

9 More co-operatives

10 Growth industries develop e.g. micro-electronics and tourism

11 Increasing numbers employed in service industries

12 Increasing industrial pollution (air, land, oceans)

Hazards

1 More problems from unstable slopes, e.g. on coasts

2 Increased soil erosion

3 Planning to deal with Fog hazards

4 Adjusting to flood problems

5 Coping with weather hazards

Urban environments

1 Fewer people living in cities

2 Decaying inner city areas

3 More office blocks in town centres

4 Travel around cities becoming more expensive

5 Redevelopment of flats and houses not in inner city areas

6 Concentration of ethnic minorities in sections of cities

7 Rich people becoming richer as a result of redevelopment

8 More out-of-town superstores and hypermarkets

9 Decline of New Towns

10 More pressure on green belts

Glossary

This glossary contains an alphabetical listing of key and technical terms used in the book. The numbers in brackets refer to the *unit* in which the term is discussed.

Afforestation   Planting trees on available land, which may have been used earlier for other purposes. (*19*)

Agribusiness   Modern intensive farming which uses chemicals and machines to increase output and profit. (*14*)

Aquifer   Natural underground water store. (*20*)

Assisted Area   An area of high unemployment which receives government help to attract industry and jobs. Most Assisted Areas are in the north and west of Britain. (*33*)

Biogas   Gas produced from decaying organic waste. (*27*)

Capacity   Maximum amount that can be contained in any given area, for example, number of people on a tourist site, number of houses on an estate, number of cars that can fit into a car park. (*11*)

Central Business District (CBD)   The city centre, with high land values, used mostly for business and commercial buildings. (*43*)

Commuter   Person who travels some distance to and from work each day, from one district or area to another. (*2*)

Comparison goods   Goods people buy occasionally, after a careful comparison of prices and value. Examples are electrical appliances such as washing machines, refrigerators, etc. (*48*)

Comprehensive Development Area (CDA)   Area of urban redevelopment, where all the old buildings in a given area are demolished and replaced by new ones. (*44*)

Conurbation   Very large, built-up area, which includes at least one major city and often several towns which have grown together over the years. (*40*)

Convenience goods   Goods people buy regularly such as food. (*48*)

Co-operative   A system where the people who work together to produce goods or services, share the profit from the business. (*36*)

Country Parks   Areas of countryside planned and organised for recreation. (*12*)

Deindustrialisation   The permanent closing down of industries in a country or a region. (*28*)

Disaster A crisis, such as a flood or a landslide, caused by lack of hazard management, or by other factors

Ecosystem   Community of organisms (plants and animals) interacting with each other and the environment in order to survive and continue. (*19*)

Employment structure   Types of jobs done in an area, or in a country. For example, how many people are employed in primary industries, secondary industries, and so on. (*28*)

Energy gap   Not enough supplies of energy (for example fossil fuels) to meet people's needs. (*25*)

Enterprise Zones   Particular areas in towns which receive special government help to create jobs and attract new industry. (*34*)

Environment   All the things that surround us such as people, buildings, natural landscape, for example. (*Introduction*)

Erosion   Wearing away of the land by human over-use, or by natural causes such as wind, or water. (*53*)

Expanded Town   Existing town which grows to take newcomers. (*16*)

Factory farming   The intensive rearing of animals, and crops. (*15*)

Flood plain   Flat area bordering a river which is liable to flooding. (*55*)

General Improvement Area (GIA)   Local government funding to improve the quality of an area by improving housing, streets and amenities. (*45*)

Green belt   Protected area round a large city, designed to prevent the city from spreading without control. (*51*)

Greenhouse effect   Overheating of the Earth's atmosphere due to gases from burning fossil fuels. (*27*)

Growth industries   Industries which are expanding and becoming more important. (*28*)

Habitat   A suitable place for particular types of wildlife and plants to live and reproduce. (*19*)

Hazard   Set of conditions which pose a possible threat to human life and which require management. (*52, 53*)

High-technology   Describes industries which involve the most up-to-date equipment (such as robots for example) to produce goods or services, also industries which produce high-tech goods such as computers. (*37*)

Honeypot sites   Particularly attractive and accessible sites which draw in many visitors. (*11*)

Housing Action Area (HAA)   Where grants are available for particular home improvements. (*45*)

Hypermarket   Large, single level self-service store selling both food and other items, with a floor area over 5000 square metres. (*49*)

Infrastructure   Property within a country or an area, such as roads, housing, hospitals, schools, etc., available for people's use. (*46*)

Interdependence   Countries and people needing each other for support and development. (*Introduction*)

Key Settlement Policy   Concentrating services in the most accessible villages in order to support a rural area. (*7*)

Leisure   Time free from work or other commitments. (8)

Migration   Moving home from one area to another. **Emigration** is moving away from the old area. **Immigration** is moving into the new one. (2, 42)

Migrant workers   People who have to leave their homes to find work in another area. (31)

Monoculture   Growing just one crop, or species of plant. (19)

Multinational   Large company with branches in many countries. (24)

Multi-racial   Describes a community which contains a number of different ethnic groups. (42)

National Parks   Large, mainly rural areas whose outstanding natural scenery and wildlife are protected for public enjoyment. (13)

New Town   Planned settlement built within the last 40 years. (50)

Organic farming   System of agriculture which uses no artificial pesticides or fertilisers. (15)

Overspill settlement   Town built to take people forced to move from major urban area by redevelopment schemes. (50)

Pedestrianise   Make streets into an area for walkers only, closed to traffic. (45)

Pollution   Harmful effect on the environment caused by human activity. This includes noise, dirt and poisonous substances. (21)

Population turnaround   People moving back into an area, and so 'turning around' the earlier situation of falling numbers. (3)

Primary industry   Involves the extraction of food and raw materials from the earth (for example, farming, fishing and mining). (28)

Privatisation   Selling off nationally-owned industries and resources (for example, shipbuilding, water, electricity) to private shareholders. (29)

'Pull' factor   Reason for moving into an area. (2)

'Push' factor   Reason for moving away from an area. (2)

Quality of life   Level of well-being of a community and the area in which the community lives. (4)

Quaternary industry   Involves providing information and advice. Research laboratories and insurance companies are examples. (28)

Quota   Amount of goods allowed. This may be a production quota (for example the amount of milk which can be produced for sale by one country in the EEC) or an import/export quota which sets limits on the amount of one particular sort of product which can be sold from one country to another. (15)

Radioactivity   Rays or particles given off when unstable nuclei break down to more stable forms. Radioactivity is harmful to humans, animals and plant life. (25)

Renewable energy   Energy produced from source which will not run out, for example, water and wind. (27)

Resources   Things which are useful to people as a means of support. Natural resources include water, land and minerals. Man-made resources include roads, buildings and machines. (*Introduction*)

Ribbon development   Building houses or factories in lines along the edge of major roads. (5)

Rural   Belonging to the countryside. (1)

Rural depopulation   People leaving the countryside, usually to live in towns. (2)

Secondary industry   Making goods, usually in a factory, for example, brewing, steelmaking. (28)

Self-sufficient   Describes areas or countries able to meet their own needs from their own resources. (50)

Service industry   Produces a service, (not manufactured goods), for the consumer, or customer. Examples are transport, health and banking. (38)

Settlement   (a) People moving into an area. (b) A built-up area, of any size. (2)

Soil creep   Slow downslope movement of soil. (52)

Subsidy   Way of giving financial help to an area, or to an industry, for example. Subsidies may be made up of cash grants from the government, or a reduction in tax. (15)

Superstore   Large, single level self-service store selling food and other household items, with a floor area of 2500 square metres. (49)

System   Means of production, such as farming, which uses various inputs or raw materials, and processes these into outputs, or products. (14)

Tertiary industry   Involves providing services for other people or industries, such as transport for example. (28)

Transnational   A company which operates beyond its own national borders, as well as within its home country. (30)

Urbanisation   Trend for people to live in towns and cities rather than in rural areas. (40)

Village constellation   Villages which group together to provide services. (7)

Water cycle   Movement of water from sea to air, to land and back to the sea again. (20)

Yield   The amount of grain produced by a crop for example, or the output produced per hectare of land.

Index